RIDING THE WILD SIDE OF DENALI

Alaska Adventures
with Horses and Huskies

by Miki and Julie Collins

EPICENTER PRESS
FAIRBANKS/SEATTLE

Epicenter Press, Inc., is a regional press founded in Alaska whose interests include but are not limited to the arts, history, environment, and diverse cultures and lifestyles of the North Pacific and high latitudes. We seek both the traditional and innovative in publishing quality nonfiction tradebooks, contemporary art and photography giftbooks, and destination travel guides emphasizing Alaska, Washington, Oregon, and California.

Editor: Christine Ummel
Cover design: Elizabeth Watson
Inside design: Sue Mattson
Proofreader: Lois Kelly
Mapmaker: L. W. Nelson
Printer: Transcontinental Printing, Inc.

Acknowledgements: many stories in this book appeared in different form in periodicals including *Western Horseman, Sports Afield, Horse and Horseman, Mushing* magazine, *Mother Earth News, Fur-Fish-Game, Small Farmer's Journal, Up Here, Trapper and Predator Caller, Horseplay, Schlittenhund,* the *Whitehorse Star,* the *Northland News,* and the *Fairbanks Daily News-Miner.*

Library of Congress Catalog Card Number: 97-078446

ISBN 0-945397-64-X

To order single copies of RIDING THE WILD SIDE OF DENALI, send $14.95 (Washington residents add 8.6% state sales tax) plus $5 for priority mail shipping to: Epicenter Press, Box 82368, Kenmore, WA 98028. Booksellers: Retail discounts are available from our trade distributor, Graphic Arts Center Publishing, Portland, Oregon; phone 800-452-3032.

Printed in CANADA
First printing, April 1998
10 9 8 7 6 5 4 3 2 1

Lilja, Julie, and the dog team at the Birch Cabin on the trapline.

CONTENTS

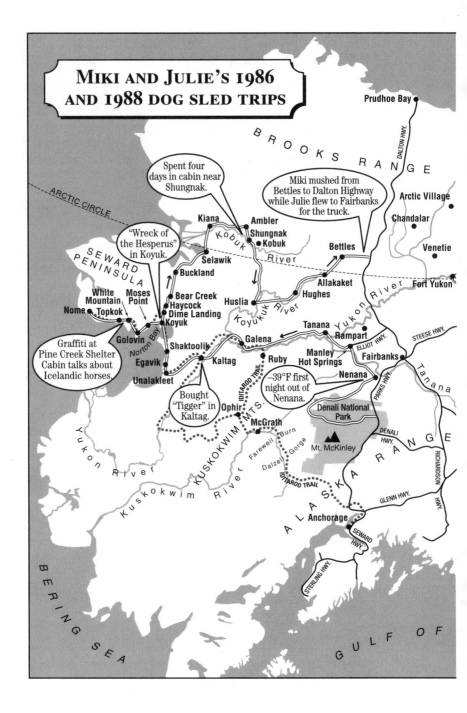

MIKI AND JULIE'S 1986 AND 1988 DOG SLED TRIPS

PRUDHOE BAY

BROOKS RANGE

DALTON HWY.

ARCTIC CIRCLE

Arctic Village

Chandalar

Spent four days in cabin near Shungnak.

Miki mushed from Bettles to Dalton Highway while Julie flew to Fairbanks for the truck.

Kiana   Ambler
               Shungnak
               Kobuk

Venetie

Kobuk River

Bettles

Fort Yukon

"Wreck of the Hesperus" in Koyuk.

SEWARD PENINSULA

Selawik

Buckland

Allakaket
Hughes

Huslia

Yukon River

White Mountain
Moses Point
Nome   Topkok

Bear Creek
Haycock
Dime Landing
Koyuk

Koyukuk River

Tanana
Rampart

STEESE HWY.

Golovin

Norton Bay

Shaktoolik

Galena

Ruby

Manley Hot Springs

ELLIOT HWY.

Fairbanks

Graffiti at Pine Creek Shelter Cabin talks about Icelandic horses.

Egavik

Kaltag

Unalakleet

Bought "Tigger" in Kaltag.

Ophir

–39°F first night out of Nenana.

Nenana

Tanana

Denali National Park

PARKS HWY.

McGrath

Burn

DENALI HWY.

RICHARDSON HWY.

Mt. McKinley

KUSKOKWIM MTS.

IDITAROD TRAIL

Farewell

Dalzel Gorge

Yukon River

Kuskokwim River

IDITAROD TRAIL

GLENN HWY.

Anchorage

SEWARD HWY.

ALASKA RANGE

BERING SEA

STERLING HWY.

GULF OF

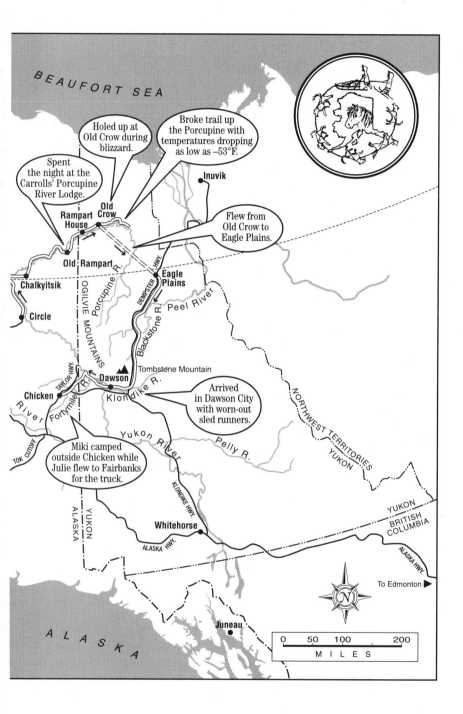

BEAUFORT SEA

Holed up at
Old Crow during
blizzard.

Broke trail up
the Porcupine with
temperatures dropping
as low as –53°F.

Spent
the night at the
Carrolls' Porcupine
River Lodge.

Inuvik

Flew from
Old Crow to
Eagle Plains.

Old
Crow

Rampart
House

Old Rampart

Chalkyitsik

OGILVIE MOUNTAINS

Porcupine R.

DEMPSTER HWY.

Eagle
Plains

Circle

Blackstone R.

Peel River

Tombstone Mountain

Dawson

Arrived
in Dawson City
with worn-out
sled runners.

TAYLOR HWY.

Chicken

Fortymile R.

Klondike R.

River

TOK CUTOFF

Yukon River

Pelly R.

NORTHWEST TERRITORIES

YUKON

Miki camped
outside Chicken while
Julie flew to Fairbanks
for the truck.

ALASKA

YUKON

KLONDIKE HWY.

YUKON

BRITISH
COLUMBIA

Whitehorse

ALASKA HWY.

ALASKA HWY.

To Edmonton ▶

N

ALASKA

Juneau

0   50   100   200

M I L E S

PREFACE

It has been ten years since we wrote our first book, *Trapline Twins*. Because not all of our adventures fit into that book, we promised another one and here it is. By the time we finished this one, so much more had happened that there still wasn't room for it all. But the important stuff is all here: how we got Icelandic horses and how we almost lost them; how we kept our huskies and how they kept us; how we use them all on cross-country treks and how we use them all at home.

We value many things in life — our independence, our family, the mutual love and cooperation we share with our loyal animals, and perhaps above all the wilderness that we call home. We have faith in ourselves and in our horses and huskies; it is the wilderness for which we fear. Our subsistence way of life is threatened as civilization squeezes a little closer each year, but we continue to harvest fish, furs, berries, meat, firewood, and other resources from this still-isolated country. We cannot retreat because there is no place left to go. So this book was not written to encourage would-be homesteaders; it is a how-we-do-it story, not a how-you-can-do-it book.

You may be confused at times reading this story because we take turns writing chapters. Welcome to our life. Being twins is confusing.

For years people have asked when we would write this book. To them we say, Life is more important. We would rather be living it than writing about it. But sharing our stories is fun too, so as time allowed we pecked away and now it is done. Enjoy.

Miki and Julie Collins

For Lilja

Our wish was a horse
and she came true

Streak and Comet swim across the river by the Birch Cabin while Miki rides Lilja, our new Icelandic horse.

CHAPTER 1

THE JOURNEY HOME

The grizzly stood elbow-deep in blueberry bushes, his tawny shoulders rippling darkly as he browsed along the treeless flanks of the Alaska Range. I watched him warily from across a brushy draw, my little horse alert by my side, her blue-flecked eyes growing big and round as she stared at the unsuspecting bear. Lilja didn't look scared, exactly, but she did look terribly impressed. Comet and Streak, my two big pack dogs, waited eagerly, ready to dash after the bear the instant I might suggest it.

Earlier in the day we had left the end of the dirt road behind as horse, huskies, and I struck out across a sixty-five-mile stretch of uninhabited wilderness to reach our home. My twin sister Julie waited there with our parents, busy caring for our team of sled dogs and doing other September chores, leaving to me and the two staunch dogs the job of getting Lilja to her new home.

Our journey had only just begun, and already I was getting into trouble. Typical.

If I went forward, I'd drop down into that brushy draw where I couldn't see the bear when he first heard or smelled me. If he approached, he'd be right on top of me before I saw him. My best bet was to get his attention while a couple hundred yards still separated us, to see what his reaction to us might be.

"Hey — ho!" I sang loudly.

His massive head jerked up. The instant the grizzly caught sight of us, he wheeled toward us, coming

Miki

9

at a swift, fluid, yet lumbering stride through the knee-high dwarf birch, not running but walking awfully darn fast.

A .45 Ruger Blackhawk revolver hung from the saddle. I snatched it from its holster, glancing at Lilja. The little horse had never been exposed to gunfire, but I decided I'd rather chase a horse bolting from a shot than a horse bolting from a charging grizzly. Gripping her lead rope tightly, I squeezed off a shot into the air.

Lilja hardly twitched as the pistol boomed, bucking in my hand. The grizzly snapped to a halt, springing up on his hind legs for a better look. I fired again, and this time he spun away, loping rapidly down the shoulder of the mountain.

I reloaded the pistol and slipped it back into the holster. Then the dogs, horse, and I picked our way cautiously on around the mountainside.

As children, my twin sister Julie and I, like so many girls, craved horses. Roaming the overgrown silt bars of the Old Channel, a shallow slough flowing near our home where wildlife abounded, sometimes we would find moose tracks and pretend they had been made by wild horses. They weren't, of course, but it was fun to dream. But as we grew up in Alaska's isolated Bush country, a land without roads, pastures, or even much wild grass, we set aside those unrealistic dreams. We could have moved to warmer climes, or even just to the road system within Alaska, but we belonged to the wilderness. Our parents lived here before we were born, and except for a few winters away getting a higher education, this vast subarctic land had always been our home.

For twenty-six years we had trapped and mushed and adventured in the remote spruce-covered lowlands north of the Alaska Range. Between running sled dogs on an eighty-mile trapline in the winter, raising a large garden and fishing for dog food during the short summers, and harvesting our year's meat and berries every fall, with an occasional thousand-mile dog sled trip for excitement, our lives were already full. Our love for horses was not forgotten, but Life marched on without them.

That is, until 1986, when we first heard about Icelandic horses and their amazing ability to forage off the land and survive the harshest winters. A scant five months later, I was traveling across Interior Alaska with a short, thick-maned palomino pinto mare.

After trucking Lilja (pronounced in the Icelandic way: *Lil-yah*) north from a farm in Canada, Julie and I had learned — sort of — how to ride and handle our thirteen-hand (fifty-two-inch) mount during a summer in Fairbanks. Now I had to get her home, and that meant a long, hazardous journey on foot across a wild land.

I'd been through this pristine area once before by dog team, and had no difficulty finding my way over the 3,500-foot bald mountain, a mere foothill of the Alaska Range. Below us a large glacial river roared through a low-walled canyon, and just a few miles to the south Denali towered to over 20,000 feet, its lower flanks already showing the white snows of September. Everything I needed for the forty-five mile, three-day leg of my journey to the Birch Cabin on our winter trapline was either on those dogs or lashed onto Lilja's stock saddle; once we were on the trapline, Julie could resupply me by float plane.

Of the more than 100 pounds of supplies we were transporting, most was animal feed. Comet and Streak shouldered thirty-pound packs for the first several miles, but soon I dismounted Lilja, tying their packs to her saddle and leading the horse while the dogs ran unencumbered up the mountainside.

Under our feet lay a carpet of tundra shrubs, dwarfed blueberries, crowberries, cranberries, mosses, lichens, and scrubby grasses, all turning vivid hues of red and gold, gray and ochre in response to the chilly fall nights. An occasional caribou paused to stare at our unlikely entourage as we crossed the high country, and by nightfall we had descended to treeline on the far side of the mountain.

The following afternoon found us down on flatter country, nearing the river crossing where the current, shallower but still racing fast, braided through a mile-wide plain of gravel bars. The water ran high for September, sweeping in standing waves over the granite cobbles. Anything over knee-deep might knock me down, but this was the best place to find a way to the far side.

Moving slowly, I used a poke stick to feel my way across one rushing channel after another, watching the ripples for dangerous spots. Lilja and the dogs followed unquestioningly.

Then my prodding stick missed a drop-off. Without warning I plunged into chest-deep water, and the current dashed me off my feet, spinning me downstream as I started to swim. Lilja stopped, standing firm as the lead rope jerked tight in my hand. Swinging me around at the end of the rope, the current washed me back against the shallow bar. I stumbled to my feet, dripping with icy water.

"Good girl," I said, shivering. "Let's try that again!" The dogs backed off and I picked my way upstream, eventually locating a safer crossing.

We camped that evening on a slough we call the Twelve-Mile, a beautiful creek lower down but here just a dry, willow-lined wash cutting through a vast plain of scrub spruce. Lilja, finished with her evening meal of sweet feed, grazed on sparse yellowing grass and bright green horsetails growing in the sand. Occasionally she poked her slender white nose under the tarp which served as my tent, making sure I hadn't slipped out on her. The dogs curled up peacefully on their nests of spruce boughs, and I slept warm and cozy on the thick saddle blanket.

One more exhausting day brought us to the Birch Cabin, right on schedule. We were down on the flats now, threading our way around countless shallow lakes and bogs, in an endless sea of scattered fifteen-foot-high scrub spruce growing from layers of deep, wet, spongy moss. Twice Lilja had sunk belly-deep in soggy, moss-covered drainages. Both times she surged forward, leaping onto firm ground, dirty water streaming down her white legs.

The homey sight of our little cabin on the bank of a wide creek revived my spirits after twelve hours of riding and walking. This was one of our main trapping camps, with a nice fourteen-by-eighteen-foot log cabin, a small cache for food storage, and a few spruce-pole dog houses scattered around the overgrown yard. Our first overnight stop on the trapline during the winter, it acted as a base for camps farther out the trail. For now, it was a comfortingly familiar shelter. I picketed Lilja where she could graze on the thick, coarse bluejoint grass growing around the cabin, and after slapping up plastic windows and lighting a fire in the stove, I took a swim in the icy creek, washing off the swamp muck that rose to my waist.

Running back to the cabin, I stopped short at the sight of Lilja grazing placidly around the cabin door. A horse! A real, live horse, right here at our Birch Cabin! A rhinoceros could hardly have seemed more out of place. Affectionately I brushed the mud from her white-and-gold coat, picking short-needled spruce twigs from the exceedingly thick topknot she wore as a forelock, a trademark of the Icelandic breed. When temperatures dipped to fifty below next winter, that thick thatch of hair nearly covering her little ears would protect them from the cold.

We spent a day of rest at the cabin, Lilja happily mowing down yellowing grass while I picked a couple gallons of cranberries to cache for the approaching winter. Julie flew our brother's Super Cub floatplane out with a resupply of feed, landing on the closest lake four miles away and hiking in to spend the night before I headed on with my little crew.

The first forty-five miles had taken us three days. But now we were heading into unfamiliar country, leaving our trapline trail to pick our way across nine miles of marsh and muskeg to hit the Old Channel seven miles from home. The winter trail followed a boggy creek system most of the way, and I decided to cut across country to the river to stay on higher ground. The nine-mile portage would be the most challenging part of the trip. With no landmarks, I depended upon a compass to find my way, and I worried about crossing creeks and bogs with Lilja. I knew I did not have enough experience to judge what was safe for a horse and what was not. I was used to traveling with dogs, who can walk across quicksand with impunity, dash through the deepest bogs, and scramble up the steepest banks. But horses aren't like dogs.

I would soon learn that horses and bogs don't mix — or rather, they mix so well as to become inseparable. Many of our bogs have a thick layer of yellow-green moss camouflaging deep, mucky water. Once a horse's sharp hooves and long, slender legs break through the spongy, overlying surface, its great weight prevents it from climbing out again, with potentially fatal results. Sometimes a horse can scurry across soft ground, but soft, safe ground is unfortunately hard to distinguish from the soft, horse-eating variety.

We struck out bravely, marching across muskeg and marsh, bog and slough. Lilja followed with a blind trust as I walked ahead, slogging through watery moss and once tiptoeing across a twisted, overgrown beaver dam. Occasionally we marched swiftly along low ridges, prehistoric sand dunes, their tops dry and firm with a game trail inevitably running along the crest. Usually, though, my feet sank several inches down into spongy moss and tussocks as we wound our way through the stunted black spruce.

Then, crossing an innocuous-appearing moss-covered drainage, Lilja fell in. Her hindquarters broke through a layer of floating moss into deep, dirty water, sinking until her belly rested in the deep red muck. This time she was too tired to struggle out.

For ten minutes I coaxed, prodded, and pulled. Finally in desperation I slapped her hard across the flank with the snap end of the heavy lead rope. With a grunt she jerked away, heaving herself upright, and several more blows drove her back to safe ground.

Trembling, I calmed her as the dogs stood by quietly. When we started again, I traveled more cautiously, seeking the firmest route in that land of moss and mire. Instead of reaching the Old Channel by evening, we camped only halfway there.

During the first part of the trip I had always been aware of Comet and Streak, of where they were and what they were thinking about. Now I was so intent on Lilja that I ignored the dogs. Yet they were always there, buoyant and cheerful when we moved along, or standing aside worriedly when things went wrong. They shouldered heavy burdens so I could save every bit of Lilja's strength, even though the weight of their packs wore them out and the horse carried little more than her saddle as I walked ahead. I counted on those two 110-pound dogs, with their laughing faces and striking black-and-white malamute masks, and they unfailingly came through for me.

The muskeg stretched on and on. Sometimes we walked "quickly" through deep, dry lichen or humpy-bumpy tussocks. Other times we trekked a half-mile out of our way, pushing through tight, stickery brush, to find safe crossings over drainages. Yet for all our caution, we had progressed only a short distance the following morning when suddenly Lilja sank again, her legs disappearing into reddish watery moss, just two feet away from solid ground.

This time I knew she wasn't going to make it out on her own. Something in her eyes told me she wasn't even going to try; something in the way her hindquarters sank to the stifle, and her forelegs were disappearing nearly to her quivering shoulders, told me we were in deep trouble.

"Get up, Lilja," I snapped. Needing to turn her resignation into fear, I struck her rump with the lead rope. She made a brief, futile effort and then lay still, shivering with cold and distress. I knew then she couldn't do it, and no amount of wishing, shouting, or prodding could help her. Groaning, Lilja shut her pink-rimmed eyes as if to say, *I'm going to die now, and there's no use making a fuss over it.*

With trembling hands I hitched her picket line to the rigging of her saddle, driving my arms elbow-deep in cold, dirty water to work it down to the heavy D ring where the cinch attached to it. Now at least I had something to pull on if she sank in deeper.

I leaped away again, dropping to my knees by the small bundle I'd snatched from her saddle bags the moment she went down. Inside, carefully wrapped in plastic and foam, lay my only lifeline to The World: a two-meter amateur radio, the size of a walkie-talkie but more powerful. At home, Julie answered my first call.

"Lilja's in a bog and I need a comealong to get her out," I said.

"Right," Julie answered, her voice tightening. "I have to gas up the plane, and then we'll be right out."

"You'd better hurry," I warned.

Julie could air-drop me a hand winch, but she'd have to find me first. In that trail-less tangle of bog and moss, taiga and marsh, Lilja and I were specks against a mottled, September-brown background.

I returned to the little horse. She had rolled onto her side and the swamp crept up to the top of her right hip, bog water turning her white coat a reddish brown. Her left shoulder lay partially exposed but her right side had disappeared, and her neck sank until the water nearly closed over it. Worst of all, her head slid back and sidewise into the water. One eye and an ear sank out of sight and as her tiring neck muscles sagged, her nostrils slipped momentarily underwater. She jerked her head up again, eyes rolling wildly.

"Lilja, Lilja!" I cried, catching her head up and lightly slapping her muzzle. "Hang on, girl. I'll get you out."

A twig of a spruce tree twisted from the nearby bank, and I tied the reins of her hackamore up to it, holding her head clear of the water. Then I tried to build a Spanish windlass, anchoring it to a nearby black spruce. Leonard Menke, a longtime trapper, had told me how years ago. But the biggest trees around were under two inches in diameter and rooted only in shallow moss overlying the frozen permafrost below. I didn't have enough rope, and I couldn't remember exactly how to make it anyway. Nothing worked.

Then I heard the familiar rattling buzz of the Super Cub. I snatched up my radio as the little plane came into sight, angling south of me.

"I am on your left," I said into the mike.

"Negative copy." The roar of the 150-horsepower engine reverberating in Julie's radio nearly drowned out her voice.

My battery was failing. I switched to my tiny reserve. "TURN LEFT!" I shouted.

"Roger."

Lilja groaned softly. I stood quivering. In the distance, Julie banked her small plane in my direction.

"Hang on, sweetheart," I urged my little horse. As Julie headed too far north, I pulled out my compass. "Take a heading of 160 degrees," I ordered.

"Roger. You're very scratchy."

Fear gripped me anew. The spare battery was failing. Julie passed by a half-mile away. "Turn left!" I cried into the radio.

"Negative copy."

"Left!"

She didn't answer. My radio was dead.

I knew she would have only taken time to dump in five gallons of gas, which that powerful engine drinks up every half-hour. And half an hour just wasn't long enough. Helplessly, I watched her circling a short distance off until at last she banked toward home.

She'd be back, but I didn't know if she'd find us in time. Horses cannot withstand being down for long, and Lilja was suffering from the cold as well. Desperately, I hurried back to work on the windlass but that proved hopeless. The trees were too spindly and the only rope I had was Lilja's fifty-foot picket, made of one-inch nylon webbing. When Julie returned, I waited until she flew abreast of me and then roared "LEFT!" into the tiny radio.

That was the last word for my radio, and put my twin sister practically on top of me, circling and circling. I slopped to the middle of the open bog, spread out my bright green tarp, and then stood shin-deep in the cold, mucky water, flagging with a red shirt, confident that either Julie or Daddy, in the passenger seat, would spot me. If I wasn't so sure that they would spot me any minute, I would have taken the time to build a fire, and the smoke would have pinpointed me immediately. As it was, they couldn't pick me out of the dappled background for over an hour.

Then one wing dipped and the plane swung down, circling low. At last! After one pass I saw Julie line up on the bog to make the drop. Throttle back. Set up the approach. Full flaps. The narrow red plane coasted down, down, coming straight toward me. The door opened and Daddy, in the back seat, leaned out. As they passed

Making a timely airdrop from the Super Cub was the only chance we had to save Lilja when she bogged down in a swamp.

fifty feet above me, he hurled out two packages. One held a spare radio battery. The other contained two comealongs and about a hundred miles of rope.

"Okay, Lilja, things are going to start popping now!" I sputtered, scrambling back up the low bank that separated the bog from stable ground. I swiftly fastened the rope onto the harness I'd rigged on her, and then tied off one of the winches to three of the stunted trees, hoping they would not uproot under the strain. Grimly, I started to crank.

The rope grew taut, and then she budged. When she felt the movement, Lilja struggled briefly, lifting herself up before lying still again. I cranked some more, and every few inches she heaved herself forward and upward. Then the comealong jammed.

I snatched up the other one. This winch had a faulty release. I could only use it once, and if that didn't do the trick by the time the cable wound in, I'd have to waste precious time fiddling with the darn thing.

"Lilja, get up!" I ordered. The rope tightened. Her body slid upward, all 650 pounds of it, and she lurched forward. Her front hooves clawed at the mossy bank. The cable shortened. I had only a few inches left. "Come on, girl!"

She jerked up, straining, and as I cranked in the last eight inches, sliding her forward, her hind legs came free and she staggered up the bank. She had been soaking in that cold bog for three hours, and appeared mildly relieved to have escaped with her life.

A light drizzle misted down as I dropped the comealong and hurried to the little mare, praising her as I squeezed the dirty water from her trembling body. I didn't linger long. We started walking again, more to warm Lilja up than to get anywhere, and we camped in the early afternoon as soon as she seemed somewhat recovered from the chill.

By then, damp from rain and my exertions in the bog, I worried about the possibility of hypothermia in myself as well as in the shivering horse. Splitting some dead standing spruce to expose the dry wood inside, I built a small but hot fire and covered the wet, chilly mare with everything I had: two burlap sacks, a sweater, a wool shirt, the saddle blanket, a large plastic bag, rain coat, rain pants, dog packs . . . she looked like a cancerous patchwork coat, but she finally warmed up. I kept back only my sleeping bag for my own safety.

I stood her by the fire, rubbing swamp dirt from her drying fur and heating water in my one-quart cook pot to soak her feed in for a hot meal. I had to make about six pans of soaked food, alternating with more pans of warmed water, each of which she swallowed in two or three mouthfuls. We were all reduced to drinking bog water, and I picked squiggly inch-long bugs and stray bits of grain out of the pan when I finally cooked my own dinner. Julie returned that evening, guided to me with the help of the spare radio battery and the smoke of my fire, to airdrop a resupply of food.

It took us four days to cross that terrible stretch. I had strayed too far west, down from the drier ground I'd been aiming for. Two or three times a day Julie buzzed out, giving me directions on how to get around the worst areas. Each evening she dropped me feed so we never had much to pack. Most precious of all were the little sketched maps she drew, detailing the terrain and labeling trouble ahead. I trekked around "Lots of Small Slu's," I backtracked down "Long Slu" to cross "Big Tamarack Marsh," and almost lost Lilja again when I had to cross a chest-deep, vertical-banked "Creek." Once in the water, Lilja couldn't climb out on the far side. Eventually she solved the problem herself, rushing off downstream and locating a better spot to haul out. Then I ran into "Big Swamp" and had to double back again, finding my way around it and tip-toeing across the last two "Slu's."

We hit the Old Channel right on track and just three days late. I laughed and cried and called Julie on the radio. We planned to celebrate our twenty-seventh birthday when I reached home, even though it wasn't the right day. (Being twins, we share a birthday.)

"Kill that chicken and bake that cake, I'm on the Old Channel!" I sang into the radio.

Comet and Streak, ever present, scented the familiar waters of their river. Knowing home was not far away, they threw open the doors of their boundless capacity for exuberant joy.

"Oh-dee-oh-dee-oh!" Streak shouted.

"Eee-dee-eee-dee-eee!" Comet shrieked, and together they hurtled their powerful bodies down onto the muddy silt bank for a good roll followed by a vigorous romp, shouting and shrieking all the while. Lilja picked up on their high spirits, lifting her head to test the air, and then dropping to her knees, plopping down to roll on the damp silt, to the detriment of her saddle and pack.

Those two devoted huskies, the pick of our "pack" for summer work, stabilized my emotions on that memorable trip. Always reliable, always strong and familiar next to the vast mysteries of the Horse, they readily shouldered heavy burdens to spare the little mare. They would have liked to chase that grizzly to Kingdom Come (or so they thought from a safe distance), but at a word from me they stayed right by my side. Oddly enough, every time I left Lilja to scout out a safe route, one dog invariably stayed with her while the other came with me — and they seemed to take turns. Now that they saw that the purpose behind our mad travels was to get home, they whole-heartedly endorsed my every move.

We still had seven miles of brush and quicksand to contend with, but this was my country now, my childhood playground, and I knew every bend, every dangerous spot. Julie and Daddy paddled up the shallow river to meet us, and we camped together that night at our annual moose camp before Daddy headed home in the canoe, leaving Julie with me to head confidently down the riverbank with our little horse and two very happy dogs.

It didn't take long to figure out that even this part was going to be hairy. Recent flooding had left quicksand all along the willow-lined banks, with nothing but endless swamps farther inland. There was no way around this stretch, yet if the horse fell in we could never pull her out with only waist-high willows to anchor a comealong to.

Lilja tiptoed swiftly over the softer spots, delicate white nostrils flaring. Suddenly one hoof penetrated the silty surface into quicksand below. Instantly the little horse collapsed in a heap. Her weight spread out, she stopped sinking, and after resting calmly for a moment she regained her strength, sprang to her feet and, wresting her leg free, scampered on downriver.

Several more times Lilja sank into the treacherous mud, and each time she saved herself by throwing herself to the ground to stop sinking until she could catch her breath and go on. Finally we reached the spot where we had to cross the river. From the far side we'd be on firm ground the rest of the way.

Julie and I swam the narrow stream first, teeth chattering in the cold, to check out the far bank. I looked it over skeptically; even though we felt this was the best spot, I wasn't sure Lilja wouldn't sink into the soft mud as she climbed out.

Julie led the horse into the water. I grabbed the mare's long, flowing white tail as she plunged in and started to swim, towing me behind. Moments later Lilja heaved herself out on the far side and stepped onto solid ground. We made it!

In triumph we marched the last mile and a half home through the golden birch forest, Comet and Streak surging excitedly ahead as Lilja strode regally behind, a raggedy blanket thrown over her wet body. As we walked into our dog yard, our chained huskies — some of whom had never seen a horse before —burst into an astonished cacophony of greeting, alarm, and incredulous exclamations. Their wild antics didn't faze Lilja. She surveyed her surroundings with a domineering eye and then placidly fell to munching chickweed as if content to live here for the rest of her life. She knew right where she was: home.

Although we knew getting horses would change everything, Julie and I never dreamed of the whole array of horsey triumphs and disasters that lay in store for us. Until now most of our excitement had come from taking our dog team on the winter trapline trails or on long-distance sled trips. We had mushed in such diverse places as Yukon Territory and the big city of Anchorage, the Kuskokwim Mountains and the Tanana River Valley. This mushing career had culminated the previous spring in a 1,900-mile excursion, following a convoluted route that took in Denali Park, half of the famed Iditarod Trail, the Seward Peninsula, and the Kobuk and Koyukuk River valleys. It was on that venture — the journey of the *Hesperus* — that we first learned of the unique little Icelandic horses that would change our lives so greatly.

Our dog sled trip through Denali Park offered sparkling views of Denali and the Alaska Range.

CHAPTER 2

THE ODYSSEY OF THE *HESPERUS*

"Get up! It happened."

I moved. Icy cold air fingered through my heavy sleeping bag, threatening my cozy security. Overhead, frosty stars were fading before a pale arctic dawn, while around me nine big huskies lay curled against the winter night. The thought of ever owning horses was far from my mind that raw morning on the Tanana River.

"Get up!" Miki bent over a thin fire, its gray smoke winding around her.

"What happened?" I asked, pushing out into the brittle air.

"It went down to forty below," Miki replied.

"What! It can't be forty below out here."

"You're right. It's only thirty-nine below."

Just yesterday Miki and I had left the small town of Nenana, fifty miles southwest of Fairbanks, mushing west toward Manley and points beyond. Thirty-below weather had already delayed our start, but this was the last day of February. The sun rose higher each day, beating back the nightly deep freeze. Spring seemed right around the corner, and we had a long way to go before breakup.

We had first decided to take a sled trip to Nome the previous summer, but in the ensuing months we had grown more ambitious. If spring held off, we'd go from Nome to the Kobuk River, where our father had worked during the 1940s. By mushing on to Bettles, we could then truck back down the Dalton *Julie*

22

Highway, which connected Fairbanks with the Prudhoe Bay oil fields in the north. Not knowing if such a long trip was possible, we planned to travel until we made it or ran out of snow, whichever came first.

"So, why do you want to go to Nome?" our friend Ray Wildrick Jr. had asked before we left.

"We've never been there before," I began, then added hopefully, "We'd rather go on a sled trip than trap beaver."

Miki smiled and nodded. Most of our income comes from the trapline, and the fur that makes money for us is marten. Beaver, trapped in March after marten season, are tougher to catch and less profitable. We preferred to skip trapping beaver, going on a dog sled jaunt instead, but now, trying to explain that to RJ, it sounded like a feeble excuse.

"We've got a map of Alaska at home," I tried again. "We draw little lines on it showing where we've gone with the dogs. We take these trips so we can draw more little lines."

Miki smiled and nodded again. I'm not sure RJ bought it, but it was good enough for us.

Sled dogs have always been the driving force in our lives. Moving to Fairbanks for high school was tough for two shy teenagers from the Bush, but the dogs pulled us through. When we returned home after graduating from college, we used our dogs to work a trapline not just because trapping was the only viable employment, but also because it allowed us to run dogs productively every day, all winter. We flirted with racing — Miki entered the Iditarod and I ran the 1,000-mile Yukon Quest race — but we already had decided to avoid the sophisticated rat race of competitive mushing and stick with our big, old-time trapline dogs instead of the sleek, tiny racing huskies. We preferred more leisurely trips deep in the wilderness, where we could choose our own route and set our own pace.

Conditioning the dogs for this journey came naturally during that winter of 1985-86. By the time we left in mid-February, the dogs had run over 1,500 miles in three and a half months on the trapline. Miki and I were in good shape, too, after long days of brushing trail, skiing sidelines, and cutting firewood. If anything, we departed overworked and tired.

The first leg of the journey was running the dogs through Denali Park to the Parks Highway where we could drive them to Fairbanks to organize the main trip. We left home February 13 with 230 pounds of dog food and gear packed into our eight-and-a-half-foot freight sled, dubbed the *Hesperus*. The long, graceful, home-built sled took its name from Longfellow's classic poem, *The Wreck of the Hesperus*, a story of shipwreck and disaster in the 1880s on the "reef of Norman's woe" off the New England coast. Our mother, whom we call Marmee, suggested the title after I smashed the sled on its maiden run.

Repaired and broken in, the sled now moved easily despite its cumbersome load. *("It was the schooner Hesperus that sailed the wintry sea . . ."* wrote Longfellow.) But disaster almost struck the second day out, when the dogs swerved past an open hole in the ice on a creek, with deep, swift water glistening black against the white snow.

"Haw, Sky," I called. Our little blue-eyed lead dog obediently swung wider to the left, but the ice began to crumble, disintegrating under the team. Our big wheel dogs, Comet and Streak, tumbled into the swirling water. The taut towline popped them out again, wet and horrified. Miki was skiing between the team and the sled to steer the *Hesperus* with a gee pole. Now she became caught between the powerful dogs and the heavy sled, with deadly water already under the tips of her skis.

"Haw, Sky!" I shouted urgently. The team quickly wheeled left and Miki threw her weight against the gee pole, skidding around the hole and leaving us breathless with relief. *("The snow fell hissing in the brine,"* Longfellow related.)

Undaunted, Miki continued "riding the gee pole," using the long spruce pole to lever the heavily loaded sled around corners. She sang loudly to the dogs:

> *I skijored on Minchumina*
> *I skijored to McGrath*
> *Skijored on the Yukon*
> *And over Sable Pass, boys,*
> > *Over Sable Pass!*

We wound over the barren crest of a high rounded dome, feeling like tiny specks on a tiny mound compared to the hulking 20,320-foot mass of Denali towering up a few miles south. A thin, icy snow cover in Denali Park left boulders and tussocks exposed, making sled travel through the spectacular Alaska Range both rough and tedious. Miki, skijoring behind the *Hesperus* now that half the load of dog food was gone, dodged granite boulders, skidded across patchy ice, twisted painfully through tussocks, and scampered with clattering skis across bare gravel. Once she lost control, shot down an icy hillside, and flew over a huge snowdrift to crash into Wonder Lake, only to rise and totter on with broken glasses and two black eyes.

Yet the brilliant white and blue of the mountains and sky, meeting in sharp angles all around, held us so spellbound that the bruises seemed trivial. "Gawking like gol-danged tourists," Miki commented as we drank in the soaring ridges of Denali rising high above jagged mountains and lower tundra hills. Sheer faces of blue-gray rock etched their features against snowy white slopes along Denali's crest. From our northern vantage point, the North Face jutted 17,000 feet above the flatlands below.

Pushing up rock-strewn Thorofare Creek, we climbed wind-swept passes and traversed snow-drifted valleys, finally following the gravel road to Park Headquarters. From there we trucked the team up to Fairbanks and spent a week getting organized for the *real* trip. We mailed boxes of non-perishable groceries and sacks of dog food to village post offices, and bought additional frozen meat for the dogs, which we shipped out air freight or left for our brother, Ray, to fly for us.

We made phone calls to determine trail conditions; purchased maps; put together first aid and repair kits; sewed harnesses, dog booties, clothing, and stuff sacks; and packed extra socks, sweaters, and gloves. During that week, the warm spell ended with a cold snap, and we realized it wasn't going to warm up anytime soon. With little Sky and big white Legs in the lead, we left Nenana facing west toward Nome, 750 miles away. And that first night on the river the temperature sank to forty below.

"After that wet thaw, it's actually kind of nice camping out in this cold," I remarked to Miki as we huddled shivering over the fire that morning. "The snow doesn't melt on your clothes, you don't sweat, and you don't have all those wet socks to dry out every night."

However, I did appreciate the forceful March sunlight which tempered the severe cold by twenty or thirty degrees each afternoon. "People will ask what we saw on our trip," I told Miki that first chilly morning. Pulling my long fur parka ruff over my face, I shouted, "We'll have to say, 'I don't know, I never saw a thing!'"

I thought a moment, then burst into song:

I've run dogs at minus forty,
I've run 'em in deep snow
Mushed against a screaming wind,
And through the overflow, boys,
*   And through the overflow!*

Days later we finally escaped the cold, but only by mushing on to the warmer coastal climate and leaving the harsh Alaskan Interior behind. Meanwhile, we camped out on the trail or stayed in villages with friends who invited us in to thaw out and dry our frosted gear: Tom Hetherington at Manley Hot Springs, Bob and Elaine Mitchell at Tanana, and Gary and Gwen Guy at Galena. Still, camping under the stars offered few hardships. We slept in the *Hesperus,* facing opposite directions so we could both fit in the narrow basket, sharing warmth and protected from wind by a tarp. With good winter gear, we didn't feel the cold during the day. Anticipating that Miki's feet might get cold in her thin ski boots, I had sewed her thick felted overboots. The ugly, ungainly "brown blobs" kept Miki's feet warm at the coldest temperatures.

The bow of the *Hesperus* rose and fell on the gentle swells of the drifted Yukon River, creaking under its heavy load as the long white-ash boards flexed over ripples in the snowpack. *"It was the schooner Hesperus, that sailed the wintry sea,"* the poem went, but Longfellow's ship sank and ours, so far, had not.

At Ruby we struck the route of the Iditarod Trail Sled Dog Race, a glossy winter highway to Nome. With the Iditarod fast approaching, spectators were crowding up from Galena to watch the race at Ruby. Camping below the village, we were awakened after dark by two youngsters trudging toward town because their snowmachine had broken. We invited the kids to warm themselves at our fire and share some cocoa while they waited for a ride. Sure enough, three snowmachiners soon roared up, stopping to investigate our campfire.

"Who's that?" they shouted.

"Miki and Julie Collins. I'm Julie — that's Miki," I said.

"Hey, I know you!" one guy burst out. "You write those stories for the *Northland News!*"

Grinning bashfully, we shook hands all around. Since the monthly newspaper went to all northern villages in Alaska, we were often recognized. After exchanging a few words, the men loaded the marooned youngsters aboard their snowmachines and raced away into the darkness like so many knights on their galloping steeds.

Following the Iditarod Trail to Galena, we learned that the front-runners of the Anchorage-to-Nome race were only hours behind us. Gwen and Gary Guy of Galena, who were leaving for the weekend, offered us their home to hole up in until the lead mushers passed. But first we had to run the dogs over to Harold's Air Service to pick up a resupply of dog food. As we mushed toward town, a snowmachiner zoomed up and shouted, "Follow me! Follow me!"

Mystified, we politely trailed the machiner, who proudly led us directly to the Iditarod race checkpoint. Perhaps he thought we were competitors, although the two of us with one oversized sled and nine heavy work dogs couldn't have looked very racey. When our team entered the throng of expectant spectators, we did not stop, but quietly drove the dogs on through, sneaking behind the post office and circling back to the air carrier office.

To avoid interfering with the race, Miki and I spent two days in Galena waiting for the front-runners to pass. Our brother Ray, who frequently provides logistical support for our adventures, flew his Super Cub ski plane out with extra supplies, and we sent two dogs back to Fairbanks with him. Buck had developed a bad back, so we dropped him from the team. Big, loyal Streak needed a rest to heal the sore feet that often plagued him on longer trips.

Following the Yukon River downstream, we found it easy to make fifty miles a day on the smooth trail. Hills and bluffs pressed close along the north bank, and we swished past the mouth of the Koyukuk River, whose headwaters we hoped to see later in the spring. On the south bank, long lines of tall, dense spruce trees grew stiffly above steep walls of frozen silt, standing like armies over the river.

As we passed snowy fish camps and villages, we noticed a slow evolution, so that those by the sea bore little resemblance to those far inland on the Tanana River. The Inupiaq Eskimos lived mainly in modern frame houses, probably because of the lack of trees along the coast, while many Athabascan Indians still dwelled in snug log cabins. Even the look of the dog sleds changed, reflecting differences in use and terrain.

In Kaltag we bought a dog. Since dropping two huskies in Galena, the *Hesperus* had been as underpowered as a becalmed ship, and before leaving the Yukon village we found a compact, tough-looking black dog named, er . . . "Nigger."

"The children named him," his owner said apologetically.

A small change worked; "Tigger" never noticed the difference.

Topping the Kaltag Portage, we coasted down through gentle, open country with small spruce groves and willow patches pooling in low areas between the mountains that isolated inland Alaska from the sea. Here we finally escaped the cold weather of the Interior, although even the warmer coastal air felt chilly with its clammy wind. Reaching the Bering Sea at Unalakleet, we

Miki followed our route with the map, pinpointing our position on the Kaltag Portage.

settled into a grassy camp and I walked up the runway to the air freight office to check on our dog food shipment. It had not arrived.

A big hand fell on my shoulder and I wheeled around to see our old friend Robbie Roberts, the "Loafer from Ophir." The gangly musher was racing the Iditarod and had come to check on a replacement sled he was expecting.

"I broke five sleds so far," he told me. "Coming down Dalzell Gorge in the Alaska Range I got stuck behind another musher on a narrow trail. I rode my sled brake until it broke. The sled tipped over and the dogs dragged me down the mountain. Broke my hand, chipped my knee, dislocated my shoulder, and smashed the sled."

A few miles farther the intrepid musher struck his head when his sled crashed into an ice-covered hole. Others found him nearly unconscious under the sled. "My God, he's dead!" they gasped, and dragged him out by the feet. Despite a concussion and a dislocated finger, Robbie pushed on, demolishing his sled yet again crossing the rough, snowless Farewell Burn. Still, he was determined to finish the race. "I owe it to my sponsors," he said simply.

Miki and I were glad we weren't racing, especially that year when poor snow conditions made speedy travel uncomfortable at best. We preferred our own slow, steady progress:

I've raced in the Iditarod,
I've done the Yukon Quest
And though I'd rather go alone,
I've traveled with the best, boys,
    Traveled with the best!

Thus ran our song, but it exaggerated. Our freight team never ran fast enough to catch up to "the best."

We waited two days at Unalakleet for our dog food. Only a few patches of grizzled snow remained around the gray coastal village, and as we explored the barren hills on foot we contemplated an old telephone line stretching up the slopes, and the rakish clumps of yellow grass, with an occasional twiggy spruce tree, too stunted to grow, too tenacious to die.

"It looks more like the Old West than Alaska," I told Miki, scanning the desert-like terrain with its low shrubs, incongruous above the distant frozen sea.

"With all this grass you could probably keep horses here," Miki added wistfully, and we both sighed.

Finally we gave up on the resupply. Our dwindling dog food might stretch to Koyuk, ninety miles away, where our next supply drop should be.

We headed up the thin strip of icy tundra that was the race trail, bumping over several miles of rough country. Miki tumbled down again and again as her skis slipped on ice or grated on exposed gravel. To avoid the worst stretches, she sometimes flung herself onto the sled, and under her weight a side railing broke, and later the other one broke too. The sled rolled down a gravel bank and a rear upright stanchion snapped. Then we lost the trail in a lonely valley of empty gray buildings called Egavik. We searched for an hour, walking across gravel and ice, looking for any faint scratches left by other sleds.

"I give up. Let's sneak out onto the sea ice," I said at last.

"Sure, Mac! Those trailbreakers stayed off the ice for a reason. I'm sure it was a good one."

"They go on the ice across Norton Bay, and that's only a few miles north of here. Besides, you're the one with bruised knees." I could see

Miki weakening. "Come on," I urged. "It'll only take a couple hours to reach Shaktoolik this way, and we'll stay close to shore."

"Okay, but if the ice breaks away and we float off and die, you're the one who has to explain it to everybody."

The team moved fast on the snowless sea ice. An open crack appeared, and we hopped over it. Another appeared, and we hopped over it, too. The next one was so wide Miki's skis barely spanned it.

"Jump!" I shouted, and Miki shrieked, but her short skis somehow flew over the open water.

"I told you!" she shouted, glowing with excitement. Then her hazel eyes popped open. "What's that? Oh, it's gone!" Then we spotted it again, a seal basking near open holes in the ice. He popped out of sight as we approached. Other seals lay sprinkled like pepper across the ice, distant black specks that vanished into the water as we came closer.

The hazardous crossing safely behind us, we chugged on to the windswept coastal village of Shaktoolik, arriving late on a somber afternoon when the sky was grim with sullen clouds. The ice, the silt-dusted snow, the grass — even the wind — all seemed washed out in bleak, chilly shades of gray, a desolate scene. Then we passed a palm tree.

It stood cheerily erect above a frozen gray lagoon near a straggling line of small houses. Never mind that it had been carved from plywood. It served as a bright reminder to travelers and Iditarod mushers not to take life too seriously.

Rather than ask for lodging at a tiny village already burdened with Iditarod racers, organizers, veterinarians, spectators, and the press, we camped several miles farther on the tundra. Our evening trek crossed so much bare ground that Miki gave up on skiing. "My knees aren't going to hold out," she confessed. We took turns walking and driving the dogs. Miki followed behind while I mushed the dogs a quarter mile and then anchored them. Leaving the team, I walked ahead and when Miki reached the dogs, she drove them past me another quarter mile before walking on. This "ride and tie" system proved faster than one of us walking alone and falling far behind.

In camp that night I spliced the sled's broken railings with driftwood scavenged off the beach near Shaktoolik, and I lashed the broken stanchion as well.

We had lined the *Hesperus* with dry grass at Unalakleet for warmth, but now we shook it out for the dogs. Our tarp kept us cozy, but the steady wind chilled the dogs and they appreciated the heaps of hay to curl up on. The evening's entertainment consisted of a showy sunset of red and gold dancing among the breaking clouds, and after dark the lights of Koyuk peeked out across the ice, some thirty-five miles north.

The next morning, Robbie Roberts and three other racers overtook us on the ice. We stopped to chat, and ended up explaining our plan to mush to Nome, Kobuk, and Bettles.

"Sounds pretty ambitious," one musher put in skeptically.

"Where'd you start from, Shaktoolik?" another asked sarcastically.

Robbie looked indignant. He knew we'd traveled 500 miles just since leaving Nenana. He asked if we wanted any dog food. "Sure!" we chorused. The *Hesperus* was empty. Robbie loaded us with excess feed, meat of the highest quality for his racing dogs. Not to be outdone, his companions packed more food over to us — chicken, turkey, lamb, fish, and liver, all for the dogs. We gave our hungry team a big feed right there, and another at Koyuk. Although our dogs traveled the same speed as these race teams, when we stopped for the night at Koyuk they pulled away and we didn't see them again until we reached Nome.

Ice glazed the slanted streets of Koyuk as we mushed through the village and climbed the hill to the runway, finding a camp spot in an isolated thicket of spruce. Ray flew out the next day, landing on the sea ice with supplies, a replacement stanchion for the *Hesperus,* and Streak. After a joyous reunion with his brother Comet, the big dog eagerly took his place in the team, refreshed by his vacation in Fairbanks. Late in the morning, we pulled out for Nome.

Sky, our main leader, had raced in Lavon Barve's 1983 Iditarod team, holding a blistering pace to finish in sixth place. Now, as we drove hard to reach a sheltered site west of Moses Point, the small, cream-colored dog became depressed and worried. Darkness was crowding the last faint light from the sky when at last we spotted a scattering of trees to protect us from the wind. Miki skied ahead to guide the dogs off the trail. "We're going to camp, you guys," she called.

A small shock jolted Sky's slim frame. He began quivering. He bounded forward, whining eagerly as he lunged through the drifts. Once loose in camp, the normally quiet dog exploded in a frenzied dance, racing crazily through the other dogs, slamming against my knees, careening and squalling with undignified and uncharacteristic abandon.

"He thought we were running straight through to Nome," Miki laughed. "Isn't he glad to camp!" The race teams rarely stopped for long on the last third of the race, and our aging leader appreciated the relaxed pace we were taking instead.

The trail now twisted through rough ice near Elim, where the wind had broken up thick blue-gray pans of sea ice and pounded them against black rocky bluffs. There the ice refroze in jumbled, tangled blocks set at every angle. After ricocheting from block to block for several miles, we finally left the sea, climbed a steep portage, and dropped back down to Golovin Bay where the ice, protected from waves, had frozen smooth and glassy enough to cast a reflection. A gusty wind whipped across the glazed surface, frequently knocking the dogs off balance. Most developed minor strains as their feet skidded on the slippery surface, but all recovered except the new dog, Tigger. He wasn't toughened yet and when his lameness didn't heal, we sold him rather than push him on.

Only a few dogs showed signs of wear. Comet and Streak worked hardest, but the two good-natured malamute crosses were tough and only their threadbare feet reflected the miles behind them. Powerful Legs, once our main leader, had been plagued with bad feet and on smooth stretches he rode in the sled to rest his cracked, swollen toes. (Later a veterinarian diagnosed a hormone deficiency which, when corrected, restored his feet.) Sky now filled in for Legs, and though he lacked the white dog's strength and drive, he took his responsibility more seriously. Our other dogs, Casey, Rusty, Amber, and Raven, all performed cheerfully, thriving on this new adventure. In fact, Rusty and Casey bred while on the Yukon, and their long-planned litter produced Reuben, a large, beautiful black dog who became a wonderful friend and lead dog.

In the next couple days we passed the hillside village of White Mountain and toiled over rolling, treeless hills that led to one last, long climb up a dome called Topkok Mountain. Iditarod racers tell horror stories about this high, treeless bluff above the sea, but with fair weather our stout work dogs, not worn down by racing, powered us effortlessly to the top.

Descending the far side was another matter. Sand, snow, sea ice, and glassy lagoons stretched out below us, but to reach it we had to bump down a steep slope of ice and gravel. Repeatedly the *Hesperus* lurched and skidded forward, only to grind roughly to a halt on bare ground. *("She shuddered and paused, like a frighted steed, then leaped her cable's length,"* wrote Longfellow, describing the ship bearing down on the reef of Norman's woe.) The jerking jolts threw me roughly forward against the handlebow, then backward to collide with Miki as she shot uncontrollably across patches of ice. Finally Miki grabbed my shoulders instead of her tow rope, wedging her skis against the sled as we rumbled to the bottom.

Crashing down the final slope, we found ourselves on a sandy beach cut by thin lagoons and heaped with rakish piles of gnarled driftwood, cast ashore by the wind and tide after floating to the sea from the tree-covered depths of Alaska's interior. With the wind rising and evening approaching, we watched for some shelter where we could camp. Miki's skis clattered over the ice and rattled as she ran across sand and scrambled deftly over heaps of sea-washed wood. Sometimes she'd fall and get mad, and shout at me to go on until I found some snow or ice or *anything* made for skis. Then she walked, carrying her short, broad skis over one shoulder, until she caught up to me waiting on a thin patch of snow. Near the end of a long day, we became tired, discouraged, windblown, and worried. The barren beaches offered no windbreaks for a comfortable camp, and the clear blue sky shifted to pink, then gray as the sun sank down.

Suddenly, a little yellow cabin hove into sight, perched between long strings of weathered driftwood and empty grass beaches. We later learned this was the Pine Creek shelter cabin, a refuge for locals and travelers alike. The local terrain formed a wind tunnel where gales raged even when nearby villages were calm, and the treeless tundra offered no refuge beyond this tiny plywood shack, open to anyone but identified by a little sign as belonging to Tom and Myrtle Johnson.

Inside, we found bunks, a stove, and a table. Graffiti patterned the unfinished plywood walls, telling of past visitors. The messages spoke of furious storms and angry bears, of local travelers and adventuring expeditioners.

"Caught in fog, blowing snow . . ."

"Had to spend the night on the count of 3 hungry bears . . ."

"On route to reindeer camp with loyal dogs Jess, Shanka & Sheea, accompanied by tireless Icelandic horses . . ."

Run that by me again?

Miki read the note twice. "I never heard of Icelandic horses. Gosh . . . I bet they're adapted to cold weather. They must be if they're from Iceland."

"I had no idea there were horses out here," I said, my interest sparked. "Sounds like a good idea, using them to herd reindeer."

Writing covered every wall, but we found a tiny spot for our own short note.

We've camped out in the snow
We've camped out on the ice
But when the wind is blowing
A cabin sure is nice!

The wind quieted by morning, and just a few hours later we stopped our team on the rough, drifted sea ice below Nome. Miki sat with the dogs while I scouted through the cluster of weathered buildings of downtown Nome, searching for the American flag that marked the post office with our dog food. I saw not one flag but several, and by the time I recovered the first sack of feed, Robbie Roberts had spotted our dogs and walked down to visit. "I saw those two big black wheel dogs and knew it was you guys," he said. (Comet and Streak were the trademark of our team for many years.)

Robbie was rooming in an apartment on Front Street that overlooked the Bering Sea. His Iditarod volunteer hosts, Ralph and Bobbie Combs, soon installed us in the vacant apartment next door. Then Robbie loaned us his visiting friend, George Rae, to fetch the rest of our feed with his truck. The dogs had three luxurious days off while we shopped and geared up for the next stage of our journey, which would take us back to Koyuk, then north across the neck of the Seward Peninsula and up the Kobuk River to Shungnak and the old cabin where our father lived forty years ago. Robbie left town shortly before we did, vowing to hang the X-rays of his race injuries in his Ophir cabin as a reminder never to race again. (He did race again, several times.)

We left Nome with some trepidation, for many uncertainties lay ahead. Some trails might not be open, or our supplies might not reach the pick-up points. An early spring could make travel slow and rivers dangerous. Knowing the stormy nature of the coast, we worried about bad weather which could obliterate trails in this barren country. Also, with the sled tarp our only shelter, we were uneasy about weathering the blizzards that sometimes screamed through. A north wind whipped up our worries the first night out, at Pine Creek, and the next day as we climbed Topkok. Nearing the mountain's crest, we looked back and saw not a frozen sea, but dazzling open water. In four days the offshore wind had broken loose the ice and driven it out to sea. Crystal blue waves, beaten frothy by the whipping wind, stretched out toward Siberia, the deep, rich water contrasting sharply with jagged white beaches. Not a trace of the ice pack remained.

"*That's* why we shouldn't have gone out on the ice by Shaktoolik," Miki told me.

That night we slept in the community center at White Mountain, and the next night in a shelter cabin beyond Golovin. "It's taken a long time, but I think we're finally getting the idea," Miki panted as she leaned lethargically against the bare cabin wall.

I lay sprawled on a bunk, gasping as the blasting wood furnace sent the room temperature above 100°. "You mean these shelter cabins? They sure beat camping out!"

We had known about shelter cabins before, but rarely bothered to investigate them. During the three-week trip from Nenana to Nome, we had camped out all but six days. After the comfort of the Pine Creek cabin, though, we started inquiring about these scattered shacks — where they were, if they were open for general use, and if firewood was available nearby. In the wooded Interior, shelter cabins would have cramped our schedule, but on the exposed coast we used them for safety as well as comfort. With the cabins twenty-five to thirty-five miles apart, they shortened our daily runs, but the slower pace made a pleasant change for the dogs. The late March days were still cool, and though we had roughly 850 miles to go, keeping the dogs happy concerned us more than beating out the approaching spring melt. We found most cabins empty, so imposing on other people wasn't the worry it could be if we stayed in villages.

"No more sleeping in the dog sled if I can help it," I said.

"No more crying over smoky campfires," Miki agreed, red-faced with heat as she sank, incapacitated, to the floor.

"Our powdered milk won't blow away before we can mix it up."

"Our tongues won't stick to the spoons on thirty-below mornings."

"No more evening prayers — 'Good night, sleep tight, don't freeze your nose tonight,'" I concluded.

From the McKinley River shelter cabin near Golovin we hopped over to another cabin east of Moses Point, and the next day we pulled into Koyuk and climbed the icy hill to our food cache above the runway. Packing the heavy load into the *Hesperus,* we started back down toward town and the trail north to Dime Landing, Haycock, and Buckland. For extra control on the steep, slick slope, we roughlocked the sled runners with wraps of chain. A side road cutting straight down the hill would spare us the intricate detour through town. With both of us standing on the runners we figured we could take that icy shortcut.

"Haw, Sky," I ordered.

The little dog glanced down the steep grade. Then he looked back at us. *You gotta be kidding.*

"HAW, Sky," I ordered.

With another doubtful glance over his shoulder, Sky obediently led the team over the drop-off. The sled whipped after them and the dogs broke into a lope as gravity took control. Gaining speed, the *Hesperus* roared downhill like a freight train. The road was steeper than it looked, and slicker, and rounded in the center so we began sliding sideways toward a ten-foot shoulder on the right. The chains lost their effectiveness in the skid, and we lost control.

"Oh — my goodness — oh — my!" I sputtered. The team would not stop. The sled could not stop.

"Ho-oly — moly — " Miki began.

The sled shot sideways over the embankment, still gaining speed and momentum.

The right runner grabbed the ground, and the sled with its 200-pound load flipped into the air. I catapulted from the left runner over Miki and crashed into the brush. The *Hesperus* rolled, shooting Miki off to land on top of me, and rolled again to crush us both. It dragged the nine dogs tumbling into the ditch, and we all landed in a broken, tangled heap.

The frame of my eyeglasses snapped and I knew I'd have a black eye, but that didn't matter. One glance told us the *Hesperus* was wrecked. Like Longfellow's schooner, she had met her reef of Norman's woe.

CHAPTER 3

THE
HESPERUS
SAILS AGAIN

"That's it," I said.

Miki and I stared in disbelief at our shattered sled in that Koyuk ditch. Between the broken stanchions, dislocated handlebow, and splintered false runner, the *Hesperus* was completely incapacitated. "We're dead," I said.

"Oh, nonsense," Miki laughed. "We're lucky it happened in town. Go down to the store and buy string, nails, wire, and hundred-mile-an-hour tape. I'll start chopping some splints."

I purchased the duct tape and other goods, and for two hours we slaved over the *Hesperus* in that ditch, the cold wind lending a bitter chill to the already sub-zero air. After nailing together the false runner and splinting broken boards with the trunk of a willow tree, we stood back to examine the wretched craft. "It'll never reach Bettles this way," I predicted.

We left Koyuk gloomily, but heading north into new and beautiful country we soon felt heartened again. Limping through the old mining camps of Dime Landing and Haycock, our big ship "drifted a dreary wreck." Two days later we stopped over in the cozy, cramped Bear Creek shelter cabin, where I overhauled the crippled sled. Miki chopped better splints from a sturdy spruce tree, shaping a stout headboard as I lashed, spliced, and struggled. After repairing and strengthening the sled, I etched a tiny mermaid and imprinted "The Hesperus" on the new headboard. The sled had truly earned its name after that baptism by fire — or

Julie

37

rather ice. When we struck out again the craft felt tight and strong, gliding smartly around corners instead of making its previous sloppy turns.

"The *Hesperus* sails again!" Miki crowed gleefully.

I was more skeptical. "It's got about 300 miles left on the back and 600 miles on the front before it spontaneously disintegrates," I predicted. Our convoluted route to Bettles meant over 500 miles more sledding, so we'd learn the accuracy of my estimation.

Crossing the wide, treeless, gentle hills of the eastern Seward Peninsula, we bucked wind and cold and great white expanses of country so blank it seemed that someone had prepared a canvas for painting and then forgotten to add any details. A frozen wind blew us into Selawik, where we learned our dog food would not arrive because St. Augustine, a volcano 500 miles south, had erupted. Blowing ash had shut down all flights out of Anchorage, including the one with our freight. Our scanty supply would have to stretch two more days.

We spent the night with Selawik elders Art and Lenore Skin, who invited these two grateful strangers to share their home and a birthday cake. In the morning, tiny, frail Lenore stuffed us with a robust breakfast of kidney-shaped "Eskimo pancakes," eggs, bacon, cereal, and leftover cake. She told us to hurry over the pass to the Kobuk River: "It's always warmer over there."

"*Quianna*," we said shyly. "Thank you."

Climbing out of Selawik's blowing snow into the stunted spruce below the Waring Mountains, we crossed through the narrow pass into a world of sturdy forests, shapely mountains, and the clean white curves of the frozen Kobuk River, an oasis in the north after the stark plains of the Seward Peninsula. Reaching the Kobuk felt like coming home. After a side trip to Kiana to pick up food and visit old family friends, we eagerly started up the pristine river, gazing with delight as each graceful bend unfolded new beauty. Unlike the sprawling, swamp-infested rivers and sloughs that we were accustomed to in the Interior, the Kobuk lay in a narrow valley with healthy evergreens marching sternly along the riverbanks below gentle white slopes rising to the sharp mountains. On this and previous expeditions we had explored much of the tangled flatlands of the Tanana River, the Kuskokwim, the Koyukuk, and the Yukon; later we would visit the ramparts of the upper Yukon and the

Porcupine, the rugged Fortymile, the lovely Blackstone, and the spectacular North Fork of the Klondike, but none enchanted us as did the Kobuk. Maybe we felt we had roots there, with childhood memories of vacations boating on the river, fishing for grayling, picking blueberries, visiting Eskimo friends, and staying in the old three-room cabin where our father lived years before we were born. Whatever the reason, every moment spent on the river filled us with pleasure.

We camped that first evening in a little gully, anticipating a warm night simply because we were on the Kobuk River, and it doesn't get cold in Paradise. In the morning, Miki prodded me awake. "Get up! I'm cold. It's thirty-eight below."

"It's the fourth of April," I protested, but the thermometer did not lie. By the time we reached Ambler two days later, the temperature had dipped to forty-one below. At the small village we stopped overnight with Keith and Anore Jones, who knew our parents back in the 1960s. We prepared for an early start in the morning, intending to reach Shungnak in time to visit friends before going up to Daddy's old cabin. Miki and I were standing at the door giving our goodbyes and promise-to-write speeches when Anore dropped the bombshell.

"Did you see the Icelandic ponies on the Seward Peninsula?" she asked innocently.

"No, but we read about them on the wall of a shelter cabin," I told her.

"They're really neat! More like overgrown dogs than horses. When they got scared they ran into a dog yard for protection, and during one thunderstorm they tried to push into a tent with the reindeer herders!"

"Horses just aren't feasible for us," we told her sadly. "We couldn't possibly feed them, and the swamps . . ."

"Oh, they just run faster to cross soft ground, and they eat any-thing," Anore assured us. "They dig through snow for grass, and browse on twigs like moose, and even munch up dried salmon!"

"How big are they? Can you ride them?"

"Oh, yes. They're almost as tall as a regular horse, and very easy to ride. The Eskimos even took them out on the sea ice. They scrambled right over pressure ridges, and the only time they had any trouble was when two feet fell into a crack in the ice."

Poor Anore! She never dreamed what she did to us. We were an hour late leaving Ambler, and we spent the entire five-hour run to Shungnak speculating about the marvelous little horses she had raved about. What if we got some? Not seriously, of course — it was out of the question — but what if? We could ride to the cranberry patches and the fish net. After the lake froze, we could ride across to the post office to meet the weekly mail plane, and haul freight home in a cute little sleigh!

Mushing into Shungnak, we parked the dogs to visit another good friend, Edna Commack. After meeting her grandchildren and enjoying a hearty lunch of succulent caribou meat stewed with noodles, we offered Edna a ride to the edge of town. She perched giggling atop the gear heaped in the sled as the dogs surged along streets of packed snow.

We swooped down a bank above the Kobuk River and hit a sharp corner at the bottom. The *Hesperus* snapped sideways, skidded, and flipped, sending Edna sailing off and rolling down the icy street. Horrified, I rushed to help the little grandma to her feet, but Edna never stopped laughing. It had been years since she'd been on a dog sled, but she hadn't forgotten how much fun it could be.

Our brother Ray and his tall friend Matt Jones flew out to Shungnak with our next resupply, and we all spent a pleasant four days there. Ray and Matt discussed saving Daddy's old cabin from falling off the high undercut bank into the river by dismantling it and moving the parts to higher ground.

"If we had some Icelandic ponies, we could haul the logs with them," Miki sighed.

"We could freight all the building materials and horse food and dog food up the river in a horse-drawn bobsled," I added.

"We could ride them here from Bettles, up the Alatna, and over the pass — "

"Or barge them to Huslia and ride over the pass by Selawik Hot Springs," I broke in.

Matt laughed. "Sounds like somebody wants some ponies," he teased.

When at last we said farewell to the beautiful Kobuk, we started south for the woods of Huslia before turning east towards Bettles. Immediately the heavily loaded *Hesperus* rolled down a snowbank and broke two stanchions in the back end. As I had predicted, the rear-end repairs had only lasted 300 miles. By now we seemed so close to home that we simply laughed and lashed the pieces together. With driftwood railings from Shaktoolik, a willow splint from Koyuk, and a spruce headboard from Bear Creek, the *Hesperus* had picked up more souvenirs than we had.

Albert Commack of Shungnak was heading up to Selawik Hot Springs, and we fell in behind his snowmachine, climbing grassy hills with patchy bare tundra and ice. A fierce wind buffeted the team as gentle slopes led us toward the low pass dividing the Kobuk from the Koyukuk, tundra from woodland, Inupiaq from Athabascan.

Behind me, Miki struggled to stay upright as grass snagged her worn skis and ice sent her

Our friend Edna Commack and her granddaughter posed for us at Shungnak.

skittering out of control. One great gust of wind shoved her clattering sideways across grass-embedded ice and then a malicious willow grabbed her ski. The tow rope jerked her forward and she flew into the air, crashing down on one knee with a dreadful shriek. She rolled over on the ground, contorting around the knee as I hit the sled brake.

"Whoa," I shouted, but the dogs, trying to catch up with Albert, didn't stop.

"Whoa! WHOA! I said STOP!" I shouted. Finally the sled skidded off the ice and grated to a halt. I anchored the team with my snow hook and raced back to Miki. "You all right?"

"Yes!" she screamed, not pausing to consider whether she really was. I could see by her face that she wasn't.

Her knee still worked, however painfully. There was nothing to do but mush on, Miki skiing determinedly, unwilling to stop. By evening the knee was swollen and stiff, and she appreciated two long soaks at the hot springs camp maintained by a rare joint Indian-Eskimo effort.

The next day we chased small bands of caribou through the
hills as the trail gradually descended toward the forested Interior. I
rolled the sled and broke another stanchion, but we pressed on. We
found the Interior much warmer, with melting snow, and our race
against spring grew earnest. Breezing through Huslia and Hughes,
we stopped only long enough to learn that our dog food had not
arrived in either place. Bill Williams in Hughes saved us with beaver meat, which tided the dogs through to a food shipment at
Allakaket.

The forest felt good after living on the open tundra so long. We
had grown up in country like the woodlands of the Koyukuk, where
the trees provided shelter from the wind and fuel for our fires. While
the wide horizons of the coast inspired us with their grand vistas,
we felt like aliens there. We didn't know the land or the weather,
and the Eskimos seemed more reserved than the Indians we were
familiar with. We couldn't pass through an Athabaskan village without being recognized, while the Eskimos, if they knew us through
our writing, were usually too polite to say so. North country hospi-
tality knew no boundaries, however; we found it widespread and
generous regardless of the region.

From Allakaket, we hopped over to Bettles, arriving at the home
of the Ketchers, outfitters and fellow dog mushers, early on a Thurs-
day morning. Miki wanted her injured knee x-rayed before the
weekend and anxiously she phoned our brother for a ride, but hung
up disappointed.

"Surprise! He can't come today."

We settled down to wait, only to learn of an early-morning flight
from Bettles to Fairbanks. Suddenly I decided to fly to Fairbanks
and drive the pickup out myself. Before meeting the plane I helped
Miki run the dogs through town to the cut-off to the thirty-six-mile
trail leading to the Dalton Highway, or Haul Road as it is known
locally. "I should meet you on the highway about six tonight," I
told her.

But between a delayed flight, a slow taxi, and a missing truck —
Ray had taken it downtown to gas it up for the drive north — I
didn't even leave Fairbanks until 6 P.M. The rocky, twisted road
discouraged breakneck speeds, especially with massive semi rigs bellowing down from Prudhoe Bay every few minutes. Whether I ran
into them or they ran into me, it would have been bad for me, so I

drove cautiously, stopping only once to loan a lug wrench to some chaps from Minto. Waiting as they changed a flat tire, I smirked to think I had all the equipment to handle that problem — a jack, wrench, and spare tire.

Cruising northward again, I drove through the dusk of the April night, finally pulling up at the Bettles cut-off past ten o'clock. Miki's tanned face beamed with relief as she walked around to my door. "What took you?" she demanded. "And you've got a flat tire."

"Great."

A couple of handsome young men would have been handy just then, but none were forthcoming so we knuckled down and changed the tire ourselves. Easing the truck off the jack, I looked at the spare tire. It was flat.

That was the start of a long night. By pure luck, this 600-mile wilderness highway had a road maintenance camp just two miles away. I trotted down there and found an obliging gentleman who repaired both flat tires, despite the late hour, and threw in some apples to boot.

In the thickening darkness, we started south. Half an hour later, we had another flat. (Someone later told us that flats are common during the spring when the snow melts back to expose metal flotsam along the road.) Sighing, we changed the tire in the darkness and plugged on with our load of dogs in their boxes, the *Hesperus* piercing the wind with its prow from atop the truck. Just as we crested a long, white hill of endless snowdrifts, we heard a familiar sound.

Poo! Blat-blat-blat! This time the whole tire flew off the rim.

"That's it!" I said. "We're dead." After two months of wilderness travel, improvising solutions for all problems large and small, we were now stuck, sixty miles from the nearest truck stop, with no options. "This is why we have dogs," Miki said. "If it was a broken dog or a broken sled, we could fix it."

The wind billowed around our truck, rocking the vehicle as we sat in the dark cab. We expected a big rig any moment, but the minutes ticked to hours and still the road stretched out mysteriously deserted. At last our luck changed at first light. As dawn blushed faintly in the east, a semi crested the ridge behind us, bearing down fast. I leaped in front of our crippled truck and boldly stuck out my thumb. I had never hitchhiked before and was astonished when the massive vehicle wheezed to a stop. "We just had our fourth flat tire," I told the driver.

"I can't pick you up," the driver said. "Rules. Insurance, you know. Get in."

"Thanks." I scrambled up to an expansive seat in the warm cab.

"We don't leave anyone on the highway out here," the driver explained. "I can't take you all the way to Fairbanks, but I'll drop off you and the tire at the truck stop on the Yukon River." He shifted gears and we flew down the roller-coaster road at alarming speeds. We talked about fools hens, Manley Hot Springs, and dog sledding, and consoled each other by confessing we had each been traveling for eighteen hours straight. He dropped me off at the truck stop and sped on his way. I had the tire fixed and hitched a ride back to Miki, and we were underway again. After a second stop at the Yukon to eat breakfast and have the other spare tire repaired, we coasted into Fairbanks, weary from the long night.

A visit to the doctor revealed that Miki had a cracked kneecap — nothing to keep her down. Three days later we drove to Nenana and hit the trail for home with our main dog team plus two yearling pups and old Loki, our retired leader, that Ray had cared for in Fairbanks. With spring well advanced, we had flown the route home to check trail conditions before deciding to give it a try. Much of the snow had melted. The rivers, stirring after their winter's sleep, yawned with gaping holes. The last stretch of trail hadn't even been broken out that winter. Yet we'd come so far that the last 130 miles didn't seem like much. If we couldn't muddle through, we could always turn around.

On April 24 we left Nenana, sledding on bare ground along a lowland route instead of backtracking through the more treacherous mountains. A few miles out the trail improved to a thin wedge of icy snow snaking across the bare tundra and still-frozen swamps. Using a gee pole, Miki held the sled on the narrow, sloping line of snow. We spent most of the afternoon touring a maze of local trails made by beaver trappers, before finally locating the right one and moving out.

"Gosh, it's good to be on the trail again!" Miki exclaimed when we camped during the hottest part of the day. After a three-day rest in Fairbanks, we were both suffering from withdrawal. It's a terrible addiction, this dog mushing!

Breakup was well under way on the last leg of our journey, but the dogs knew they were almost home and not even obstacles like this spruce-pole bridge could slow them down.

Because of soaring afternoon temperatures, we traveled mostly at night when the mushy trail froze up and the dogs worked better. Sledding through the short April nights, we tiptoed across log bridges, waded through overflow, and raced against breakup to get home. With just fifty miles to go, we entered the trapping domain of the ambitious Duyck family, and lost ourselves on their wide-ranging loops of beaver-trapping trails that petered out at various beaver ponds. After circling, backtracking, and reconnoitering, we gave up. The main trail didn't go much farther, anyway, so we decided to cut across country.

Bad mistake.

First we tried to go south to an old tractor trail. Impenetrable thickets of birch saplings, willows, and alders laced their skeletal fingers to block our way. We tried to follow a creek and almost fell through the rotten ice. To the north, a river ran our way and we slogged across open tundra and slush to reach it. The ice wasn't safe this late in the spring but timidly, and then with growing determination, we started upriver. My rubber boots leaked, and for miles I waded through freezing overflow, feet numb with cold as ice water pumped in and out at every step. Gaping holes in the river ice stretched black and treacherous, ready to swallow a person or an entire dog team. A year later this stretch of river actually did gulp down an intrepid traveler. He shucked off his backpack, bumped his way downstream under the ice, and crawled out another hole. Finding himself still healthy, he climbed back into the original hole and drifted downstream a second time to retrieve his pack!

But he was lucky. The strong current could spell disaster if we weren't careful. We steered wide of all but the last hole, which we had to cut past to intersect the nearby Cat tractor trail. As Miki walked ahead to examine the long hole, she spied an otter reveling in the open water. Noticing Miki, he stretched his head above the surface, staring curiously and hissing in his queer otter way, before bobbing off with the current.

Miki didn't like that hole. In some places if we fell in, we'd hit underlying ice. In other places, Miki's long pole stabbed through snow into swiftly flowing water that yanked her stick downstream before it hit bottom. She scouted out a safe route and tiptoed across, pulling the loose pups along. We all sighed with relief when the team hauled the sled ashore. From here we knew we could find the Cat trail and follow it to a creek near our trapline.

A trapping cabin, owned by our neighbor Jonathon Blackburn, stood back in the trees and we paused there to warm up. Handfuls of dried grass stuffed in my boots helped warm my wet feet as we slogged down melting trails and across more open tundra. Then we crossed one last river to intersect the creek that flowed down from our Birch Cabin.

Recognizing their old stomping ground, the dogs surged forward. Eighteen miles of firm overflow ice made a solid trail to follow, and that night we made a pleasant camp on the dry, bare bank under sheltering spruce trees. The dogs lounged on crispy leaves and we barefooted around camp as our wet socks dried.

"Traveling in the cold has some advantages, but in spite of being wet all the time it sure is fun when it warms enough to camp without bundling up," I mused.

We did not stop at the Birch Cabin. "Sorry, boys," I said, but the dogs didn't care. They knew home lay ahead. After five long, wet days with no food left, we were all ready to dry our toes for good.

Miki and I knew this trail intimately. When we ran into knee-deep water and ice, we cut inland to intersect an old overgrown parallel trail. When we encountered a second, larger flood, we crossed a willow flat to hit a slough that led us to the Old Channel five miles from home. Miki, slogging through water and willows ahead of the dogs, stopped on the riverbank. The team crowded up and stopped. I walked up. We all stood together and looked at the river.

Miki walked ahead of the dogs to guide them home across miles of mud flats, while migrating geese and swans flew overhead.

Thick brown runoff water churned from bank to bank. There had to be ice under that flood, but how much? And would it have holes? And how deep was the water under that ice? We knew this country, and we knew we had to cross this powerful flood. I tied the loose pups to the sled to be sure they followed us. Miki looped a rope through Sky's tugline. "Ready?" she asked.

I nodded grimly. "Whatever happens, don't let go of that rope!"

"And don't *you* let go of that sled!"

Miki plunged into the water, dragging Sky and the team in as the muddy bank fell away. The dogs scrambled along readily, knowing they had to cross to reach home, and the *Hesperus* obediently plowed in behind them. Water gushed into my boots, first through the leaks and then over the tops as the water rose to my hips. Concentrating on controlling the sled and my footing on the icy, irregular bottom, I didn't notice the cold. I was prepared to swim if I had to. The sled, lightly loaded with sleeping bags and trail gear, floated up and swept downstream as I steadied it.

*"It was the schooner Hesperus, that sailed the wintry sea
..."* Our *Hesperus* did not sail, but at least it floated, which is better than Longfellow's ship did. And the reef of Norman's woe in
Koyuk had not proved so deadly as the one in the poem. Buffeting
across the river, we reached the far side and climbed ashore, laughing with relief as we helped the dogs heave the dripping sled up the
silty bank.

"Five miles," I said, stomping around as water squirted from
the holes in my boots.

"You'd better patent those boots," Miki told me.

"Why?"

"They're self-draining!" she laughed.

We had five miles to go, the last five miles of almost two thousand. Two miles of wading through sodden, overgrown marshes
along the flooded river. Two miles of wading down a flooded slough.
And one mile of slopping across ankle-deep mud along the bay. The
final creek crossing had flooded and refrozen. Miki, who could not
ski through mud, had been walking ahead of the dogs but now she
took the sled while I followed to help the young dogs on the ice.
Blue-eyed Sky tiptoed onto the glassy surface, followed by gangly
Rusty. As the team dogs started out, the ice suddenly broke.

The dogs were swimming and floundering. Sky, with his light
build, scrambled to stay ahead of the crumbling ice. Rusty fell in,
and Sky pulled him out. "Hike!" Miki roared. "Hike, Sky! Hike!"
More dogs fell in, then the sled. It floated up and began to roll. Legs,
riding in the basket to spare his tender feet, struggled to stay above
water. Rusty broke through again. Sky pulled him out.

"Help me, help me!" Miki shrieked. If the sled rolled, Legs would
be trapped underwater, but with the handlebow floating up near
Miki's shoulders she had no leverage to steady it. I pushed forward,
helping the struggling pups through waist-deep water, but I couldn't
catch up with the sled.

Half the dogs were swimming while the taller ones clawed at the
ice under the water. Somehow Miki held the sled upright and Sky kept
the team moving. He reached the shore and dragged Rusty out one last
time. Rusty dragged the team out, and they dragged the sled out. I
splashed ashore, pushing the pups through shards of floating ice.

We slopped across the last mile of mud and grass and slush and
ice. The fresh air smelled rich and sweet, alive with the wet scents

of spring. Migrating geese, ducks, cranes, and swans erupted from the mud flats, rising to swirl overhead, loudly protesting our intrusion. Then, at last, the dogs climbed the bank to our home. The lawn lay bare and brown, the dog yard dry and vacant. Winter was over. In fact, breakup was nearly over. Our trip, 1,900 miles in all, ended on April 26. Miki hurled her skis under the eaves and rubbed her still-sore knee. "Boy, I'm glad it's spring!"

The dogs lounged on their houses, licking mud and water from their fur as smoke from the dog food cooker boiled up. Muddy harnesses hung drying in the sun along with wet boots, socks, and sleeping bags. Across the bay, ducks and geese settled back down in the swamp grass, muttering quietly about the disturbance.

We sat with the dogs on their houses, unable to break the close bond of the last two and a half months. We talked about the trip. We talked about where to go next: the Kuskokwim Delta, perhaps, or the Porcupine River. Then we began talking about Icelandic horses. And we couldn't stop. We became obsessed. What if — seriously, what if?

"This is crazy," I said at last. "We know it would be a mistake to bring horses out here, no matter how bad we want them. It's simply insane. What we have to do is tell Marmee. She'll see what a stupid idea it is, and put a stop to this nonsense for us."

Later we called our mother into our bedroom. She sat on Miki's bed, listening to us rave about these incredible little horses that could cross bogs and eat twigs. "And they sound so sturdy and easy to keep that we're thinking about getting some," I finished. Then we waited for an incredulous laugh, a loud protest, the voice of reason.

But Marmee didn't laugh or look shocked. She didn't protest. She didn't say anything. She just sat there with a funny look on her face.

One month later we were on our way to the Icelandic Horse Farm in Canada.

We take precautions to protect our horses against accidents or injuries. Here Julie checks Lilja's hooves before a ride.

CHAPTER 4
HORSES AND HUSKIES

Actually, the decision to get horses came neither simply nor easily. Being deeply entrenched in our bush way of life, Julie and I tend to resist change. Buying horses offered plenty of potential for that. To us the big animals were a dream and a mystery. We didn't know how — or if — they might fit in. We did know they would change our lives, which until now had been stable and comfortable, though far from monotonous.

Growing up in a vast, roadless chunk of Alaska north of Denali, we spent our childhood in a community of roughly thirty people scattered around the shores of a large lake. The village was served by one telephone and a weekly mail plane, but had no school. First living in Federal Aviation Administration housing near the runway, we later moved to a cabin Marmee and Daddy built six miles away. Our only companions were an older brother, Ray, an inevitable pet dog, and whatever wild critters, playthings, or imaginary characters we had on hand.

With an endless "front yard" of mud flats, glacial streams, swamps, and lowland spruce, outdoor adventure early became a way of life. After seven years of correspondence home schooling, we spent nine unhappy winters in Fairbanks attending high school and college, but the Bush has always been home. Even after graduating from the University of Alaska with degrees in biology and journalism, we rushed back to our roots to pick up where we had left off. Instead of applying our book-learning

Miki

to nine-to-five jobs, we put to work the skills we'd learned as children: trapping, hunting, gardening, berry-picking, sewing furs, and fishing with gill nets.

In some ways Julie and I never grew up. We still live in the same two-story log cabin with our folks, although we are all home together only intermittently. Neither of us ever cared to accept the drastic changes marriage would bring. Before we got horses, only the needs of our sled dogs (and sometimes our lack of funds) tied us down, and wherever we wanted to go the dogs came along as our transportation. This gave us tremendous freedom to roam, whether around Alaska, into Canada, or simply throughout our vast 800-square-mile "front yard."

By using all our resources, and by working day in, day out, we scratch out a living from fur trapping, making and selling handcrafts, and on-and-off writing and photography. (I am always amused by people wanting to move to the country so they'll have time to enjoy nature. While we deeply appreciate our wilderness, we usually lack the time to pause and enjoy its beauty.) When fur prices soar or animal populations boom, we make a good living, at least by our standards. We don't need much money: our parents provide us with room and board, while we supply them with moose meat, garden vegetables, and berries, putting up enough for year-round use. Because we've never been overly concerned with appearances, clothing expenditures are minimal. That leaves the upkeep of our ten to fifteen sled dogs, our biggest single expense, and part of that is offset by catching fish to feed them.

Since trapping provides the bulk of our income, from November until mid- or late February catching furs is all-important. Our family inherited a vast trapping area from Slim Carlson, an old Swede who had trapped the land since about 1918 until a few years before his death in 1975 at the age of eighty-nine. People told us we couldn't make a living off a trapline — not a couple of girls in an increasingly modern era. But we proved them wrong. Of the 130 miles of trails reclaimed from Slim's old, overgrown lines, we trap fifty to ninety miles each year, rotating areas to ensure healthy animal populations.

Before buying horses, we often traveled together, each day mushing from one cabin to another, checking traps as we went. Other times we split up to cover more ground. Our parents took care of the house, and when they left on vacation we let the place freeze as our trapline journeys took us away from home for up to two weeks at a stretch.

How could we manage if we had horses to care for? We knew horses couldn't travel the winter trails with the speed and efficiency of a dog team, and how could one of us manage the entire trapline while the other stayed home to horse-sit? Could we afford to feed them all winter and give them the best of care? We had been mushing sled dogs for twelve years and had a good feel for animal husbandry, but that didn't mean we could handle horses. Then, too, our work kept us so busy, would we even have *time* for horses?

"If we get horses, we'll spend so much time just earning money for their feed, we won't ever have time to *ride* 'em!" I complained.

"We'll just have to get more efficient," Julie countered. "We can use the motorboat more often, instead of the canoe, and use a chain saw instead of cutting wood by hand."

I didn't like that idea. I hate the sound and smell of a chain saw, and I hate packing it around in the dog sled with all its gas and oil and parts and tools. Besides, I couldn't fix the darn thing when it broke, which it *always* did. (Julie has since become a little more adept at repairs.) Still, we did spend a tremendous amount of time each year cutting eight to ten cords of stove wood with a bow saw.

Horses . . . one of the few childhood dreams we'd completely given up. Now we had a chance to rekindle that dream, make it a reality. Besides, if things didn't work out, we could always sell them again, right?

In the end, insanity prevailed. We'd just have to overcome inevitable problems as they arose.

So, scarcely a month after the triumphant if soggy end of our grand dog sled expedition, we drove 1,800 miles from Fairbanks to the Icelandic Horse Farm in Edmonton, Alberta, the closest place which sold the rare little horses. There we learned more about the breed.

Although not well known in North America, Icelandic horses enjoy great popularity in Europe, and most of the Canadian stock descended from animals imported from Iceland and other parts of Europe just one or two generations back. The horses arrived in Iceland centuries ago in the open vessels of Viking settlers. Around 1,000 A.D. Icelanders banned the importation of any more livestock to prevent the spread of disease, effectively isolating the breed and keeping it very pure.

The subarctic region proved so harsh that only those animals highly adapted to cold climates and scarce forage endured. Ashfall from periodic volcanic eruptions wiped out vast areas of grassland, causing countless horses to starve. Only the toughest ones, able to survive on small amounts of coarse feed, and those trusting enough to turn to humans for help, lived through such disasters. Instead of predators, which do not inhabit the isolated island, the horses had to deal with quicksand, turbulent rivers, jagged lava rocks, and deep bogs. Instead of the typical equine tendency to spook and run from danger, the Icelandic horses developed an instinct for carefully sizing up hazardous situations to determine the best approach. Over centuries in the subarctic, they adapted to life in the cold climate by developing long, dense manes, extremely thick winter coats, compact bodies, and short legs. Like Julie and me, they are short, stout, and built to last.

Although the farm we visited supported several dozen horses, the owner, a cheery lady with the unusual name of Robyn Hood, kept most for breeding and show. She could only offer three which matched our level of ignorance. Mosi, a gray gelding, proved to be chubby, unattractive, and poky. Lilja, a palomino pinto mare with a young colt at her side, looked slight and unattractive with pink-rimmed eyes, a pink nose, and a skinny neck.

The third horse was Katla. Although her dusky-black coat was dull and unkempt, I wanted her as soon as I touched her and looked into her glowing dark eyes. And she wanted someone of her own, too, instead of being just another horse in a big herd. She also proved to be the best riding horse, with a swift, easy "tolt," the running walk or smooth gait that made the breed famous.

Three days of riding lessons and general assistance from Robyn, her husband, Phil Pretty, and their helpful trainer, Christine Schwartz, convinced us to buy the two mares, plus the young foal, Bjarmi. We purchased a rickety second-hand horse trailer, made out an enormous check to Robyn, loaded up our new charges, and headed north in a state of shock.

After two days on the road we felt a little more competent loading and unloading the quiet, willing horses at overnight stops. Then, late one evening near the Alaskan border, Katla slipped as she backed out. One hind leg jammed against the trailer partition, opening a gaping four-inch gash on her hock.

Miki and our pet dog Pepper share a close moment during a summer trek below the Alaska Range.

That's when we discovered a major difference between horses and dogs. A husky probably would have healed without any treatment at all. We had the wound treated by a veterinarian as soon as we reached Fairbanks the following evening, but in spite of professional care and our own dedicated ministration, an uncontrollable infection set in.

For the entire summer, we took turns living at our parents' "town house" outside Fairbanks, taking care of Katla and learning to ride Lilja. Although the black mare improved enough to ride in July, she had a second freak accident, smacking her healing hock and chipping a bone in the joint. The infection became systemic by early September, unresponsive to an array of antibiotics, hospitalizations, and operations. Katla continued to deteriorate until finally, after three months and three thousand dollars in vet bills, we had to accept the veterinarian's last option: euthanasia.

That heart-breaking blow did little to boost our confidence. Nevertheless, just before we made the final decision about Katla, we sold Bjarmi the colt, and I made the treacherous trip with Lilja over the mountains and across the bogs to her new home.

Our slightly used little horse settled right in, adapting to a very different life with confident ease. Always a loner and low on the pecking order in her old herd, Lilja didn't mind being away from other horses. We penned her for a few days to be sure she didn't roam too far, then let her run loose. At first one of us always supervised her, but we soon realized that this was the home she'd always wanted. Like most of our new sled dogs, she had sensed that her stay in Fairbanks was only temporary. Even when that wait stretched to three months, she never seemed fully settled. Yet after just a few days here, she knew she was really home. She adopted the dog team as her new "herd," sleeping in their yard, surrounded by her protectors. She grazed on the lawn and dozed in the forest against a backdrop of golden birch leaves drifting softly down to match the big golden patches on her white coat.

By the time I returned home from Fairbanks after saying goodbye to Katla, we had only three days of moose hunting season remaining to get our winter's meat supply. We left our ever-willing parents in charge of all our assorted critters: Pepper, our big black pet dog, the sled dogs on their chains, meat poultry waddling around the yard, and our brave little horse foraging loose. Heading up the shallow river, we made the seven-hour paddle to our moose camp, arriving nearly exhausted. Just at dark I got lucky and shot a big bull, and by the following afternoon we beached at home with the first load of precious meat.

"Come on, come on!" Julie called as we paddled up.

Pepper heard us and came rocketing down to the beach. Just behind her, honking and squawking, rushed the three young geese, followed closely by a turkey, fat and waddling as fast as he could.

Then came Lilja, trotting down to welcome us back. I didn't notice her pink-rimmed eyes or scrawny build; I only saw a wonderful horse, *our* horse, hurrying down to greet us, her people.

We put her to work right away. Although not yet harness-broken, she helped us pull wheelbarrow-loads of moose up to the screened meat shed, working with just a strap around her chest. Load after load, hundred-pound quarters, ribs and backbone and neck, she carted up. The smell of freshly skinned wild game never bothered her. At the time, we failed to appreciate this calm willingness characteristic of the breed.

When Lilja first came to live with us, she didn't have much spirit. Drained by nursing a foal, the stressful transition north, and the exhausting cross-country journey, she poked along, never traveling faster than a slow jog, and didn't have much opinion about anything other than eating. But during that first year, when she lived alone and learned to pull a sled and pack a load, slept with the sled dogs and traveled as far as the Birch Cabin sixteen miles out on our trapline, Lilja changed. The additional training, of course, helped. She was only green-broke when we bought her, and her inexperience coupled with our own ignorance made her progress seem slow. But as the months and later years slipped by, she muscled out and blossomed into a fun-loving (as well as food-loving), spunky (but not *too* high-strung) little charge. Although selfish and tyrannical with other horses, she can't hide her affection for us, and usually gives her poor uninformed owners the benefit of the doubt when asked to do something unreasonable. It would take many horse books and equine magazines — and many misadventures — for us to become more learned in the ways of the horse.

Over the coming years we would buy and sell a few more horses, even raising a couple of foals, before finally hitting upon a good combination of animals suited to our unique needs. Yet Lilja still can't be beat for knowledge of our country. She shows the new horses the best places to eat, deciding when to go for the bluejoint grass growing rich and green on the beaches and in the woods in early summer, and when it's time to head for the marsh sedges during the fall, winter, and spring, when they retain more nutritious greenery. She can test the river for quicksand or weak ice, blazing the way for bigger and stronger horses. She knows where we store the carrots, and how to cross beaver dams, and how to brace against the shafts to keep a sled from overrunning her on a hill. She knows that our dogs are safe but that strange huskies sometimes bite!

Initially we worried about what our eighty-pound sled dogs would think of horses. After all, huskies are natural predators, ready to tackle any moose, bear, porcupine, or other critter that moves through the woods, flies across the sky, or swims in the deep.

Comet and Streak, our big, loyal half-malamutes, met the horses first. Sons of Loki, our fierce old leader, they weighed well over a hundred pounds apiece, with nearly identical glossy-black and pure-white masks, and for years they powered our team with tremendous strength and boundless enthusiasm. During the summer we spent nursing our ill-fated black mare Katla, I crammed Streak into our little Cessna 140 and flew him into Fairbanks for his comforting company. His first reaction to the horses proved typical for most of our dogs. His head snapped up. His eyes popped out. Then he pretended they didn't exist. Apparently, the idea of animals the size of yearling moose peacefully coexisting with us was simply impossible. He seemed to pretend the horses just weren't there. Even if a horse walked across his line of vision, he looked right through it, not even following its movements.

But after spending a month away from his canine companions, Streak bonded to the horses as none of the other dogs ever would. If I rode Lilja away, he

Lilja and Barki wait patiently as Miki makes notes in her diary during a break on a pack trip.

screamed and cried hysterically unless I brought him along. When the vet or farrier came, he fiercely made all sorts of rude vocal threats to those villainous intruders fiddling with *his* horses. Even after we returned home, the sight of a bridle in my hand sent him into the same ecstatic tizzy of anticipation as a dog harness.

Comet arrived in Fairbanks a couple weeks before I brought Lilja home so he could become accustomed to her while I conditioned both dogs to carry the heavy packs they'd shoulder on that difficult trip. The first time he saw the adult horses, Comet pretended they did not exist. Then he spied a smaller, less intimidating creature: Lilja's four-month-old foal, Bjarmi. Nearly as big as the colt, Comet lunged at Bjarmi's throat.

Anticipating his actions, Julie and I quickly deflected him. After that, the big dog pretended all horses did not exist, and wouldn't so much as glance at them. His attitude eventually wore off, as had Streak's, and by the time we parted with Bjarmi and brought Lilja home, the colt had delighted in chasing Comet around the corral.

Of all the dogs, our big brown leader Toulouse proved the most aggressive, leaping at Lilja with fangs bared the moment he laid eyes on her. His quick, tentative nip just glanced off her tough hide, and she ignored his uncivil greeting. Intimidated, Toulouse backed away, and then he, too, pretended she did not exist. Although he never again challenged an adult horse, Toulouse did maul one future foal who needed several stitches, a job we had to do ourselves. (The foal recovered and did not even fear dogs after the attack.)

Sometimes the horses started it. Liking the dogs' fish-and-rice dinners as well as her own pelleted feed, Lilja often helped herself as the dogs cowered aside — all except for old Loki. Ancient though he was, he screamed and snarled with rage when Lilja approached his food, even flying at her face with toothless jaws. Once or twice Lilja stomped on him to drive him back into his house, but he refused to be intimidated by this animal eight times his size. She had met her match, and turned to harassing more benign dogs instead of tackling the old monarch of the team. Eventually we had to ban Lilja from the dog yard at feeding time: dog food is just too expensive!

The dogs quickly learned normal horse behavior, and any deviation caused them to sound the alarm. Late one night I heard them all barking and dragged myself out of bed to investigate. At first I didn't see what was wrong. The dogs stared toward the corral above the garden fence, but all seemed quiet. Then, scanning the jungly growth in the garden, I realized Lilja was on the wrong side of the fence, munching up our winter's supply of vegetables! Even though she'd only gone from one side of the fence to the other, the dogs knew she was in the wrong place and loudly informed us. (Sometimes, though, the dogs let us down. One year the horses got into the garden and pulled up all our carrots, devouring all two hundred pounds of them. Another time they bit off most of the young broccoli plants we'd started.)

Pepper, our big black pet dog, never quite overcame her initial shock over the horses. Even now, when she hears Lilja's approaching cowbell, she gives at least a quiet growl, if not a five-bell alarm. Pep's vigilance paid off one night as I camped out on the winter trail with her and a couple horses. As she lay curled against me for warmth, she began to growl. I thought she was nervous about having a horse picketed so close, but when she persisted, I poked my head out into the cold and saw that Lilja was a few feet off the end of her picket; the snap had popped off, letting her loose. I don't know if the horse even knew she was free, but Pep sure did.

Normally the horses can wander freely without causing a fuss as long as the dogs know it's all right. But if the horses start galloping around in a fit of spring happiness, the dogs join in with a great cacophony of envious barking.

One spring when we hadn't been working Lilja much, she blew off steam by rushing out the woodlot trail and then galloping back as fast as her short little legs could go. Each time she ended up in the dog yard, where the amused huskies watched from their chains.

Then Comet got in Lilja's way as she came roaring up the trail. When he dodged sidewise to avoid her, his chain snapped tight between him and the stake. The chain caught Lilja right on the knee as she was in mid-air and at top speed.

Her legs swept rudely out from under her, Lilja fell flat on her chin, hitting hard. She hopped up, glaring. Comet had dodged back to his doghouse, leaving the chain lying innocently on the ground. With an enraged little buck, Lilja spun around, galloping away. I had been horrified to see her crash to the ground, afraid she might have been hurt. But I was laughing so hard at her astonished expression that I couldn't have helped her anyway. As for Comet, he never let himself — or his tie-down — get in her way again, and Lilja sure learned a little respect for the unpredictable behavior of dog chains.

For some reason horse tails fascinate the younger dogs. Maybe they feel a little braver assaulting that end of the horse, and the tail does make a handy handle to grab onto. I once watched our mild-mannered gelding, Jim, lying peacefully in the yard, quietly enjoying the late-winter sunshine, when Rosie, a half-grown, twenty-five-pound husky pup, ambled up and grabbed his tail. First she tried to rip it off. That failing, she tried to *chew* it off. When she couldn't penetrate his long, thick tail hairs, she clambered onto his broad rump and tried to eat him. Not once did he object. When he finally tired of her antics, the big white horse carefully stood up and strolled away, Rosie wildly barking at his heels.

All the horses proved good with dogs, but Lilja is not quite as forgiving as some. When blue-eyed Joni was young, she was worse than most pups. Many times I saw her spring up on her hind legs, place one paw on either side of Lilja's rump, grab the mare's tail, and try to forcibly rip it off. Lilja usually ignored her, rarely bothering to even move away. But she didn't forget, and one winter day as she came prancing home from foraging, she spotted Joni's litter of half-grown pups milling around. With a crunching clatter of hooves on bitterly cold snow, the little mare dashed forward, scattering the pack. Spying Joni, she humped her back and, mouth agape and short neck snaking, she chased the little miscreant into the closest doghouse. The fact that it was sixty-eight degrees below zero had not the slightest chilling effect upon her wicked glee.

When we first bought horses, a lot of people asked us, "Are you getting rid of your dogs?" Good grief no! Horses give us galloping excitement, heartwarming companionship, and charming pastoral scenes quite out of place in Bush Alaska. But they could never replace our sled dogs in our lives or in our hearts.

Our team is indispensable. Trapping is our primary source of income, and the dogs are our primary method of travel along our trails. Some of the country we trap through is too rough or too wet for snowmachines, even though they are faster and often more economical than a dog team. Machines can't climb over three-foot-high piles of deadfall, scale vertical banks, or cross thin ice or half-frozen marshland. Horses, too, have their limits, impeded by bogs and quicksand during the summer and by deep snow and hazardous ice in the winter. No horse could travel the distances our dogs do on soft, snowy trails. Our dog team travels six to eight miles an hour, covering up to fifty miles a day if we aren't stopping for trail work.

That's not to say our horses are useless! Far from it. Although we bought them more for recreation than work, they pull their own weight. In the winter we sometimes use them on shorter distances along the trapline. More importantly, they haul cords of firewood from the forest and drums of water from the lake, hitched singly to a homemade sled with birch pole shafts. Sometimes they haul freight — mostly groceries and feed arriving on the mail plane — home from the runway, although the punchy, snow-drifted trail across the frozen lake often slows our speed to a trudging walk. The twelve-mile round trip can easily eat up four or five hours, and I must confess we make more trips with Daddy's snowmachine than with the horses. Still, they save the dog team, which is often overworked on the trapline, from lots of routine grind.

While the dogs lie panting on the roofs of their houses during the summer, the horses are still hard at work, packing home groceries, chicken feed, gasoline, tar paper, library books, mail, fish from the net, and other supplies from the boat landing half a mile away. Occasionally the water is high enough to boat or canoe to the house, and sometimes Daddy's motorcycle or Lilja's two-wheeled cart carries the goods, but usually a pack horse provides our near-daily transportation.

We soon learned the differences between working with horses and dogs. With a dog team, I work with perhaps 700 pounds of bone and muscle, about the same as one of our small, thirteen-hand horses. But that 700 pounds of dog comes with eight different brains, all thinking in different directions. The 700 pounds of horse has only one small brain, which, being not much bigger than one dog brain, does very little thinking at all.

Dogs are predatory animals, curious, aggressive, and quick to respond. They have a much stronger attachment to humans, making them easy to train because they want to please so much. An encouraging word or quick pat is often enough to make a responsive dog tackle the most challenging problems. Horses, on the other hand, are prey animals, timid with a more tentative curiosity. They may be just as happy grazing alone as socializing with humans, and a pat and encouraging word is all very nice but just doesn't have the same thrilling effect.

Striving to please, dogs try hard to figure out what we want. Sometimes they try so hard they stop listening, concentrating instead on what they *think* we want, right or wrong. Dogs can also be hard to direct. They want to go, act, move, respond, or run so much it can be extremely difficult to control all eight of them at once, especially at the start of an early season run when they are fresh and excited. Unlike dogs, horses usually prefer to walk, and their quiet pace seldom results in an upset sled or abandoned driver.

We harness-train both horses and dogs by hauling firewood, something that has to get done anyway. The trips by dog sled are full of hair-raising crashes as half-trained youngsters dash through the trees and sprint up the wrong trails. The sled flies along, half out of control, scattering firewood far and wide. With only vocal guidance for directional control, and an ineffective brake for speed restraint, we are at the mercy of our leaders, who may or may not force the pups to obey. With a horse, we have reins for directional

Icelandics forage aggressively for wild grass even in deep snow, but we supplement their feed once the snow is over knee-deep.

guidance and braking. We stroll along, concentrating on steering the power supply rather than the sled, which the horse can lever around with the shafts.

That is, until the horse spooks. Dogs generally don't spook, but horses, being prey animals, can get explosively defensive when startled. With dogs, we have more of a chance to regain control over at least a few of those brains. When a horse explodes, only one brain is in residence, and often it isn't functioning at all. The whole 700 pounds is off for parts unknown, with or without the unfortunate driver. It is a tribute to the Icelandic breed that our horses survived their first few winters of harness work with their ignorant new owners without catastrophic accidents.

Most sled dogs more or less train themselves, working instinctively within minutes of first being harnessed. The trainees are hitched in a small team, and away they go. Of course they don't travel too fast or too far during their first year or two, but if things go wrong, it's not a major crisis. Tangles may be momentarily frightening, but after a quick hug, the pups are wiggly and happy and ready to go again.

But horses have that prey instinct. When hitched to a sled and started forward for the first time, they can be appalled to realize that the innocuous-looking sled is bent on running them down. The faster they go, the harder the sled chases them, and when a horse gets too excited you simply can't control all 700 pounds at once. As horse people are fond of saying, it's much easier to control a few pounds of brains than the remaining 697 pounds of horse. We learned to break down every lesson into the smallest possible fragments, circumventing the ultimate task as long as possible before putting the entire thing together and actually getting some wood hauled.

First we teach the horse to drive without the sled, and then the harness is introduced. The first load is usually a spruce pole that the animal hardly feels, and gradually he understands that he can pull bigger loads, and that they aren't *really* chasing him.

Then we slowly introduce shafts, which control the sled on corners and steep hills. (Lilja first learned to pull a sled without the benefit of shafts. After getting run into a time or two by a misbehaving sled, she learned to keep an eagle-eye on her treacherous load.)

Finally we put all the pieces together: driving reins, harness, shafts, and sled. The entire affair may take several weeks, and we haven't even hauled any firewood yet.

Ultimately, though, with a horse we have only one harness to put on instead of eight, and can use a sled three times as big as a dog sled, while traveling at a leisurely, controlled pace. Long-distance travel is still left to the dogs, but by using horsepower for chores at home, we save the hard-working team many a burdensome day.

The Icelandic horses have lived up to their reputation, flourishing on minimal feed and living off native grass much of the year. Although they run loose to forage, we often corral them at night. During the winter this protects them from ranging wolf packs, and in the summer it keeps them from becoming obese. (When on rich grass, Lilja can get fat on just four hours of grazing per day.) Over the seven-month winter, with deep snow and temperatures sometimes plummeting to fifty below or colder, we feed each horse one-half to three-quarters of a ton of imported pelleted feed. That's a lot of feed to mail in parcel post, but even on a straight commercial diet three horses don't eat as much as fifteen of our big, hard-working sled dogs.

From April or May until November or December our horses rustle for themselves, living well on wild grasses and sedges, willow leaves, shrubs, and even wild rose bushes (stickers and all), nettles (stingers and all), and roots they paw from the ground. They occasionally nibble on plants shunned by wild critters: dwarf birch, low-bush cranberry plants, blueberry bushes, and other such unpalatable brush.

Then there are the fish. Because we feed fish to our dogs daily, we always have some on hand. We knew Icelandic horses in their native country ate salted fish for additional protein, and during lean years they even patrolled ocean beaches searching for dead fish. Even though our freshwater fish have no salt, the younger horses often munch on them, especially when half frozen. Whitefish eggs are a treat for them, and the horses annoy us no end by pulling down our stacks of frozen fish to nibble on. The first time I rode one young horse alone to check a net set under the ice, he acted nervous and uncertain, but his concern changed to contented delight when I pulled the net out and he found flapping-fresh fish to munch on!

When we go riding, we always take a few loose dogs along; the Icelandic horses don't mind a bunch of eighty-pound huskies tearing wildly around. Only occasionally will a horse take offense when a dog hovers irritatingly close to its heels, kicking out to tap the offender lightly but pointedly on the nose.

The first winter Lilja lived with us, we spent three weeks in early spring with her and all the dogs at our Birch Cabin trapline camp, cutting firewood for the following year. On the trip home, Julie took the team, leaving five dogs behind. When I departed a couple hours later, I brought them running along loose, all dancing and barking and bouncing around as I trotted the little mare up the creek. With sixteen miles to go, Lilja knew better than to travel fast, but we were heading for home and she'd been cooped up for most of her stay at camp, so she eagerly stretched her short little legs into a brisk jog.

Julie would have the home cabin warm and dinner ready by the time we arrived. A dog team is so much faster than a horse! Julie would be less than two hours on the trail; I'd be almost five.

We soon left the icy creek to portage to another marshy drainage, following the sled trail over low spruce-covered hills lying dark against the glistening spring snow. In the open wind-blown areas my horse sank deeply into the drifts, lurching and struggling through brisket-deep snow while the dogs scampered merrily across the packed surface. But in protected areas where the trail lay hardened and icy Lilja moved right along, little white ears flicking this way and that, her thick, stiff mane bouncing softly with every quick step.

After mushing dogs for years, the peacefulness of traveling horseback gave me a sense of awe. I had only one mind to guide, one body to control. The physical contact with Lilja's warm bare back beneath me tightened the bond in a way I hadn't experienced working with sled dogs. Horses are not generally as devoted and affectionate as dogs, but the attachment can run just as deep in other ways.

Even with no saddle, Lilja's gentle jog was easy for me to ride, and her warmth kept the cold at bay. All the mucky spots in the swamps seemed frozen up tight, but as we approached a beaver dam I spied a hole now frozen, just below the dam. I slowed Lilja and just as she was stepping down near the fresh ice, she froze. Pausing, I heard the sound of water gurgling swiftly under the ice. The upwelling flow from beneath the dam had thawed the ice as it swirled turbulently upward.

"Oooo, good girl! Let's go elsewhere," I said, sliding off and thumping her solid white shoulder fondly before leading her around the dam. Falling in a little hole like that meant nothing to the huskies, but if Lilja broke through, I might never get her out.

Right below the dam a little patch of grass showed through the melting snow on the bank, and I stopped to give Lilja a pocketful of grain and let her graze while I ate my moose meat and crackers. After she licked up the last of her sweetfeed, my little horse collapsed into a heap of gold and white, rolling onto her back to kick out luxuriously as she scratched herself in the granular spring snow.

At the sight of the vulnerable, convulsing horse, my five big dogs instantly transmogrified from delightful domestic companions into slinking, stealthy, hunting wolves. Splitting up, they swiftly circled to close in for the kill from all angles.

Just as I leaped up, Toulouse darted forward, ready for dinner. Lilja never noticed him. As she rolled vigorously in the snow, one solid hoof accidentally clipped the big brown dog right in the nose. With a pained yelp, he leaped back and the others retreated with more respect. The horse, they decided, was not in the throes of death, and dinner would have to wait.

Some miles on, I slid off her back once more. "All right, Lilja." Ahead of us lay the Old Channel, an expanse of glassy overflow ice, and I counted on her rubber horse galoshes, complete with ice studs, to keep her upright on the slick surface. With their hard hooves, horses can't walk safely on ice, and because of their large size on toothpick legs, when horses do fall, they can easily tear tendons and break bones. If I had studded boots on all four of her feet, Lilja could have trotted right across, but with just one pair for her front feet, she knew she might slip. I figured she'd balk if I let her, and I caught her long, goat-like winter beard in one hand to look her in the eye.

"We have to go across that ice, and we have to go *now*. I have my little stick — " her ears twitched as I showed her the willow wand I carried as a quirt — "and you know I shall use it if I have to! So come on."

I marched across the ice, and she knew she had to follow. Lilja tiptoed out, nostrils flaring in nervous concentration. I held her at a very slow walk so she wouldn't slide, keeping up a steady chat to rivet her attention on my voice rather than her own fear. By the time we gained good ground her faith in me — and my faith in her — had strengthened. Later, experience would teach us what was safe and what was not, and she would trustingly move out with cautious determination across anything I asked her to tackle. By being careful not to lead her into danger, Julie and I boosted her faith in our judgment, and by paying attention to her concerns, we learned to tell when she felt something was too dangerous. The other horses were no problem: where Lilja went, they would follow.

Finally we broke out of the last line of willows, and only a half-mile of deep drifts lay between us and home. I looked out across the narrow bay at the curl of white smoke rising from the cabin, then hopped down, slipping off her hackamore. She deserved a break. I hoped she'd walk that last distance over the rough drifts to cool off, but no; as soon as I walked ahead, she broke into a gallop. Clattering past me, snow flying in every direction, she sped toward home, blasting right through the heavy drifts.

The dogs hurtled away after her, and all six beasties tore out across the bay, Lilja racing with the huskies like the big dog in the pack. Over the drifts they flew, running abreast to the far shore where they singled out to rocket up the narrow trail, two dogs, the little palomino pinto, and three more panting dogs.

I grinned, slung the bridle over my shoulder, and headed for home. You just can't beat life with horses and huskies.

Our new horse Kopur was the undisputed boss, but Lilja was the leader. Where she went, Kopur would follow—as long as it wasn't too far from home.

CHAPTER 5

COPING WITH KOPUR

Most horses don't fly. For that matter, most otters don't either. But there are exceptions.

Lilja spent her first year with us as the area's sole equine resident. As Miki and I learned to love and care for her, we became convinced that we needed a second horse, and that she needed a companion. Despite Katla's disastrous accident and Lilja's traumatic journey home, we made plans to buy another Icelandic horse. Instead of making the hazardous overland trip, maybe we could charter a plane and fly him out. He'd still have to cross several streams and swamps on the journey home around the lake, but that was nothing compared to the overland trip.

Miki and I arrived at the Icelandic Horse Farm with eager expectations, only to be disappointed by the selection Robyn and her husband, Phil, could offer. With the popularity of Icelandics booming, many horses had already been snapped up. Robyn's trainer, Christine, showed us two quiet geldings on consignment, but both had flaws and were overpriced. One sweet young colt looked just right, but we lacked the experience to train him.

The only other horse, a handsome black and white pinto named Kopur (pronounced *Cow-per*), struck us as a fine, likable chap. We rode him several times, and he tolted swiftly down the road, his hooves beating a rapid, even time as he pelted along. He cooperated when Christine worked him around the yard, even when he was pulling something behind him. He was easy to

Julie

catch, and stood quietly for saddling. But Kopur had one serious flaw: he could be skittish. Once he bolted, and proved too strong to stop promptly. Phil Pretty told us frankly, "He's either very good, or a complete idiot."

Kopur had wide, soft brown eyes, which we took as a good sign, and a shiny black, finely chiseled head with a muscular, rounded white and black body. His mane, black with a few bronze strands, lay long and thick over a powerful white neck. He walked with a swift, springy gait, hooves flashing easily over the ground. Although friendly, he didn't especially crave companionship. Born fourteen years earlier at Varmilækur, Iceland, he arrived green-broke in Canada at the age of seven, but hadn't been used much since. We hoped that with consistent use and our talent for handling spooks (spooky dogs, anyway) we could give Kopur more confidence and mold him into a reliable horse. Icelandic horses often work into their late twenties, so he couldn't be called old, but we worried that as a mature horse he wouldn't quickly work out problems he had carried in him for so long.

"Can we do it?" I asked Christine.

She screwed her eyes shut for a moment and then replied, "I *think* so."

With no good alternatives, we decided to give Kopur a chance. The 1,800-mile trailer ride to Fairbanks didn't faze him except for during one break when he tangled badly in his picket. Leaping to his rescue, Miki and I convinced him that we had saved his life. He began taking a real interest in the adventure, but on arriving in Fairbanks his insecurity got the better of him. He was all alone, worried, and nervous. Once he bolted and escaped for several hours. While waiting for the veterinary inspection and import papers, we also learned that he had sensitive, tender skin and he hated to be crowded.

Meanwhile, I searched for an air charter outfit willing to fly a horse. The first company didn't have a large enough plane. The second said, "A horse? Never!" The third, Wright's Air Service, owned a vintage single-engine de Havilland Otter that could carry a horse plus additional freight. Would they take Kopur? "Sure, anytime!"

The Otter looked like a World War II relic with the features of a good Alaskan bush plane: tail wheel, powerful engine, and the large wings needed for short-field takeoffs.

Kopur's reluctance to enter the small de Havilland Otter delayed the loading until midday when the increasing summer heat made the air turbulent and the horse panicky.

The orange and brown plane's cargo door was set chest-high behind the wing. It measured forty-six inches tall. Kopur stood fifty-two inches (thirteen hands) at the shoulder. During his week in Fairbanks, we gave him a preflight training course that included walking up a narrow ramp and ducking under low poles. We also spent a couple of days back at home, and brought Lilja around the lake to the runway the day before the flight.

Miki and I both felt queasy about putting a horse — and this horse in particular — on a plane. We considered building a crate, but no crate would fit through the door. Our veterinarian gave us sedatives instead, assuring us they would keep Kopur calm.

We arrived early at the airport, giving the medication to our worried horse and leaving him quietly in the trailer until it took effect. The drugs made Kopur absent-minded and he forgot to watch his feet as he climbed the narrow ramp to the Otter. Twice he stepped off the edge and crashed to the pavement below. After half an hour of coaxing, we managed to stuff him through the low door into the little plane. With his thick black topknot brushing the fabric of the low ceiling and his sides cramped by plywood, mattresses, and other freight, Kopur stamped nervously as we tied him in. We had a second dose of sedatives but I feared it would make him unbalanced in turbulence, and Miki knew he'd be impossible to unload if he was too doped up. We cross-tied his head in the open bulkhead just behind the cockpit and as I ran a third rope toward the back of the plane, the pilot poked his head in.

"I can't tell you how important it is that he doesn't run into the back of the plane," he warned.

Pilots ourselves, we knew that would upset the plane's delicate weight and balance, perhaps causing a stall and crash. We tied that third rope to the bulkhead instead. Miki slid into the copilot's seat, turning to offer a bucket of oats to the pinto. He dug in, chewing grimly, quivering and flinching as the engine roared to life. I sat in the rear, taking the only other available seat, separated from Kopur by a mattress on its edge.

Kopur stood frozen rigidly during takeoff, his powerful muscles bunching as he fought the sway. I sat stiffly, staring at the horse as the pilot gently lifted the craft. Once we were airborne, I began to relax as the plane steadied and the harsh engine noise abated a bit. It looked as though Kopur would cooperate despite his anxiety.

We'd hoped for an early start, but the loading delays had pushed our takeoff to late morning. The hot June sun sent air currents swirling upward, shaping billowy cumulus clouds as the plane climbed. At an altitude of barely a thousand feet, the Otter hit turbulence. Kopur started with alarm, his head jerking up. His forehead connected sharply with the gray fabric snapped across the ceiling. The drapery popped loose and three yards of the quilted material fell down onto his face and back.

Kopur decided that he did not like to fly. He wanted out. He wanted out *now*. And the only direction he could move was toward the cockpit.

Lurching forward, he drove powerfully against the restraining ropes, lunging halfway into the cockpit. The windshield looked like an exit, so he aimed for that. Hooves pounded the floor near the controls as he fought to free himself. The pilot dropped the yoke and seized the berserk horse's head, trying to push him back. He couldn't do it. Miki grabbed Kopur's nose, shoving desperately. She couldn't do it, either. Jumping, stomping, and kicking, Kopur was determined to get out of that plane and no human strength could stop him.

Meanwhile, nobody was flying the plane. It nosed downward and from my seat in back I saw downtown Fairbanks rising to meet us. In a moment of panic I considered grabbing Kopur's tail to drag him back, but I knew that would only terrify him into trying to leap forward away from my clutches. In another minute we would be splattered across the biggest mall in Fairbanks, but I sat unmoving and helpless; doing anything else would only make matters worse.

In the cockpit, Kopur strained toward the windshield as the pilot threw his weight frantically against the thrashing horse's shoulder and Miki clung to Kopur's head. Then her fingers found his nostrils. She pinched them shut. Unable to breath, Kopur backed away, pulling clear of the cockpit to stand dancing and quivering with terror.

The pilot seized the controls, wheeling the plane back toward the airport. I gently pulled the offending fabric away from Kopur's head. Miki held up the second syringe, meeting my eyes with a silent question. I shook my head. The sting of the injection might trigger another rampage, and we'd be on the ground before the sedative took effect anyway.

Landing safely, we taxied back to the hangar. The pilot should have thrown us all out, but he didn't. Leaving us to regroup, he simply strolled off looking rather white. Miki and I gave Kopur another shot and tied him down fore and aft, side to side, up and down, until he could hardly move. The pilot had a cigarette. Then we took off again.

Kopur weaved stuporously in the turbulence, but he didn't panic. The seconds passed interminably as miles of green spruce, willows, and marshes slid by, broken only by the gray lines of glacier-fed streams. The Alaska Range pushed up sharp and white in the south, its foothills stretching below: there was the mountain Lilja had climbed, the glacial rivers she had crossed, the green sucking bogs and gray quicksand she had braved. That journey had taken days, and now Kopur was making the trip from Fairbanks — three times as far — in an hour. The early afternoon chop jogged the plane constantly, unbalancing the sedated horse, but he did not panic again. After a tense, bumpy flight the lake spread wide and blue before us.

"Do you want to buzz your cabin so they'll know you're here?" the pilot asked Miki, but she shook her head. Our folks and all the rest of the tiny community would already be gathered at the runway, awaiting the arrival of the airborne equine. Sliding gently down from the sky, the pilot made an exquisite powder-soft landing on the gravel field.

Our neighbor Ray Wildrick backed his ancient yellow pickup to the cargo door but Kopur, still groggy, refused to duck out. Our faithful pilot waited patiently as we coaxed and bribed, but Kopur refused to budge. Finally we led Lilja to the door, hoping she would perk him up. He didn't even notice her.

But Lilja! Oh, my! She didn't know whether to be positively thrilled or absolutely outraged! The nerve of this handsome stranger invading her territory! Lilja's winter alone had made her independent — and spoiled. She was not just A horse. She was THE horse. Squealing and stomping, she tried to bite him while shrilly declaring the violence that would be done if he didn't leave *now*. Finally we took her away.

Two hours passed while the sedative gradually wore off. Finally we maneuvered Kopur to the threshold and I slid a strap behind his left pastern. Miki picked up his right foot and bumped his shoulder, knocking him off balance. I jerked the left hoof off the threshold, and Kopur tumbled out to the truck bed as the bystanders cheered. Ray gently backed the truck against a steep bank so Kopur could step down. He was glad to be on the ground again. Actually, we were all glad to be on the ground. Our pilot immediately took off and probably never flew a horse again.

Riding Lilja, Miki led Kopur around the lake. He crossed the rivers and streams and hurried along when the mare scampered across sagging quicksand. Once home Lilja and Kopur fought for hours, eventually reaching an uncertain truce, the beginning of a close dependency that never quite matured into true friendship. He was the boss. She was the leader. If he glared at her, she moved away. But Lilja decided where to forage and when to come home. They didn't fight often, but occasionally got into kick-boxing matches, especially if Lilja was cornered and unable to move away.

One day Kopur lost his temper and chased Lilja all over the yard. Trying to escape, the little mare scurried past the dog yard . . . into, around, and out of the corral . . . down toward the wood lot . . . and back into the corral again with Kopur, ears pinned, hot on her heels. Miki ran to the corral gate. "Lilja, Lilja!" she called. Lilja spun back and scampered out the gate. Miki slammed it in Kopur's face, trapping the angry horse. Pleased with herself, Lilja smugly ran loose until the gelding calmed down.

Most of the time, the two horses gave each other mutual respect if not actual friendship. Occasionally they sidled up to each other to trade scratches, nipping and digging with strong teeth at withers and manes, but usually they simply tolerated each other.

Miki and I worked all summer rehabilitating our new horse. We rode Kopur five days a week. He learned to carry a pack, and every other day he packed fish home from the net. After we gradually, gently broke him to pull in harness, he dragged poles and small logs from the forest. We hitched him to a dog sled once or twice, but never put him in shafts because of his sensitive skin and tendency to spook when crowded. Kopur wasn't as lazy as Lilja and we enjoyed riding him, but occasionally he freaked out and bolted.

As time went on he panicked less often, but the damage was done. The all-important trust between human and horse had failed to solidify. We had learned from dogs that to build trust we had to control every situation, but Kopur's strength and our limited ability made that impossible. Kopur didn't blame us for his fear, but instead of looking to us for reassurance, he simply bolted for home, finding security in his corral instead of in us. We taught Kopur to relax on rides, so we could travel with a loose rein instead of always pressing the bit on him. We could even ride him bareback if we were careful, but he never felt safe the way Lilja did. I learned to always grip his mane, so if he did spin and bolt, throwing me off, at least I would land on my feet.

By summer's end, Kopur was more reliable and we felt he would be safe on a pack trip. Our plans started out big — packing out to a trapline camp and building a little cabin to replace a tent camp, which itself had replaced one of Slim's old cabins that was now unusable. The wall tent, while a comfortable home, was inconvenient for handling fur and unsafe in severe cold when cinders from the roaring fire sometimes landed on the canvas roof. Now that we had horses, they could do the gut-popping work of hauling cabin logs, but moving the horses out to the trapline in the summer, when the swamps and rivers weren't safely frozen, would be a real challenge.

For days we scouted a trail through the first ten-mile maze of swamps. At first we started out on foot and if we hit a large marsh we simply returned home to fly over the area, taking notes and sketching potential routes around the obstacles. Later, as we pushed farther, the horses joined us to carry camp gear. Of course some dogs, usually Comet and Streak, came along to keep us company and warn off wild animals.

The dogs made themselves useful in other ways, too. Once Miki was scouting far ahead of Lilja through terrain so brushy and monotonous she wasn't always sure she could find her way back to her horse. Luckily, the dogs kept better track. "Let's go back, you guys," Miki would suggest, and they obligingly led her straight to Lilja every time. (Fortunately, they somehow realized that Miki meant "Let's backtrack," not "Let's go back home.")

Another time I reached a fork leading to one of our camps where we had left some food cached high in a tree. Comet and Streak, ranging ahead, suddenly stiffened, dropping their heads and staring intently through the trees toward the cache. Some big creature had caught their interest. Tying up Lilja, I followed cautiously as the two big dogs stalked forward. I scanned the forest, suspecting a bear in the food cache. The dogs suddenly surged ahead and a rumpus ensued. Hurrying warily toward the fray, I spotted a small black bear perched in a spruce tree, broken feed sacks scattered below the cache, and my dogs bouncing and hurling obscenities treeward.

Seeing that this bear posed no immediate danger, I turned round to look for others. The bear looked small enough to be a yearling, which meant he could be traveling with his mother. With one eye on the bear and the other on the woods, I cleaned up the wreckage and called off the dogs, pleased with their performance.

Despite our best efforts to find a safe trail, we had to make occasional compromises to blaze our way through the swamps. To cross one deep creek, we found an overgrown beaver dam which seemed fairly solid. Comet and Streak trotted cheerfully across. I walked slowly, shoes in one hand, sinking to my ankles in the black muck but feeling a solid surface of roots, logs, and beaver poles below. Lilja followed me, cautiously testing the footing at every step but still pausing to snatch a bite of grass growing on the dam. Kopur followed carefully in her tracks. One misstep upstream and the horses would tumble into deep water; one step downstream and they'd sink into the dense, grassy marsh below the dam.

Elsewhere along the creek, beavers had undermined the mossy

banks with tunnels, and we rode slowly so the horses weren't hurt when they punched through. Another spot of soft ground didn't look too bad, the thin tamarack trees growing over it suggesting there wasn't much underlying water. Still, to be sure the horses didn't sink in too deeply, we built a corduroy surface of parallel spruce poles. Kopur carefully stepped on the poles so his hooves didn't sink into the muck. Lilja carefully stepped between the poles so her hooves didn't slip on their round surfaces. Neither horse sank in very deep, even after several crossings churned up the wet moss.

One pleasant, warm evening I stretched out in camp after a long day blazing trail, and turned on my little radio to check in with Miki, who was home tending the dogs and garden. When she answered my call, I reported making good progress with the trail.

"Well," she said bitterly, "You needn't have bothered. We won't get the permit this year."

"Oh — oh!"

The cabin-building permit which we had applied for from the federal government had required officials to complete reams of paperwork, plus do a survey for rare plants and archeological evidence, and even hold a public hearing. The appropriate government offices had dutifully accomplished all this, typed up the permit, and added the envelope to the outgoing mail. Then someone filed a lawsuit — not against our cabin in particular but against cabin permits in general. Unfortunately, the person who had granted our permit was exceedingly scrupulous. He plucked the envelope out of the mail and tore it up. Our plans were derailed for five long years until the lawsuit was settled.

Instead of calling off our whole excursion, we decided to make a late-August trip with the horses anyway. It would give Lilja and Kopur packing and camping experience, and be a good vacation to make up for our otherwise pointless efforts. Leaving our dog team with neighbors, we loaded packs on both horses and also on three of our four dogs: Comet, Streak, and their father, old Loki. Pepper, being a pet, didn't have to carry one. She appreciated her special status and felt demeaned, punished, when we made her work, even though she had a fine build for it.

Kopur sensed our nervous anticipation that precedes expeditions, and he decided the whole thing was a bad idea. We had hardly left the yard when he tore away and raced home. After the second start he calmed down some, but by then we were all on edge. Our nervousness fueled his, and his fueled ours. We gladly camped the first night in a small, park-like clearing under tall spruce trees above a swampy creek that provided unpleasant but usable water. Firm silt ground underfoot made a fine surface for the horses to roll on. Although we found no safe pasture for grazing, Miki and I did cut grass from the swamp to supplement their soaked pellets and grain.

Twilight fell softly over the creek as the horses munched their dinner. A muskrat swam quietly downstream, sending a quivering wave behind his long oscillating tail. He paused, floating, by a patch of tall marsh grass before diving to leave the dark water flat and still. Farther upstream, the slap of a beaver's tail echoed; three ducks whirred past, wheeling skyward when they saw us, and then silence settled again. Pepper lay in our little tent to escape the mosquitoes and no-see-ums, and Miki and I soon joined her. The other dogs, used to sleeping outside, lounged easily despite the bugs — Comet by the tent door, Streak near the horses, and Loki off on his own.

We passed a quiet night, but in the morning Kopur grew rigid and jumpy as we threw a diamond hitch over the tarp that protected his pack, pulling the lash rope extra-tight to hold the load securely in case he started bucking.

"He's only scared because we're scared, but I can't stop being scared knowing he might try to run home and fall in a bog," I complained, frustrated. I pointed at Lilja, who was already loaded, standing in the morning sunlight with sagging ears and half-closed eyes. "Look at her. She's not scared. She's bored."

Then we saw the light. We tied Kopur behind Lilja instead of hand-leading him. He tuned in to her instead of us. Trailing behind the plodding, sleepy-eyed mare, his tension drained away and he began to relax. That solved the whole problem and we turned our attention to navigating.

Our new trail guided us through the swamps to the relatively firm riverbank near the Old Channel, and from there we picked our way around potholes and through dense willows and alders until we reached a year-old forest fire burn. We boldly pushed ahead, struggling through stiff, blackened spikes of burned spruce, climbing over fallen logs, and wading through ashes still soft and fluffy. The spear-like scrub spruce stabbed and ripped the canvas pack tarps while fresh charcoal blackened our skin and the horses' white legs.

This black landscape continued for miles. Some people might have found it oppressive, but I thought it both depressing and uplifting. With burned standing trees stripped of needles and twigs, we enjoyed unusually fine views. In most spruce forests, you can see only a few yards ahead, but here we could see distant ridges and ravines, which gave us a feeling of greater freedom and a better understanding of how the land lay. With good visibility, accidentally bumping into a bear was much less likely, too. Signs of new growth lent excitement to every hollow and ridge. A few grasses braved some wet areas, and widely scattered fireweed added a flashy red touch to scorched black slopes. In other places, the intense heat had seared through the topsoil, leaving a sterile, sandy clay with no organic material left to support life. Liverworts and fireweed might return readily and cottonwood groves would quickly take root where the moss had burned away downwind of existing cottonwood trees, but the ancient spruce forest would take a century or more to grow back.

Far below the Burn, the river lay in a canyon of sandy banks, and deep ravines sent us detouring inland where boggy little creeks and potholes made traveling difficult. Meeting these challenges with horses for the first time was hard, and two days later when we reached a fork in the river that marked the southern limit of the Burn, we were battered and bruised and ready to stop.

"Never again!" I declared. This route was just too rough. Yet it turned out to be the only route possible, and in the years to come we followed it with horses several more times, to reach our trapline and the higher country of the Alaska Range.

A nice island lay just upriver, and a long period of low water had dried out quicksand that otherwise could have posed a danger. Crossing the waist-deep channel to the island, we found a lovely campsite with enough grass to keep the horses happy. We spent two blissful days there, lazing in the tent, picking cranberries, and riding the horses. Lilja and Kopur stood tied at night, but foraged loose on the island during the day, with Lilja's big cowbell sounding out their location when they wandered from sight.

One morning Pep set up a violent bellowing that started the other dogs to their feet. As we looked around, a large black bear broke into view on the far side of the river. To test his temperament, we fired the rifle to see if he spooked. The shot exploded in the still air, shattering the cool serenity of the morning. The bear was not alarmed. The horses were. Deep in the thicket behind the tent came the rumble of hooves.

"They've bolted!" I cried, but I was wrong. Lilja was racing back to camp to investigate the noise, Kopur following her lead.

"Only an Icelandic would do that," I told Miki confidently. The truth was that while we often said that, we didn't know enough about "normal" horses to draw a reliable comparison.

The bear nonchalantly continued upstream, and as our ten-day vacation drew to a close we wound our way back downriver, fighting through the Burn, slogging through the swamps, and finally climbing the birch-covered hill back home.

On the last day of our trip, Kopur's saddle slipped sideways and, like a normal Icelandic, he did not buck or bolt but simply stopped and wouldn't move until we fixed it. We arrived home well satisfied with his performance, feeling that he had passed an important test.

Kopur may have passed the test, but the gelding did not graduate. As a flurry of fall chores distracted us from the horses, we rode Kopur less often. Throughout the winter, we realized that when he wasn't ridden hard and regularly, his progress backslid. With persistent daily workouts he showed gradual improvement, but then went rapidly downhill if he wasn't worked, becoming flighty and worried once more. When we began trapping full-time, we couldn't spare the hours necessary to keep him a safe, happy horse.

We began to see how poorly he fit into bush life, too. He lacked the versatility and courage to be reliable in all situations. I could ride Lilja bareback without reins, but I wouldn't dream of doing that with Kopur. I could vault onto Lilja's back, but Kopur sometimes bolted if I even poked him sliding my boot in his stirrup. As time passed we used him less in harness, too; the potential for injury if he ever exploded was too great. Camping out on the trail or at a trapping cabin took him away from home, the only place where he felt truly secure, and he needed that security even more than he needed Lilja; he would leave her at the first opportunity to head home alone. Miki and I had to make several long horse hunts that winter when he escaped from the Birch Cabin or bolted on the trail.

Kopur's problems and our own inexperience made a bad combination. By January, when we realized any improvement was only temporary, we'd already had enough spills, rodeos, and horse chases to know that an animal like Kopur was dangerous in an isolated setting without doctors or veterinarians to patch us all up after accidents.

The decision to sell Kopur came slowly because we still liked him. It was hard admitting that we had failed him. We eventually realized, though, that keeping him would have been a mistake for him as well as us. In the hands of an experienced rider, with a stable home, daily attention, and regular workouts, Kopur would be happier and safer. And we would be happier and safer with a horse we could count on, a horse we could trust with a pack, a sled, or the neighbor's children.

Our bad experience with Kopur shook our confidence, but it still didn't put us off horses. To the contrary, Kopur taught us far more than a quiet horse ever could have. From him we learned to calm a horse by keeping a hand pressed to his side while we worked on him. We learned about shaking the neck, rubbing the mouth and forehead, and working the tail to help him relax. Kopur taught us to sit quietly in the saddle and hold a slight tension on the rein when he grew afraid, just to show him we were (we hoped) in control. On his back, we developed balance because he got scared if we felt unstable. We learned to respond calmly in frightening situations — even if we were inwardly terrified — to avoid fueling his fear.

We also learned that horses were not so much like dogs as we'd hoped. If we were to have horses, they couldn't be just any horses; they had to be carefully selected. The myth of the indestructible, unflappable, totally reliable Icelandic horses was not entirely true. Many Icelandics are very quiet and reliable, but some are incredibly fast and spirited and a few, like Kopur, are not good family horses at all. In the years to follow, we met several other novice riders who bought untrained Icelandics on the basis of the breed's reputation. Many of these aspiring riders were turned off and their fine young horses ruined by this unfortunate combination.

Although determined to replace Kopur, we didn't want to repeat our experience in the airplane so soon. (Later we did fly quiet horses with complete satisfaction.) This meant Kopur had to leave home overland, and the new horses had to come back overland, too. But that is a story Miki gets to tell.

CHAPTER 6

THE LONG, LONG TRAIL

Lilja paused, gazing enraptured with blue-flecked eyes out over the snowy valley below us, the northeastern reaches of the Kuskokwim Mountains standing rocky and windblown just beyond. After puffing a moment, I walked on, my two willing pack horses in tow as I pushed upwards.

Cresting the 1,700-foot ridge, the horses and I viewed the far side of the birch and spruce hills dropping away to a fifty-mile-wide plain of lowland spruce, dotted by lakes and lined with streams, stretching away to the Alaska Range. A warm late-March sun lit the northern mountain walls for the first time since September, gilding the snowy flanks and turning the vertical granite buttresses a deep blue-gray.

Julie and I had hoped to bring Kopur out the fall before, backtracking the cross-country route I'd taken with Lilja, to trade him in on a better model. High water in late summer made that plan just too hazardous. Then, in March, runway construction crews planning to upgrade the local airstrip brought out a Cat tractor train of heavy equipment, packing down a solid winter trail that twisted across 150 miles of desolate terrain to Nenana, on the Parks Highway near Fairbanks. It offered us a one-time shot to make the trip relatively free of hardship.

A chest-deep layer of snow covered every particle of forage, so the two horses carried virtually all the food they'd need for the expected ten-day trip, leaving me afoot. *Miki*

On the winter Cat trail, our horses and huskies traveled together for a couple of days before Julie went ahead with the faster dogs.

Julie would leave with the dog team two days later and catch up with me halfway, bringing along a half bale of hay to supplement the horses' pelleted diet. Except for that and a few small essentials I carried in a light pack, everything I needed was loaded onto the two horses. Lilja's pack weighed about 150 pounds, but I kept Kopur's to 90. I didn't want to risk him blowing up and running all the way home when I loaded him in the morning — not when my back trail would stretch out over a hundred miles.

I headed out on March 23, well before breakup but after the weather had warmed from the dead of winter. To spare me ten miles of a mighty long hike, Julie led the horses out the first morning, and I caught up to her with the dog team in early afternoon, covering in one hour what it had taken her three to walk. Julie returned home with the dogs, and I was fresh for the long climb to the top of that high ridge. Underfoot, the trail lay hard-packed and wide, ideal for walking, and nightfall found the horses and me twenty miles from home.

Not wanting Kopur to have any excuse for spooking, and needing to spare the weight of more feed, I had not brought any dogs with me, and I felt lonely and vulnerable without their companionship and acute wilderness senses. We camped just below treeline in the wide path that the bulldozers had pushed through the scrub spruce. Except for collecting firewood, I never left that trail. With the snow so deep and no snowshoes, I had to struggle every time I ventured past the berm. Fortunately, with no traffic it was safe to camp in the middle of the road.

As I strolled down my private highway the following morning, the two previously quiet horses suddenly blasted past me at a wild gallop. Leaping to one side to avoid their clattering hooves, I set myself against Lilja's lead rope. The little Icelandic mare snapped sideways and stopped. Dropping her head, she half-closed her eyes. *Oh well, running away is just too much trouble.*

Tied to Lilja, Kopur also snapped to a stop. Then he started bucking. I could see his saddle had swiveled halfway around his body, frightening him. Even though I had carefully tightened his cinch before loading his pack, he'd been so tense that it later loosened as the walking relaxed him.

"NO!" I called sternly, and he stopped, rigid and trembling. Then I heard the airplane. It was Daddy, flying out to check up on me. I had to get my radio from the little backpack I wore, but any wrong move would turn this into a rodeo event for an airborne audience.

Daddy circled back, rechecking the area behind me; he hadn't spotted me yet. That gave me the thirty seconds I needed to get the saddle off and calm the alarmed horse. I dug out the handheld ham radio just as Daddy flew up and spotted me.

"I'M FINE!" I shouted into the transceiver.

With a cheery tip of the wings, the little Cessna 140 twirled away. Daddy would arrive in Fairbanks in just over one hour. I still had more than a week of walking.

Half an hour later we were reloaded, cinched up double-tight, and on our way. Lilja's lead rope swung from my hand, and Kopur trailed her, tied on by a break-away string which would part should they have a serious accident.

A hundred and fifty miles is a long hike, and we soon fell into a pleasant routine. After walking several hours every morning, the horses and I camped, resting for the afternoon before resuming our march at 4 or 5 P.M. and walking another three or four hours, until nearly dark. At each stop I unloaded the horses, built a fire, and melted snow for us all to drink, lacing my own with cocoa mix. The sub-zero nighttime temperatures warmed quickly each brilliant sunny morning, reaching fifteen above by afternoon.

On the fourth evening Julie caught up with me, Pepper and a pack of mostly grown pups scampering along loose behind her team. The horses relished the hay she brought, and for the next two nights we camped together. Although the dogs traveled over twice as fast as the horses, Julie didn't want to stress her youngsters. She took it easy, spending the morning in camp and then catching up to me for a leisurely lunch before mushing on to set up the evening camp. For one afternoon she took part of Lilja's load so I could ride.

What joy! To sit restfully atop Lilja's empty Decker pack as the little mare jogged briskly down the spruce-lined trail, watching the miles slip by instead of pushing every inch behind me myself! The spirit of the trail hit her, and Lilja couldn't wait to find out where we were going. Kopur trotted easily behind, our routine accepted if not embraced. Fortunately both horses were well accustomed to our dog team, and not even our poor old spook minded the sight of fifteen large sled dogs careening up behind him.

When Julie pulled ahead for good, I'd been on the trail for six days and had just over a day of traveling left. Kopur carried all the remaining feed, leaving Lilja only my meager camp gear: a pot, spoon, sleeping bag, change of foot gear, and little else. In spite of having nearly 140 miles behind her, she was so frisky I rode her occasionally. The total 200-pound load should have been about her limit, but she just wanted to trot all the time, moving steadily at her gentle little jog-pace. Although not showy like that of the better-gaited Icelandics, her pace felt pleasant to ride, and that's all I cared about.

"It ain't over til it's over!" I kept warning myself. The trip seemed too easy, and Kopur's previous escapades left me wary. I could just see myself chasing him 148 miles down my backtrail! I spent one last night out, Lilja's thick, double-length saddle blanket barely protecting me from the cold of the sub-zero ground below.

Walking along just a mile from the little river town of Nenana on the morning of the eighth day, I heard a shout from behind, and I didn't have to look to know it was a musher ordering his team to pass us.

Our horses might stand placidly watching our own team pass within three feet of them, but a strange pack of dogs whizzing up out of the blue was too much. Kopur bolted.

He careened into Lilja and they both galloped past me. Dodging the bolting horses, I set myself against Lilja's lead rope. She snapped around and stopped, dropping her head. Kopur hit the end of his rope, whiplashed around, and stopped.

The dog team dashed past. Kopur bolted again. Lilja bolted. I leaped aside, set myself, and snapped Lilja around, and she snapped Kopur around and they both stopped. The musher looked back and waved. I waved. Nenana was just around the corner.

Julie reached Fairbanks a day ahead of me — which was fortunate, as it took her half a day just to dig the old horse trailer out from under a near-record snowfall. She met me in Nenana and, my goodness, when Lilja saw the trailer that had carried her north three years earlier, her little eyes popped right out. She couldn't convince herself it was real until she reached out and touched it with her nose.

Several days later, during the medical check required for Kopur's return to Canada, our veterinarian expressed surprise at the excellent condition of our horses, pointing out the extra roll of fat over Kopur's shoulders. Apparently, many horses in Fairbanks were still lean after an intense cold spell that winter of 1989, when temperatures plunged to fifty and sixty below for two weeks. Our little Icelandics had weathered it with impunity, even maintaining their weight during the long hike to Nenana. In fact, since arriving in Fairbanks, Lilja had been on a diet because she'd started gaining weight on the plain grass hay we bought for her!

Leaving Lilja and the dogs in care of our ever-obliging brother Ray, we made the long drive back to Edmonton, giving Kopur back to the Icelandic Horse Farm on consignment. At last he was out of the Bush. Our troubles were over but, sadly, his weren't. Kopur changed hands several times, traveling first to California, then Ontario, then to several farms on the East Coast. The last we heard, he was serving as a lawn ornament and not being worked at all.

Our new horse was twelve-year-old Jonaton, a gray gelding built like a draft horse and, at fourteen hands, large for an Icelandic. With a temperament the exact opposite of Kopur's, this horse could do anything we asked of him. Although a bit timid at times, his main reaction to being startled was to give a big jump in place and then freeze up to stare wide-eyed until satisfied that everything was safe after all. Because the Icelandic pronunciation of his name sounded something like "Yawn-a-tawn" — not an easy word to get your mouth around in a crisis — we just called him Jim (or Jimmy, Jimbo, or Jim-Bob, as fancy hit us).

Then insanity struck again. We had decided to breed Lilja, but instead of towing her to a stallion clear down in Edmonton we decided to buy a colt. That way we could keep either three or four horses, or sell whichever ones didn't suit our needs.

With his patchy, shedding coat, the colt didn't look very attractive, but his face shone with sweetness. Later, his deep red summer coat, with its white shoulder patch and legs, would come in as glossy as could be. From the narrow star on his forehead came his Icelandic name, Dropi: Raindrop, or Horse-With-A-Star. Although he had run practically wild for the first year of his life, and had been unapproachable when Robyn Hood bought him from a breeder in British Columbia, Robyn had done a little gentling and he had quickly become friendly and open-minded, willing to be loaded into a trailer, have his feet handled, and accept other basic training.

"Do you think we can train him?" Julie asked Christine.

She screwed her eyes shut for a moment and then replied, "I *think* so."

Still, we were skeptical. Buying Kopur had been such a big mistake that we wondered whether we knew enough, after just three years of owning horses, to train a green one, much less handle a three-year-old stallion. Once again, insanity prevailed. Dropi came home with us, and we never regretted it, even though we could not ride him for another year. Icelandic horses mature very slowly, which decreases the daily nutritional demands of the growing youngsters. Consequently, they should not be ridden until turning four or even five. During the long summer to come, Dropi would tag along without so much as a saddle on his back. Lilja was thrilled to meet her new companions, especially when she found she could boss them around — even big Jim, who was simply too polite to argue.

I kept reminding myself, "It ain't over til it's over!" We still had to get the horses home again after breakup. After a few weeks in Fairbanks training our new horses for their upcoming travels, we

made the long, bumpy drive to the end of the road, just as we had
with Lilja three years earlier. Pepper, big black Reuben, Streak, and
Amber came along to serve as pack dogs and bear protection.

Once again Lilja and I climbed into the foothills of the Alaska
Range, more confident now that Julie and two more horses were
backing us up. Marching in the lead, Lilja knew just what we were
doing, and come heat wave or high water, she was headed for home.

The heat wave came first. Mid-June brought temperatures in
the seventies and eighties, and we knew the glaciers of the Alaska
Range must be melting fast, sending floodwaters down the river
ahead. Even in the shallow stretches high water could turn us back,
forcing us to wait until colder weather.

Up and up we climbed, pushing through scattered alders and
glossy-leafed dwarf birch before breaking out onto a high plateau
covered with low tundra plants shimmering under the hot summer
sun. We paused now and then at rare patches of sparse grass, letting
the horses graze while we rested among the cool tussocks. Her mouth
stuffed with greenery, Lilja often lifted her head to gaze out at the
silvery river winding through the bottomland below us.

Camping on a high ridge that evening, we sat enthralled looking across the valley to the startling slopes of Denali shooting
skyward, 17,000 feet higher than our airy site. Thin wisps of clouds
hovered across its face, occasionally cloaking the peaks while a three-
quarters-full moon slipped softly up the mountain's eastern flanks.
Although the freezing line was at five or six thousand feet, the steep
upper ramparts caught and held no snow, leaving blue granite bare
to the lingering summer sun on this, the longest day of the year.

Just thinking about such a scene gives me a shivery feeling. Some
people say such vastness makes them feel small. Not me. I feel bigger, stronger, just knowing I am a little part of it all, my heart
encompassing the whole great land at once.

A day and a half more brought us to the crossing of the braided
glacial river. As we suspected, the water was rising, but the first few
channels didn't seem too bad. Although each ran deeper than the
one before, our two pack horses, the colt, and the four dogs forded
them easily.

Then we paused, and from the safety of a wide, cobbled gravel bar,
we stared out at the gray silt water rushing past, frigid and hip-deep.
The swiftness of the current could easily knock one of us off our feet.

The big gelding Jonaton, nicknamed Jim, quickly made friends with Lilja on the trip home.

Grimly, Julie headed out first, leading Jim and gripping his mane for stability. The sturdy gelding walked close behind her, with the red colt tied to his pack saddle with a break-away string, and dogs scattered ahead, behind, and between the horses. Leading Lilja, I grabbed Dropi's tail for support as I followed them into the icy water.

Just as Julie pushed into the deepest part of the cobble-bottomed channel, the current caught Amber, swimming with her light pack, and swept her downstream, slamming her into Jim. Startled, the white horse lurched forward, knocking Julie down into the foaming gray water. His lunge jerked Dropi ahead, wrenching the colt's tail from my grip just as Julie disappeared into the channel.

Without the colt's support, I started washing downstream. Only by clinging to Lilja's halter could I stay upright and struggle forward, quartering with the forceful current. The mare strode ahead, stabilizing me, and by the time I regained my footing in shallower water, Julie was straggling onto the gravel bar with Jim and Dropi. She had been stomped underwater by the rushing horses.

"The only thing worse than being trampled by stampeding horses, is being trampled while you're drowning," she said sadly.

The last channel looked like the most dangerous yet. Surging water, pushed along by run-off from the rapidly melting glaciers, raged in standing waves past our sandbar, looking six feet deep as it boiled over alder sweepers. Scouting it carefully, we found one spot that, judging by the swirling water, was a bit slower and perhaps four feet deep. Just downstream lurked some positively wicked sweepers, spruce stumps and large willows raking through the boiling water, waiting to snag any unfortunate person, dog, or horse that didn't succeed in making the crossing. Nearly out of horse feed, we counted on reaching our Twelve-Mile camp, eight miles away, by the following evening. With rain starting to fall, the water could only rise higher.

We stopped for a quick supper to think things out, although with the specter of that crossing hanging over us, we had to choke down our food. By the time we finished, the water had risen on the marker stick we'd planted at the edge of the sandbar. Clearly, if we were to cross, we had to do it right away.

Julie and I dared not walk across that channel, choosing to ride the more stable horses instead. Lilja's homing instinct seemed about to pay off. As I perched atop her near-empty pack saddle, she gamely plunged into the water.

It was deeper than I thought. Chest-high, the water tore at my dangling feet and slammed into the broad side of the little mare, threatening to wash her away. Without warning, she dropped into a hole, her nose dunking underwater.

I snatched at her lead rope, trying desperately to turn her back to the relative safety of the island. Ordinarily easy to control with just a lead rope for a rein, this time she stiffened her neck and drove ahead: *she was going home.* Stubbornly, she regained her footing and rushed for the bank. Jim, with Julie aboard, hurried after her, followed closely by the colt. Pack dogs were washing far and wide, only to scramble out just before the sweepers snagged them. Then, abruptly, we all stood on solid ground, laughing and shouting and trembling.

We camped in the alders, with nothing but a scattering of horsetails for forage. Rain poured down all night, and the river rose a foot in twelve hours, reaching a mad flood stage. There was no turning back now. In the morning we gave the horses the last of the feed; the scrubby alders and spruce and moss offered little even for open-minded Icelandics. Following a rapidly rising slough, we reached our Twelve-Mile trapline camp, and the food cached there the winter before, by late afternoon. Rain pelted us all day and when we reached the camp, the normally knee-high creek ran waist-deep. The next day found it flooding bank-to-bank, and the Birch Cabin and home were on the opposite side.

The wall tent we used for a winter shelter had been taken home for the summer, to safeguard it against bears and mildew, but by throwing a tarp over the collapsed roof of Slim's old abandoned cabin, we were able to light a fire in the little camp stove and dry out a bit. Sitting in the cramped quarters, we contemplated our fate.

"Too bad we don't have a cabin here," I commented. "We could dry out a lot better. And the dogs could come in."

In reply, Julie chanted:

"Here we sit, the river's flooded
All dreadful things that we have drudded . . ."

"Drudded?"

"Dreaded doesn't rhyme," she pointed out, continuing:

"All these things just can't be true
That happened here to me and you!"

The following evening found us six miles downstream, waiting for the water level to drop so we could make the ford and regain our trapline trail. We sat there for twenty-four hours, until the water fell and the current slackened. In the evening, we finally mounted our faithful steeds and, perched atop their packs, rode across. Although almost swimming, the horses had no trouble in these calmer waters. Seven exhausting hours of slopping through deep moss, over tussocks, and around countless potholes of the horse-eating variety brought us to the Birch Cabin, grateful for the twenty-four-hour daylight that had allowed us to travel past midnight. If Lilja hadn't known where she was headed, we would have had some mighty unhappy little horses. Fortunately, the others picked up on her determination, following her stoically until the cabin's grassy yard came into sight.

Two glorious days at the Birch Cabin revived us all. Julie and I cleaned up, doing summer chores while the horses mowed a wild pasture nearby. Then, taking a deep breath, we plunged on into Bogland, the last frightful distance of the trip, following a different route than on my disastrous first efforts. Although home lay only sixteen miles away by winter trail, our contorted path dodging swamps and marshes would add at least four miles. We planned to take three days, traveling in easy stages. After what had happened to Lilja on her first trip, I wanted the horses well rested, so if they did fall in, they might have the energy to get themselves out.

"It ain't over til it's over," I sang as we boldly headed through the wilderness. Pink bog rosemary and cranberry blossoms, white leatherleaf and spirea and Labrador tea and other tiny wildflowers brightened our path, but we only had eyes for the dangers under the feet of our trusting horses. Making countless detours, we crashed through miles of stunted black spruce that snagged and tore the canvas pack tarps. We tromped across endless soft, deep moss, and checked out a multitude of boggy crossings by poking a long stick down to see if the overlying moss rested on solid ground or floated over deep, horse-gulping water. Our efforts deflected trouble for a day and a half.

That was when we reached the one obstacle that we couldn't detour: a 200-foot beaver dam spanning a swampy creek of red-brown water that flowed slowly between steep, grassy walls. The water varied from one to four feet in depth; the goo beneath was another five feet deep or more. The stick-and-mud dike provided our only bridge.

The dam lay just eight miles from home. Lilja gamely slid down the grassy, eight-foot bank to reach it and boldly started across. But within ten feet she was in trouble. Her hard hooves slipped on freshly peeled wet logs and punched down through the new construction the beaver had thrown up when the water rose during the recent flood. Helplessly she slithered sideways into mucky water, lurching back up only to fall again. This time she rolled over the lower edge of the dam to crash down onto her side in the green marsh below, her legs cast upwards against the bulwark of sticks and mud.

Ordinary horses have trouble regaining their feet when cast on one side with the legs higher than the body, and being in a swamp doesn't help. But Lilja is not an ordinary horse. Wiggling, rolling, and squirming, she clawed her way back onto the dam and made a beeline for the safety of the bank. Immediately she stepped in another soft spot which sent her tumbling into the muck.

After a momentary struggle, Lilja groaned sadly, laid her head down, and shut her eyes as if to say, *That's it, folks, I'm going to die now.* But wait! Just as her eyes closed, she spotted a blade of bright green grass. Stretching out her skinny neck, she plucked it, munched it down, and lay back, once more ready to die. But she wasn't fooling us.

"Lilja, GET UP!" we shouted. Heaving on her empty pack saddle, Julie and I rolled her upright and with an effort she crawled forward, scrambled to her feet, and bounced back up the near-vertical bank.

Desperately we cleaned up the dam, removing loose, slippery logs to make it as safe as possible. This time we tried with Dropi; at least he was small enough to pull out more easily. The poor little fellow followed us trustingly onto the dam, but it was no good. He never quite fell, but after fifteen feet of stumbling and sinking, we dared not go farther, and turned him back to solid ground.

For a day the horses grazed the lush grass along the bank while we searched the creek for a safe crossing. We found nothing but bottomless muck and other beaver dams even less stable. Finally I walked home, catching a ride with Daddy in his outboard boat the last few miles, and flew around in the Cessna to scout out the area from the air. Boggy creeks sprawled like penetrating cancerous growths in the lowlands, endlessly intertwined. If we walked clear around the headwaters of this one, it would shoot us against other drainages farther north. After four days we admitted defeat. I rejoined Julie, and we retreated back to the Birch Cabin with its plentiful wild forage and supply of cached food. While Julie babysat the horses, I returned home to care for the garden and fly the rest of the dogs home from Fairbanks, where our brother Ray had been caring for them.

A second heat wave brought on another flood of glacier melt, delaying our tentative plans to try another route home. Then a long rainy period prolonged the high water. For two months Julie and I took turns caring for the horses at the Birch Cabin and tending the dog team, garden, fishnets, poultry, and berry-picking at home, and attending a couple weekend craft bazaars in Fairbanks to make some money.

Frankly, I much preferred the quiet life at the isolated trapline camp. Life there quickly slipped into a pleasant if solitary routine. Every morning I rode Lilja across the creek, leading Jim and allowing

Dropi to skip along loose. Then we galloped down the sandbar, trotted into the woods, and headed for the pasture, where I left one horse on a picket to be sure of finding them later. Returning to the camp, I waded the waist-high creek and filled the day with chores: writing, sewing, cutting wood, building doghouses, or working on the cabin or corral. Sometimes I fished for grayling as a treat for myself. I also shot squirrels for the dogs to eat with their boiled rice, and, after hunting season opened, grouse for myself.

Although I had no visitors during my stay, Julie had several when she took my place. Streak alerted her to the first, baying deeply one morning at some large animal down by the river. When Julie heard a loud, rumbling roar, she knew Streak had cornered a moose in the creek. Loping down to the sandbar, pistol in hand, she saw a cow and calf facing her from about thirty feet across the water. The cow's roaring snarls warned Julie to stand back because they were coming ashore.

Julie didn't want the mother moose to come close where the dogs might chase her, possibly getting trampled. "Go away!" she shouted.

The cow didn't know what to do. She shoved her calf with a huge nose, turning in a circle, growling in the strange way that they have. She was about the ugliest moose Julie had ever seen. Her face was exceedingly long and narrow, bigger around the nose than the eyes. Her tongue kept flicking out as she growled, and, rolling her head to glare at Julie, she flashed the whites of her eyes. The calf, belly-deep in water, looked robust and healthy but confused.

"Go away!" Julie shouted.

The cow shook rainwater off her coat and indicated that she wanted to come ashore.

"Go *away!*" Julie shouted sternly.

The calf shook raindrops from his eyes, then his whole body. Julie was getting wet, too, and she didn't like the way that cow kept glaring. The big brute clearly didn't intend to back down.

Julie fired a warning shot into the air with her .44 Ruger revolver.

The cow allowed as how she might find business on the far side of the stream after all, and shoved her calf back to the distant shore. Streak was a good boy and did not chase her. The moose's growling

With lightly loaded horses, we could ride across streams. As Miki perches on top of Lilja's pack, Dropi leads the way and Streak and Reuben follow behind.

had upset Jim, who thought it must be a grizzly at least, but the other two horses seemed disinterested.

A couple days later, as Julie saddled the horses to ride downriver to a pasture, the dogs came alive. They stood on the riverbank testing the southwest wind, tense as they keenly pulled a fresh scent from the air. Julie didn't see anything across the river, but before riding on to the pasture, she took her pistol just in case. Leaving the horses to graze, with the dogs voluntarily standing by to guard them, she walked back to camp alone.

"Well, strike me down if there wasn't a bear in the yard!" she told me later. "His coat was just as black and glossy as could be — Miss Clairol could take a few lessons from him."

As Julie stepped up, the bear panicked and fled, crashing through the barbed-wire horse corral *("Sproi-oi-oing!"* Julie said) and heading for parts unknown. The last she saw was his glossy black rump hightailing it upriver. He had thoroughly sprung one wall of the small corral, which Julie had to repair; she later rebuilt the whole fence, replacing the hazardous wire with spruce poles.

The bear didn't come back, although some bear did tear down

some red surveyor tape she had hung four miles away. So many black bears tear down our red trail flagging that Julie once commented, "Have you noticed bears' affinity for red tape? They should be in the government."

Summer flew by as we took turns vacationing at the trapline camp and slaving away at home. Scouting by air, I plotted a fifty-mile escape route from the Birch Cabin. By following the high bank of a small creek for twenty-five miles, we could make a short portage to reach the very site where we'd vacationed with Lilja and Kopur two summers earlier. But the weather alternated between heat, with subsequent high water, and rain, with subsequent flooding, and we just didn't trust any river crossings. Horses, with their large bulk perched on long thin legs, tend to roll if a fast current hits them broadside when their feet are in quicksand.

Finally, as autumn weather cooled the higher elevations, the glaciers stopped melting. The rains stopped falling, the rivers dropped, and at last, after a two-month wait, Julie and I joined at the Birch Cabin to prepare for the week-long trip home.

With grass yellowing and unknown land ahead, the two adult horses would have to carry heavy loads of grain in addition to our own food, dog food, and camp gear. Of course the dogs could shoulder a little weight, and I planned to pack our sleeping bags myself to cut down on the bulk the horses had to smash through the close-knit alders bordering the stream.

"I'll bring my .22," I suggested. "There are lots of grouse and squirrels around, and we can leave this canned meat and dog food."

Julie looked skeptical; risking any sort of survival situation is strictly against our policy. But at worst we'd all be just a bit hungry for a few days, and she acquiesced. "All right. But only if *you* carry it!"

Julie led the pack horses, the colt scampered along loose, and three ranging pack dogs, each loaded with ten to fifteen pounds, completed our entourage. I took the lead, carrying my bulky if lightweight pack and resting my old .22 single-shot over my arm, its back sight held in place with strapping tape. The sights were so far off I had to aim an inch above a grouse's head to hit it, but I downed a squirrel that evening for the dogs, and almost every day after that we were blessed with one or more grouse. We ate the succulent meat simmered with noodles, or, our favorite way, roasted slowly over the evening fire. Every day I also picked several cups of rose hips, reddened by the August sun, as a nutritious treat for the horses, especially Lilja, who we hoped was now in foal.

For three days and twenty-five miles we pushed along, heading almost directly away from home, a course that did not please Lilja one bit. Sometimes the creek bank spread out like a park, lovely with towering white spruce scattered on a carpet of dry mosses and lichens, and no undergrowth to slow our progress. Other times we had to push through nearly impenetrable thickets. (Have you ever seen a five-foot-wide loaded pack horse try to squeeze through a one-foot-wide gap in the trees? Not a pretty sight.) Although we circled the worst thickets, they often forced us into vast expanses of hummocky tussocks, or, worse yet, Bogland itself, slowing our progress considerably.

On the morning of the fourth day we arrived at an old trapping cabin which, according to my aerial reconnaissance, marked the spot where we had to portage over to the river.

Taking a deep breath, I led the way cross-country through a light obscuring rain, hoping to cross a featureless, mile-wide expanse of black spruce, tussocks, and taiga and hit the next river near our little island camp from two summers before.

Marching ahead, I relied solely on a compass heading. But half a mile later, I realized with a start that the metal barrel of my .22 was drawing the compass needle to one side. We were going the wrong way!

"Here, *you* carry it!" I ordered, shoving the mischievous rifle at Julie. Making a slight course adjustment, I plunged on, Julie following with the pack horses and Dropi ripping up mouthfuls of wiry tussock grass as he trailed along.

The flatlands rose slightly to better ground, and suddenly we broke out on a thirty-foot bank just a short distance above our target. As we gazed through stout cottonwoods to the silvery river below, a few grouse exploded up. I snatched my rifle back and moments later had our supper in hand. Dropping down the tall, overgrown bank, we made the shallow crossing to the island.

Lilja had not been pleased with our progress, knowing we were heading farther from home. But when she marched out onto that familiar sandbar, her gloomy outlook on this summer-long expedition reversed itself. She tossed her head, stiff white mane surging like the whitecaps of a breaking wave. She recognized this place! From here she *knew* she could get home. We stripped off the saddles, turning all three horses loose to buck and roll delightedly in the soft sand. Thoroughly pleased, they grazed on the fading grass, horsetails, and willow leaves as we dried our damp clothes under a fresh new sun. Roasting our grouse to perfection, we gnawed them down to the bones, which the drooling dogs quickly polished off. Satiated, we sat back to rest, greatly relieved to be on familiar ground.

Of course we weren't home yet! The major river crossing ahead was the one we'd dreaded all that long summer of high water. Even now, with the river lower, we weren't sure about it; dropping water is slower and calmer, but often leaves quicksand behind.

We tried it the following morning. Lilja's delicate nostrils quivered, her mouth set in a tight line as she determinedly felt her way, stepping gingerly or rushing when the bottom sank under her hooves. Jim and then Dropi followed close behind, and we safely reached the far side, dripping, chilly, and ecstatic.

"The hard part's over and vacation time begins!" I warbled as we reloaded the packs. Climbing the steep bank above the river, we took a deep breath and entered the twelve-mile-long Burn.

A day and a half later we staggered out at the lower edge, tattered and blackened. The Burn had gobbled us up, chewed and torn and bruised us, only to spit us out as unpalatable. Snags and deadfall battered our gear and tried our patience, but we fought back with extra cord and triple-diamond hitches over each pack.

Streak caught a porcupine — his fourth that summer — but fortunately we carried pliers for quill removal, and we skinned and cooked the prickly beast for the dogs' dinner that afternoon. Between squirrels, grouse scraps, and the porcupine, the dogs only needed half of their meager food supply during the trip.

We walked a couple more miles on the riverbank and then cut over to Bogland to avoid more quicksand downriver. Those inland swamps still had us worried. Two years had passed since we'd marked that scanty path through the maze, and if we lost it, we'd probably disappear forever. But we got lucky, only really losing our way once in a spot where we could just cut across relatively dry ground to reach a creek ahead.

We spent that last night at an old camp in a park-like bench above the swampy little creek. As beaver slapped their tails indignantly at our intrusion, the horses peacefully grazed the sparse, coarse grasses. We spread our damp, tattered gear out to dry in the evening sun, and then it rained all night. We didn't care. We were almost home and could even hear the distant grumble of heavy equipment rebuilding the airstrip eight miles away. We had only one more challenge: another beaver dam.

We hadn't crossed it with horses for two years, and the dam had deteriorated since then. When we reached it the following afternoon, we paused. At most questionable spots we led Dropi first. He was the smallest, and the other two, being harness-broken, could pull him out if he fell into serious trouble. Inexperienced though he was, he had trustingly stepped out on the most wretched footing, crossed the worst rivers, and clambered over the most frightful deadfall. Until now.

The poor little fellow took one look at that dam and broke into a sweat. He trembled as he stepped after us, only to balk at the very edge, recalling all too vividly that other awful dam of two months ago.

Tied to a nearby spruce, Lilja pawed impatiently. This journey to trade in Kopur had been a long one; we'd been gone from the end of March until today, the last day of August. She knew home lay only three miles away, and no beaver dam was going to stop her now!

I untied her lead rope and Lilja stomped forward as if to say, *I'll show you how to do it!* She marched right out onto that dam and straight across to the other side. Impressed by her audacity, Jim followed with just a little hesitation, and then the red colt tiptoed tentatively across. They made it!

We hit the birch-covered hill, and the horses thrilled at the feel of dry, solid ground beneath their feet. Usually placid Dropi went a little crazy. He ran and bucked and shook his thick neck until his mane flew. He'd never been there, but somehow he knew he was almost home. Even steady, quiet Jim seemed relieved.

I never saw Lilja so happy as when she stepped out onto our grassy lawn. We turned her loose and she was so excited she could hardly eat — and that's really something for our little glutton. She galloped up and down the trail, raced over to see the sled dogs, and then came charging back again, Dropi hot on her heels.

Home! she seemed to cry out with every fiber of her being. *Home at last!*

The following spring Lilja gave birth to a beautiful pale palomino colt. We named him Trausti, which means "Trusty" in Icelandic. Although thrilled, we had hoped for a filly so we could have two breeding mares. We bred Lilja once more before having Dropi gelded by a vet who flew out to our homestead. Even as a four-year-old stallion Dropi could be led around by the forelock, but in our isolated area having a new foal every year wasn't feasible, and since the horses all ran loose together, gelding was necessary for birth control.

A month before Lilja's second foal was due, we sold Jim and Trausti to families in Nome. Although a great horse, strong and willing in harness, Jim was too much of a kid's horse. We hoped to keep the new foal, and as we didn't want more than three horses, those two had to go. Splitting the cost of a charter with the new owners, I flew them in a Sky Van to Anchorage. Both horses behaved impeccably during the flight — quite a relief after the scare Kopur had given us. At Anchorage International Airport, I transferred them to a horse trailer which was lifted, horses and all, into a Hercules cargo plane bound for Nome. Despite a small earthquake and a long delay in loading, the transition went smoothly. Sadly I said goodbye to my friends as they departed for another life. Trausti grew up to be a gorgeous dark palomino stallion, and happily, both he and Jim have done well with their new families.

In early June, when the grass was greening and wild roses filled the air with their perfume, Lilja gave birth to another colt, the cutest little red and white pinto. Sitting with the newborn in the soft glow of 3 A.M. summer light, Julie and I studied a list of Icelandic names, settling on Andi, a word easily pronounced by Americans and meaning "Spirit."

Watching the little fellow testing his wobbly legs, we admired the large red patterns on a background of white, with smaller red spots splattered across his snowy back and sides. As he tolted and loped around just two hours after his birth, the breaking sun struck a spring shower across the bay, and magically a double rainbow materialized against the dark clouds. Inspired, we lengthened his name to Regnbogi Andi — Rainbow Spirit. Dropi and Lilja had done us proud once more.

CHAPTER 7

FALL
FOLLIES

"RUN FOR YOUR LIFE!" I screamed.

The ground had exploded with yellow jackets buzzing furiously beneath my feet. Miki, two steps ahead of me, had just walked over an underground nest cleverly positioned under the trail we followed to fetch the ranging horses.

We raced beyond the raging mob of hornets and down to the marsh where the horses grazed on sedges and wild grass. Trausti was just a few months old that fall, and Dropi barely green-broke, so I jumped onto Jim's broad bare back and Miki piled onto Lilja. "We'll have to gallop past the hornets and hope the horses don't buck us off into the swarm if they get stung," I told Miki.

"RUN FOR YOUR LIVES!" I screamed as we rode toward the humming nest. Kicking Jim, I charged the still-swarming mob, Miki galloping close behind.

No luck. Jim gave a surprised grunt and slammed his nose against his chest, trying to knock away the stinging hornets. I kicked him hard. Normally slow and lumbering, the strong white horse shot forward with alacrity and we bombed past the outraged insects. After that, we galloped over the hornets every day, the horses fearless but aware of the need for speed. Even a year later, when the nest was long gone, they still rushed past that awful place.

The hornets are at their peak in August, when some years they rival our armies of mosquitoes, and they even strip the flesh from our drying fish. A bucket of fresh fish left outside is soon crawling with hornets. Luckily they aren't vicious when they're away from the nest seeking food, and a gentle tap on

Julie

the bucket with my toe will disperse them. The way to rile a hornet is to offend his nest. When the dogs accidentally trample one of these sacred havens, they're usually moving too fast to get caught, but sometimes a hornet burrows deep into a dog's thick coat and stings him. Unable to scratch the hornet out, the unhappy dog runs to us instead, crying and squirming as we gingerly dig the barbed insect from the dense fur.

Horses pose a greater problem, because they're programmed to bolt when unexpectedly hurt. Icelandics rarely run blindly, but in the case of hornets it's best to leave in a hurry without actually bolting. Lilja once stepped on a nest while I rode her bareback down a steep hill. We both got stung as I heeled her into a quick run. She charged down the slope in big jumps, head down and back humped. I sprained my hands with a death-grip on her mane — no way was I going to spill off into that rabid horde!

The worst encounter occurred when Jim was hauling logs for a new shed in the horse corral. As I led him down the hill through the forest, the log hitched to his harness jammed on a fallen tree. Turning to free it, I recoiled in horror when I saw a stream of hornets bubbling up from the dry leaves beneath the horse. He was standing on top of a nest. The furious little beasts attacked his legs and belly but he was hopelessly stuck. Unable to flee, he could only jump up and down. On the nest.

I rushed to free the log, but couldn't reach it without being stung. Jim frantically whacked at the excruciating stings, but he never tried to bolt.

"Get up!" I shouted. "Get up!" I didn't care if he broke the traces. I wanted him out of there.

Jim dropped his head and rammed into the harness with a powerful lunge. His log smashed through the fallen tree and careened after him. "Run for your life!" I hollered, racing behind as the bees trailed angrily after us. Once out of range, I jerked off my outer wool shirt to shake off the hornets drilling through the heavy material.

"Whoa, whoa," I shouted, but Jim didn't stop. He galloped through the open corral gate, whipping the log around to park it with the others before stopping to wait for me. I doctored my stings and we hauled a few more logs so Jim wouldn't finish the day brooding over an alarming experience.

Sometimes the hornets are on the receiving end of an attack. These days we only remove nests from critical locations, like the outhouse, but as kids we burned lots of underground nests with diesel fuel. Way back before Marmee let us play with fire we had fewer options. Once Ray found a nest in the most awful place — the strawberry patch in our front yard. He declared that we could incapacitate the villains at least temporarily if we sprayed them with whole powdered milk. We all filled our mouths with the sweet powder and tiptoed up to the nest. Ray stomped on it to bring the hornets out in a frenzy of rage and POOF! All together we blew the milk at them. And you know what? It worked!

A painless way to eliminate hornet nests is to have a small bear around. A nice little bear that only comes out at night, who will dig up nests to eat the larvae. One bear destroyed dozens of nests on our hill, some within a few yards of home. Of course, you want a black bear, not a grizzly. Grizzlies are even more scary than hornets. A grizzly is what we got one year during the dark nights of September.

A moonless September night can be the darkest of all the year. Even as the nights lengthen in August, we usually have enough twilight to spot a lurking bear, if not to read a book as we can in midsummer. By October, a skiff of snow will reflect any light from the night sky, making the background gray instead of black. In September, though, nights are long and black without any snow for contrast, and you can walk right into a tree — or a bear — without seeing it.

Very late on one of those black nights, our normally quiet dogs became especially noisy. Of course, the cool fall nights make them more vocal than usual, as they impatiently anticipate the arrival of ice and snow, sledding and excitement. Then, too, I knew a little fox had been sneaking around, so I brought only a flashlight when I checked the dogs. They looked excited but not angry, and I peered into the darkness without much concern, my light flashing across brush below the dog yard. There! Small green eyes reflected the light, but I couldn't see the critter who owned them. To be safe, I turned loose the big guys, Comet and Streak, to chase it off. We walked below the dog yard, where they picked up the trail.

The crashing chase that followed sounded disturbingly like it involved a bear, but I wasn't convinced. When the dogs returned from their errand, I tied them up and went back to bed. An hour later, the dogs started up again. "Your turn," I mumbled to Miki. She checked it out, then came back for her rifle.

"Sounds like a bear," she reported. I grabbed a flashlight and a .45 automatic and followed her out. We heard the animal slopping through soft mud and water in the shallow, silt-filled bay in front of the cabin.

Miki fired a few shots to speed his departure while I held the flashlight. "I think he's a grizzly," she said. "He looked light-colored, and he had tall shoulders."

"I'm scared," I whispered.

"Me, too," she whispered.

Checking the beach where we had left a moose head from the fall hunt, we found the hundred-pound head and massive antlers gone. Big, wide bear tracks led to the water. The bear had dragged the head, with its sixty-inch rack, out into the muddy bay.

We stood looking at the tracks and listening to the silence of the dark night. One thought stuck in my mind: tomorrow I would be home alone, because Miki and our folks were flying to Fairbanks to attend a hearing. A bear that comes back usually returns more than once, and we had plenty here to interest a bear: moose meat hanging in a screened shed, split fish drying on racks, young turkeys in a pen, horses in the corral, and trapline bait rotting in sacks.

"Are you sure you want to go to town tomorrow?" I asked hopefully. I didn't want to face a grizzly by myself, but Miki said, "I have to go." We had learned that no matter how inconvenient, boring, frustrating, or downright stupid politics could be, we simply had to get involved. Politicians were always trying to ram unwanted projects down our independent and unsuspecting throats, and we had to stay abreast of them or be washed away in the flood of development and industry.

Alone the next evening, I tied Comet and Streak on the beach by the pole fish-drying rack. I staked Hector and young Reuben near the meat shed, and moved toothless old Loki to the horse corral. Barring the door, I laid my pistol, rifle, headlamp, and spare shells on the table. At 1 A.M. the dogs started barking.

Not wanting to mess with the bear if he minded his own business, I hung out the window and listened to him walking down the bay, *globbety-slop, globbety-slop* in the black mud.

An hour later he came back, and again I leaned out to listen. *Globbety-splut, globbety-splut.* Closer this time. I walked down to the beach and stood with Comet and Streak as they loudly dared the intruder to venture closer.

"Go away! Go away!" I shouted. The bear looked at me, eyes glinting in the lamplight. Then he went away.

I left my socks and sweater on when I went back to bed. The bear returned even sooner than I expected. Young Reuben began barking, almost under my bedroom window. At first I thought the big pup was being paranoid, because Hector didn't join him. At ninety-five pounds Reuben was a big dog, but he didn't have much experience. Then I heard the meat shed straining. The bear had torn the screening and was trying to drag down a quarter of hanging meat, and the ridgepole along with it.

Heart sinking, I crept outside and circled the shed warily, rifle ready and headlamp pinned on the small building. The bear backed out through the torn screening just fifteen feet from the dogs and thirty feet from me. My sights were locked on him, but as he fled through the heavy brush my headlamp glittered across dense trees that blocked a clean line of fire.

"Oh — he's black" flashed through my mind as the light briefly exposed the bear's body. He looked small, with low shoulders. Then he was gone. I edged closer to the dogs, nervously scanning the forest and wishing I had shot him. Seconds later the bear's eyes winked through the trees behind me — he had silently circled me, and now prowled back and forth in the darkness.

"Time to call in the SWAT team," I thought. Hurrying to the beach, I unsnapped Comet and Streak. Because of their size and courage, these two were our best bear dogs. They worked well together and had the raw nerve to face a bear, but the intelligence and skill to not push too hard. "Get him," I said as they started up the hill. The dogs located the bear, but they wouldn't chase him. They came back to me.

"Get him," I urged. They left, growled and barked at the bear, and then hurried anxiously back. *"Get him,"* I ordered sternly. They left. This time the growling sounded more serious. With an effort the two dogs drove the bear back up the hillside.

I didn't like this. A black bear should have bolted or climbed a tree; this animal had stood up to the dogs. Maybe it really was a grizzly. Retreating to the house, I listened to the fracas as the dogs grimly battled to drive the bear farther away. Twenty minutes later they all started circling back again, still growling and snarling!

"Time to go again!" I steeled myself, packing my rifle, pistol, spare shells, and headlamp back outside. As I walked down the hill, my beam caught the bear's eyes when he looked up from the thick swamp grass along the shore. Raising Daddy's vintage World War I automatic pistol, I let seven shots fly into the night like so many tiny glowing rockets. The blasts sent my dogs scuttling for cover, but the bear, unconcerned, shuffled on through the mud. *Globbety-splat, globbety-splat.* Then he looked back.

"Go away!" I shouted. Suddenly it seemed funny — or maybe the strain was making me nervous — and I started giggling. "Go away!" I shouted again, and it came out like a shriek.

That shrill tone had an instant effect. The bear turned and cut swiftly toward me. He circled downwind to catch my scent, probably wondering if I was vulnerable. Although almost close enough to shoot, the bear warily avoided entering the full view of my light. I angled closer. So did he. I knew I had to shoot him if I could, but I wanted to see his body, not just his winking eyes. A few more feet should do it.

Then Comet and Streak charged out of the brush. They cut fearlessly between the bear and me, furiously driving him back. They weren't going to let him get me, no sir!

The bear reluctantly retreated to the woods and the dogs returned to my side. The bruin didn't come back, and the next day I walked along our pasture fence pulling long brown hairs from the bottom strand of barbed wire where the bear had pushed under the fence. The brief glimpse of him I'd had made me think he was a black bear, but his prints looked like those of a grizzly. Miki had thought he was a grizzly. He acted like one, and the dogs treated him like one. And when I pulled those long, grizzled hairs from the fence, I had to admit that maybe he *was* a grizzly.

Fall adventures usually aren't quite that exciting. Chores keep us at home harvesting vegetables, berries, and fish, and the only real break in the grind is our fall moose hunt. This brings anxiety as well as excitement, since we depend upon the meat for our winter supply and finding a moose is not always easy. Most people in this area hunt from motorboats, but we usually use a canoe, paddling and poling far up the Old Channel where no outboards can go, to find hunting areas of our own. A little tent houses our sleeping bags and gear, while a big tarp overhead protects us from the frequent rains and shelters our boots, dry firewood, and the little one-burner gas stove we use until we catch a moose. (Smoke from a fire might scare off the moose, who otherwise will sometimes peek curiously inside our tent.)

Along the silty gray river, the autumn air carries rich scents of summer mingling with winter — the crisp but humid smells from dank swamps and river water and the yellowing willow leaves wet from rain. Now and then the thick, musky odor of a fox or mink drifts along the riverbank. Most important are the sounds. Here in the dense willows, you can be a hundred feet from a moose and unable to see more than the gangly legs or a graying antler tine, so we listen for moose instead of looking for them. A twig snapping, a far-off grunt, or the scrape of an antler in brush can set your heart pounding.

It takes a keen ear to locate, identify, and follow a distant moose, because the land is alive with other creatures hurrying to complete their own fall chores. Beavers push through alder thickets, dragging branches to store underwater, and the crack of their tails on the water carries far. Rabbits (snowshoe hares, actually) with feet and ears strikingly white as their winter coats start to replace brown fur, scurry down narrow aisles in the grass as they flee dangers real or imagined. Often we hear wolves howling as their scattered clans, broken up for a summer of small game hunting, rendezvous to form the packs necessary for taking bigger prey during the winter. Ducks drop in on swamps for a hasty feed, then take off with a great whirring of feathers, while the clear musical honking of trumpeter swans drifts in from faraway lakes and ponds. Overhead, giant flocks of sandhill cranes float by hourly, trilling ceaselessly as they whirl in slow dances around the updrafts to gain altitude for their southern migration.

The wind, too, whistles, murmurs, and roars as it sweeps in from the northeast, then shifts to southwest as fall storms do battle with an approaching arctic cold front. The continuous racket clogs ears that strain to filter out all but the faintest faraway *sshhh* of a moose gently pushing through brush.

Each autumn has the same kaleidoscope of sounds, the same swampy smells, with sunlight glancing off the river and shimmering in the leaves, or rain misting down to dampen the crunch of dead twigs underfoot as we range along sloughs, searching for sign — a moose bed, fresh tracks, the trampled, pungent ground or shredded saplings left by a rutting bull. Every year is similar yet unique, each kill so intense that it is branded in the memory like an unforgettable dream.

One year we hunted day and night without crossing any good sign. We were getting scared. A nasty cold kept me in the tent on rainy days, which was every day, so Miki went out alone. One dark evening she came in drenched and empty-handed.

"Well?" I asked.

"We're failures. Is that what you wanted to know? Failures!"

A few hours later, morning dawned brilliantly clear and Miki shot a fine small bull just a couple hundred yards from camp. She had lured the bull across a deep swamp by scratching a tree with a little antler to imitate another moose, which only sweetened her success. She named the moose Archie, and pranced jubilantly around all day singing saucily.

Another year we knew moose were scarce so we began hunting extra early. Day after day we ranged across forests, rivers, and swamps. The only day we delayed hunting was when the forecast called for a solid freeze and we frantically harvested our root vegetables so they wouldn't be lost. Unseasonably cold weather and snow hampered our hunting, but we didn't admit defeat until after dark the night hunting season closed, when we met on the riverbank to go home.

"I kept waiting for you to shoot," I said reproachfully.

"*You* were supposed to shoot the moose," Miki retorted.

"No, *you* were," I said. We stood in the dark for awhile, and then we both sighed and went home. Since we had taken over the family chore thirteen years earlier, that was the first year we failed to find a moose. Fortunately, Miki shot a black bear that fall, and with a moose haunch from a neighbor and meat from grouse, lynx, beaver, and fish, we stretched our meat to last the year.

Rabbits jinxed another hunt. It started when I heard a small bull swim across the river. I don't like to shoot moose in the water — it's

Miki demonstrates how we scratch a moose antler in the brush, often a startlingly effective way to draw out bull moose.

hard enough to butcher a 1,500-pound animal on dry ground — so I cut upriver to head him off. Sneaking after his wet track, I heard a soft thumping as he quietly trotted off to the left.

Or was it a rabbit? I wasn't sure. I've never been good at distinguishing the tiptoe of a moose from the pounding dash of a panicked snowshoe hare. A moose throws a faint vibration into the ground, but otherwise they sound oddly similar. Hoping to find my moose, I silently followed the sound into a grove of alders.

It was a rabbit.

"Dang rabbits!" I swore.

Then I heard it. *Rattle, scrape — tap.* The poetic sound of an antler dragging through the brush. Ah! Meat for the pot. I tiptoed forward. *Tap . . . rattle.* A cautious moose, I see. Carefully, I stalked the sound until it broke into view. It was Miki, rattling the bushes with her little antler, hoping to pull out a moose. She thought I was the moose. I thought she was. By then, it was dark.

At first light we set out again, splitting up to cover more ground, each carrying our prized hunting tools — "Mooseless Antlers," we called them. My goodness, the bushes were crawling with moose that morning! Grunting, rattling, thump-thumping away. I couldn't decide which one to chase. The rabbits were out in force, too, ready to decoy me away from my objective. Finally I zeroed in on a likely-sounding beast moving around a big marsh — Archie's Swamp, we called it, because we got Archie there. I skillfully stalked my target until it materialized again into Miki.

"Any luck?" she whispered.

"No, too many rabbits," I replied.

"Dang rabbits! I'm going to bring up my .22 and trim the population after we get a moose. If we get a moose."

Then we heard a bull for sure. He was rumbling right toward us, so we rattled the bushes to draw him out. He came so close we could see tall willow shoots whipping above his driving antlers. Then a loud snort sounded, followed by total silence. The moose had winded us and quietly vanished. It was right at 8 A.M. anyway. After 8 A.M., the moose disappear to sleep and it's hardly worth hunting again until dusk.

So at dusk we tried again. Moose swarmed the thickets, and time after time we came close only to be distracted by those *dang rabbits!* This continued for several days. At night we chased each other and bunnies. At dawn we chased bunnies and bulls that vaporized precisely at eight. One night Miki returned to camp after dark. "I heard Daddy Twelve-Antlers way back in the swamp. We'd better go in at first light and try to find him."

"Do we want to shoot a moose that far off?"

"It's better than not getting one at all," Miki said gloomily.

Very late in the night we heard a moose prowling around a mile-long island in the river across from camp. The Big Island, of Hawaii, we called it. Lying in the cozy darkness of the tent, we discussed this new development and devised a fresh strategy. Miki would search for Daddy Twelve-Antlers, while I took the canoe over to look for this guy.

Before dawn, we reached our respective positions and settled in to wait for daylight and a sound from the moose. Black trees with lacy twigs etched thin lines against an ashen sky as I stood on a sandbar inhaling the cool morning air. Behind me the river whispered around sweepers and stumps, interrupted occasionally by the startling whack of an alarmed beaver. Overhead, the winnowing of a snipe drifted down from the calm overcast sky. A duck whistled past, a fast flier judging by the sound — perhaps a goldeneye. It landed on the water with a *shirr,* detected my presence, and leaped straight up to fly away.

Only a few minutes passed before I heard the determined crashing of a mature bull far off in the brush. Trembling suddenly, I tentatively raked my Mooseless Antler through a dead alder clump. The bull responded vigorously, marching aggressively toward me, intent on driving this little runt into the river. Suddenly I knew no bunnies would confuse me today. Miki would not lure me away with her own bush-rattling. Eight o'clock would not come too soon.

He came swiftly, angrily, to my call. Bursting from the brush, he saw his mistake and faltered, but too late. He fell on hard ground not far from the river.

We butchered the moose and spent two days ferrying the meat home in the canoe. By taking two loads, we made room for the hide, extra scraps for the dogs, and entrails for trapline bait. We even brought out the rack, the last item to go since we rarely find a use for it. With the winter's meat secure, Miki went rabbit hunting with her little .22. She was out for revenge — and the dogs could use the meat.

Butchering a large moose can be challenging. Miki is lucky because this moose, unlike "Archie," fell on solid ground, and close to the river so we didn't have to pack the meat too far before moving home by canoe.

Hours later she returned empty-handed. She shoved the .22 into its case and swore. "Dang rabbits!" The bunnies had cleared out.

When the horses have pulled the last of our moose meat up from the beach to the meat shed and the quarters are hanging behind the screening, safe from flies, birds, dogs, and smaller varmints if not from bears, we turn to other fall work that has been neglected because of the all-important hunt. We clean out the garden, leaving only a few vegetables to flirt with the coming frost, and Miki layers the refuse with horse manure in her compost cribs. We move the dogs to the winter dog yard, and I repair the doghouses, stuffing them with straw and shooing away greedy little horses that try to steal the bedding to munch on. We build a new trapline sled or overhaul the old one, also working on harnesses and winter clothing. Miki makes our hats from lightweight, soft marten fur, and I make mitts from heavier, wind-proof beaver pelts. We each sew our own fur or canvas mukluks, knit extra-heavy wool socks, and attach new wolf ruffs to our parkas to fend off bitter winter winds. Some years

I hang a new fish net before the fall whitefish run, a pleasant but time-consuming task. From morning until night I sit on the floor of Slim's old cabin, now our workshop, twirling twine into tight knots that hold the filmy netting to the lead-core bottom line and the top float line which suspends the net in the water. Then we set the eighty-yard net under the lake ice, hoping to catch a few hundred fish to feed our dogs during the winter.

The fur money from last spring has been spent by now, but freezeup is still our richest time of year, for we have been harvesting and stocking up supplies at a frantic pace all summer. Piles of seasoned birch firewood stand stacked against the coldest winter. By our feed shed, a pole shelf sags under the weight of hundreds of frozen whitefish for the dogs and sacks of bait for the trapline — moose bones and guts, fish heads, chicken and grouse feathers.

The potato room in our stone basement is stuffed with boxes, bags, and buckets of potatoes, carrots, beets, onions, cauliflower, cabbages, and sometimes pumpkins and squash along with the last of the tomatoes, lettuce, celery, and cucumbers. Against one wall of the basement, tall stacks of wooden gas crates serve as shelves now loaded with food, both store-bought food from town and the food we have preserved over the last four months. Jam jars by the dozen crowd two shelves: strawberry, blueberry, cranberry, raspberry, and sometimes currant, high-bush cranberry, or crowberry. And Mason jars, cases of them, packed with moose meat, whitefish, rhubarb, pickled beets, and maybe pickled cucumbers or carrots. Various tins and jars contain dehydrated vegetables and berries to be eaten while camping or out on the trapline. Cranberry juice, squeezed from gallons of cranberries picked in September, fills old ketchup jars.

We store another five to ten gallons of cranberries in the porch, where they stay cool until winter arrives to freeze them. In the meat shed, we leave one or two quarters of frozen meat hanging, ready for a roast to be sawed off for dinner, although most of the meat is packaged and stored in Daddy's homemade, battery-operated freezer. Not all the meat will fit because the big box is already stuffed with garden vegetables and berries, along with chickens and turkeys raised over the summer.

Surrounded by these riches, we aren't so troubled if cash is tight, but there's no time to relax and bask in the warm feeling of finished labor. Between these major chores we fill handcraft orders, meet writing deadlines, finish summer projects, fly to Fairbanks for shopping, haul boats up from the freezing lake ice, clean stovepipes, deworm and vaccinate dogs and horses, trim the horses' hooves, and store away summertime gadgets like rototillers and water pumps.

This whirlwind of fall chores doesn't give us much time to play with the horses. Now and then we hitch up one to haul moose meat, potatoes, fish, firewood, water, or freight, but we don't do much actual riding. So we were tickled one day when our young neighbor, Becky, wanted to spend the afternoon riding with us. This was a perfect excuse to horse around, and luckily we had three riding horses that fall, Lilja, Jim, and Dropi, so we could all go.

Sitting astride Jim, I led the way up the hill through the forest of mature birch and stately spruce trees. Only a few songbirds remained, mostly chickadees, red polls, and juncos, and they were feeding quietly, gathering strength to face the long winter. The forest, barren of leaves and scantily clad in lacy patches of soggy snow, had better visibility now with the branches bare, and we could often see the flat gray water of the lake far below the rolling slopes. The two-mile climb to the top of the hill had the horses puffing a little despite switchbacks that eased the grade.

At the very top, in a pocket of black spruce and wild grass, the dogs crossed an exciting scent and trailed it to a leaning tree where they apparently had found some small critter cornered under the roots.

The horses needed to catch their breath anyway, so I slid off to investigate. Amber and Pepper backed off to make way for me, but Streak hovered at my side, urging me to look. Under the low hummock I saw a den formed by the roots, but the partly frozen ground had not been tracked upon since the last snow. I squatted and bent my head to peek inside.

In the darkness I glimpsed a soft movement. As my eyes adjusted to the dim light I realized it was a bear. He lay curled up an arm's length from my face, his heavy muzzle turning slowly toward me as he peered out with sleepy little eyes. I could have easily reached in and touched him, but I didn't.

"It's a bear den," I reported loudly, standing up. Then, to be sure everybody understood, I added, "With a bear in it."

The bear didn't come out. He had settled in for hibernation and probably felt safer in his hole.

"I think we'll leave now," I said, and we did. Pepper and Amber fell in behind the horses, but Streak stayed by the den for a long time hoping the bear would make an appearance.

We thought about going back later to shoot the bear for meat because we weren't catching enough fish to feed the dogs, but we didn't. I thought this little bear had been eating hornet nests earlier in the fall. He never bothered us, and we decided not to bother him.

Amidst the hectic schedule, and between bouts of grim weather that often settle over this area in late fall, I try to fit in one last flight to town to tidy up our affairs for the winter. One memorable year when I wanted to fly the plane in for its annual inspection, the weather stayed bad throughout freezeup and the ice was so thick we could cross the lake with horses before the sky began to clear. As cold winter air gradually forced back the clouds, the moisture condensed into fog and haze that obscured visibility despite a weak sun that filtered through the lingering ice crystals.

For three days I crossed the lake to heat the plane's engine, hoping the haze would burn off. Three other pilots arrived daily with the same idea. The weather here gradually improved, but over Fairbanks it was still marginal. Finally an incoming pilot reported reasonable visibility en route. Within minutes, all four planes were in the air.

Our little Cessna 140, which Marmee and a friend had bought in 1950, didn't fly as fast as the other planes, and dusk was just starting to thicken the hazy, overcast sky as I approached the small city of Fairbanks. Knowing the flat light on the snow made it hard to judge altitude when landing, I considered diverting to the well-lit main airport, but my pickup was parked at Phillip's Field near downtown. I decided to make an approach to the narrow little gravel strip, and if I couldn't see the runway clearly, I'd pass over it and swing around to International.

I let the Cessna down cautiously, using enough power for a speedy go-around if it looked bad. But it looked fine. I could make out tracks on the runway. Throttling back, I let the plane settle to the ground. The plane contacted sticky snow and slowed down abruptly. One moment I was rolling out, and the next snow was flooding the windshield in a flashing whirlwind of movement and confusion.

I looked around, bewildered. I wasn't moving anymore. Worse, I was hanging upside-down! The plane had flipped, somersaulting to land in deep snow off the runway. The unexpected maneuver left me dizzy and disoriented, but unhurt. Then, realizing what had happened, I pulled myself through the shoulder harness, popped the seat belt, and fell in a heap on the ceiling of the plane. Squirming upright, I popped the door latch. For a horrible moment the door stuck, trapping me, but when I pushed hard it ground open and I tumbled out.

Mercy!

The runway was plowed narrower than usual. While I had seen the cleared runway, in the poor light I *hadn't* seen the snow berms encroaching on either side because they blended in with the snow everywhere else. The sticky, wet snow had made steering awkward, and when the plane drifted slightly to the left, one wheel had grabbed the berm and snapped the plane on its back. The Cessna wasn't badly damaged, but any damage to an airplane is costly.

Gloomily, I jogged down to Jess and Ann Bachner's aircraft hanger for help. The mechanics hurried out with their jeep to right the little plane and tow it in.

"I was bringing it in for an annual anyway," I told them.

"It's going to be an expensive annual," they said sadly. These mechanics had been with Bachner's Aircraft since I was an airsick baby, and they felt for me. That evening I raced frantically around town doing what errands I could before catching the weekly mail plane home again the next morning, leaving town for the last time until spring.

It's always a relief to have the chaotic fall work over and winter dead ahead with new work — the harvest of furs — a less complicated job than the lists of chores that must be juggled around during the other seasons. That fall I was more glad than ever to be done with the exciting but perilous season.

Trapline tent camps are handy but not as safe as cabins, and it's hard to care for pelts properly in them. Here Miki and Reuben take a break at the West Line camp.

CHAPTER 8
TRAPLINE
TRAILS

"Here we are," I mused to Julie one pleasant November evening at home. "Two thirty-four-year-old, college-educated twin girls, near the end of the twentieth century, sitting on the floor of our bedroom, skinning beaver. Isn't there something a little incongruous about that?"

Indeed, trapping is not an occupation most modern women aspire to. But outside opinions and expectations bounce right off of us, and we consider ourselves lucky for many reasons. Most importantly, our upbringing in this remote area allows us to pursue a wilderness lifestyle and profession that very few places worldwide have enough undeveloped land to support. We harvest wild renewable resources which provide us with a cash crop — raw furs — as well as subsistence foods and products for our own use. The subarctic Alaskan Interior is not a rich country, especially around here where we no longer have the great herds of caribou or the rich runs of salmon that fed the area's original human occupants. We drain an uninhabited area of hundreds of square miles to meet our needs.

At the same time, we are less isolated and have more outside resources than Slim Carlson and other trappers who preceded us. Weekly or even daily mail planes fly in fresh food, medicine, mail-order goods, and the tons of horse and dog feed we must buy. We also have the money needed to take advantage of air transportation. Our income trickles in year-round from several sources, and we don't have to spend every waking hour fighting to meet our needs and the needs of our animals — not quite, anyway.

Then, too, we are lucky that in our unlikely profession we work alone. What others think that we,

Miki

as women, can or cannot do matters not at all. There are no higher-ups anxious to keep us "in our place." As adolescents we wanted nothing more than to live here in the Bush, but we were told we would probably have to depend upon seasonal work away from home to make ends meet; jobs in the Bush range from scarce to nonexistent.

That didn't stop us from trying. Freed from college, we set out to live, and have been doing so very nicely ever since. Through hard work and the good fortune of having a trapping area rich in marten, our mainstay, we make trapping pay off. The fact that we still live in our parents' home has helped immeasurably. We provide them with everything we can gather, hunt, fish, or grow off the land, and they provide us with most of our other groceries, from powdered milk and cereal to peanut butter and crackers. Daddy maintains all things mechanical and electrical, from outboards and water pumps to the generator and satellite TV, while our mother takes on the chores no one else wants: cooking, washing dishes, housekeeping, laundry, and worrying.

Of course Julie and I have to put up with a few skeptics. When I told a mechanic in Fairbanks that I was a trapper, he stared at me with a patronizing mixture of doubt and disgust before demanding, "Do you catch anything?"

Another man who was trapping himself asked us how many marten we had caught so far. Although it was early in the season, that year unusually large numbers of hungry marten had headed for the smelly fish and rotted moose guts we used as bait. We rarely volunteer specifics, but when he pressed for a number, Julie said gravely, "Right now, forty-two."

He stared at us, gobbling wordlessly at the idea that we had seen more luck than he. "Well . . . well . . . I'm ahead of you because I've got thirty, and there's two of you," he finally sputtered. Then, without thinking, he blurted, "Besides, you're just girls!"

Girls or not, opening day on the first of November finds us out with the dog team, making tracks and setting traps. The dogs, working in harness since the first snow allows us to start sledding, toughen up quickly; with good trail conditions we might run them 150 or even 250 miles in the first fourteen days of November. Every round trip to check the sixty to ninety miles of traplines, loops, and spurs means traveling 120 to 135 miles, and that distance is covered every two weeks or so all season, barring severe cold or an impossibly deep snowfall. Small cabins or wall tents scattered every ten to twenty miles along the trail serve as lunch stops or overnight stays. The Birch Cabin sixteen miles out is our first main cabin, with a second one, the Spruce Cabin, being either forty-five or fifty-three miles from home, depending on which route we follow. At these places we might stay several days or even weeks, running side lines and loops into rich fur country.

Of course, the weather doesn't always play into our hands. A late fall delays everything if open water doesn't freeze on schedule. The dogs can slog through half-frozen bogs, but the waist-deep to neck-deep creek in front of the Birch Cabin can stop us cold. Although it's often frozen by the first of November, we can't count on it, and several times we've had to camp out under the tall spruce on the wrong side of the creek, unable to reach our little cabin.

One year we reached the creek on November 1, prepared for a long stay on the trapline breaking out the snowy trail, setting traps, and opening cabins that had stood empty over the summer. With neighbors caring for the horses, and our folks at home to keep the house — and its year's supply of root vegetables — from freezing, Julie and I had the chance to travel together. Because we don't keep enough dogs to each run our own team, I frequently skijor behind the sled, towed by a rope tied to a back stanchion. This time, though, anticipating the difficult conditions typical of most early season trips, I rode a second sled tied behind Julie's. Our suspicions were confirmed; we found the trail rough from lack of snow and wet with half-frozen bogs. But nothing seemed impassable until we hit the creek just in front of the cabin. It was wide open.

Standing on the snow-covered gravel bar, Julie and I studied the clear, forceful current swirling past with its load of clotting snow pans. Shelf ice closed in on the open channel from both sides and great clots of sandy slush stuck to the gravel stream bottom, but the main channel ran free and turbulent. The dogs hung back, eyes following us reproachfully. After breaking trail all day they just wanted to get to the cabin, but not one was ready to go through that dangerous black water. Sky's blue eyes rolled worriedly as we reconnoitered; the little leader would brave anything for us if we insisted, but he did hate getting wet.

With that fast water and moving slush, and shelf ice reaching out to deep water, we couldn't safely wade across. We were prepared to camp out, but that seemed hard when our little cabin stood just a hundred yards away.

"Let's build a bridge!" I exclaimed. Julie looked skeptical.

Walking the length of the bar, we found a large island of ice that had formed over a shoal in the center of the stream. With channels of open water only twelve feet wide on either side of the island, we might be able to span them with logs. Hunting up some driftwood logs, we threw down four poles, making a rough bridge two feet wide lying just above the surface of the water.

"Are you sure that ice will hold up?" Julie asked, eyeing the fragile island suspiciously.

"No-o-o," I replied. "But we'll find out!" At least the water alongside the island didn't look too deep.

Gripping a walking stick, Julie started across. The logs sank beneath her weight until the current slapped at them, painting each one with glassy ice. Reaching the far side of the bridge, Julie stomped on the island with one foot, then tested the thickness with her ax before edging onto it.

"I guess it'll do," she called back dubiously.

I turned the twelve big huskies loose and they crowded around, anxious to cross until they approached the rushing water. Toulouse, then only two years old but already a bold leader, dared the structure first, tiptoeing determinedly over, toenails digging into the wood. The others pushed toward me again, and I eased one out onto the bridge. Once committed, he rushed forward only to freeze up halfway across, trembling so violently that the bridge threatened to fall apart beneath him. Julie stretched out, grabbed his collar, and hauled the grateful fellow to safety. One by one each dog inched across as the poles became more and more heavily coated with ice.

Meanwhile, the ice island itself was threatening to either sink or disintegrate beneath the weight of our cavorting huskies. I followed the last dog over, and we hauled the poles to the far side. Although narrower, the channel here was deeper and Julie helped each dog across with a rope. The rushing water knocked most of them off the sagging, icy bridge, but Julie quickly towed each victim ashore.

I was no different. In the back of the pack, I stepped out onto the bridge, and as the slick logs shifted and rolled, I slipped off into waist-deep current. "Eeek, eek!" I shrieked, and then gasped as icy water shot through my heavy clothing. Julie towed me ignominiously through the slushy stream, helping me up the steep, overgrown bank.

We spent three hours huddled around a blazing woodstove in the cabin, the rough wooden floor carpeted with soggy dogs. Then, armed with the tall ladder from our cache, we returned for our two sleds. With one log on either side, the spruce-pole ladder made a fair bridge, even if it did bend precariously. We pulled both sleds across to the island, but on the final crossing the first sled, loaded with 150 pounds of dog food and trapping gear, slid partway off and one stanchion hung up on a ladder rung. I heaved the front upward as Julie shoved it forward from behind. The sled didn't budge. When I lowered it back down, the current caught a runner, trying to roll it off the bridge. Meantime, the ice island began to crack up.

Julie scrambled over the sled to reach the bank, and as the ice edge broke, the ladder tipped sideways. Together we dragged the sled, ladder and all, ashore. Throwing down our portable bridge on a remaining spot of strong ice, we retrieved the second smaller sled. At last everything was safe, if not quite dry, on the cabin side.

"Bet you couldn't get a snowmachine to do that!" Julie declared.

Just as bad was the year Julie made it across the creek with the team, only to be stopped the following day by another open creek ten miles on out the trail. Returning to the Birch Cabin, she found that creek now flooded with three feet of water — on top of questionable ice — trapping her for several days until the creek froze up safely again. If she hadn't trapped a beaver and a couple of muskrats, the dogs would have been pretty hungry by the time she made it home.

One of our favorite spots is the tent camp set on the picturesque Twelve-Mile Slough. The eight-by-ten canvas wall tent, heated with a tiny shepherd's stove and lit by one of our typical Coleman gas lamps, wasn't as safe or convenient as a cabin, but it did keep us comfortable most of the time. One especially frigid morning I was supposed to head up there from the Birch Cabin, en route to the Spruce Cabin, but the idea of spending the night in a tent in such severe weather didn't appeal.

"You'd better go, unless it's colder than thirty below," Julie told me. After all, for us trapping is serious work, not strictly pleasure.

Usually minus forty degrees F is our cutoff, but we often fudge on that if our evening's destination is a tent camp. Flashlight in hand, I crept out into the dim predawn of that late December morning. Tiny bits of frost, collected on the underside of the porch from humid air swirling out the door, sprinkled down on my head as I peered at the thermometer: twenty-five below. It *had* to be colder than that! But I grimly loaded my sled, packing an additional huge down sleeping bag, and headed out. Thirteen chilly, snowy miles later I arrived at the Twelve-Mile camp. I headed straight for the thermometer: it was forty-eight below! By the time I called Julie on the radio that evening, the temperature had dropped even more.

"It's fifty-four below!" I shouted into the mike.

"Yes, I know," she retorted. "You looked at the wrong thermometer before you left. That one is broken and always gets stuck at twenty-five below!"

Although worried about cinders starting a fire, I kept the stove stoked all night, and inside two sleeping bags I slept warm and cozy. But I felt badly for the dogs, curled up in the snow without even any doghouses. If I had been in a cabin I would have brought them all inside, but with the hot stove in the tiny tent even one rambunctious dog was too dangerous. By morning the temperature had sunk to fifty-eight below, too cold to continue on the trapline without serious risk of frostbite or freezing should I have even a small accident. Instead I broke trail through deep snow a couple miles out, then fled back to the Birch Cabin none the worse for wear.

Our Twelve-Mile camp was an easy place to call home. It stood under tall, protective spruce on the far side of the creek from the main trail system, facing south toward the snowy flanks of the Alaska Range. Sometimes the wind came down from the north, howling through the treetops and occasionally dodging down to shake our canvas tent and rattle the stovepipe. So pervasive was the sound that at least once I dreamed that the distant roar of the wind was the rush of water flooding the slough.

During one early season trip, when I cut a water hole through the ice the water boiled up out of the hole so fast it just about flooded the slough. After I went to bed that night, I lay listening to the ice boom and crack. That had never happened before, but I figured the ice, freezing and expanding rapidly, was putting pressure on the water below. Sprawled limply on my makeshift bed of spruce slabs, I also heard the distant roar of the wind, coming closer and closer. I kept waiting for it to swoop down and rattle the tent walls, but it never did.

Then I heard water splashing.

Oh! That hadn't been wind! I sprang out of my sleeping bag, pulled on my boots, and ran outside in my long johns, flashlight in hand. From upstream came a dull roar mingled with the rush and gurgle of swiftly flowing water, a scene straight out of my most disturbing dreams. For a moment I thought the ice was actually breaking up and going out with the current, but then in the dim light I spied a low wall of water speeding downstream, flowing over the solid ice. In seconds it passed by, the water behind it coming up nearly two feet in five minutes.

I immediately prepared to flee to higher ground. Arthur and Beau, two big young dogs I'd left loose, knew that creek blocked our trail. They whined anxiously, running up and down the shore as they stared at the surging water pushing along its load of branches and sticks, slush and flotsam.

The water finally stopped rising, and during the night it started draining away. By morning several inches of water and slush pans still flowed down the creek, but with bold Toulouse in the lead, we crossed without difficulty. Running loose, Arthur, Beau, and old Hector didn't want to follow. I mushed out of sight, then stopped to wait until the two pups braved the water and caught up. The last dog, Hector, ranged the far bank, whining wretchedly, afraid to step into the drifting slush, and finally I walked back for him. I thought I'd have to wade over to coax him into the water, but Beau dashed back through the clogged current, bounced up to Hector, and then raced across to me again. He did that twice, pausing once in mid-stream for a drink as if to prove how harmless it was. Hector got the message. As I cheered him on and Beau danced delightedly about, the aging dog crept across the water. My team complete again, I gave the sled a push and the dogs shot forward up the trail, leaving the treacherous little stream behind.

Most northern trappers travel with snowmachines, which enable them to go faster and farther than a dog team. Since Daddy purchased a relatively reliable, easy-starting machine several years ago, Julie and I have used it occasionally for convenience and to spare the dogs. But snowmachines can be less dependable, or even unusable, on extremely rough trails, during severe cold, or when traveling through water, overflow, or on dangerous ice — all of which are common circumstances on our trapline. We prefer our dogs, anyway, with their quiet powering of the sled, their companionship, and their vigilance in alerting us to scents and sounds we might otherwise be oblivious to.

On the trapline, I can let go of the sled to walk behind as the dogs drag the load up a hill, confident that they will stop when I call to them. A few might prefer to keep going, but we always have a couple of dogs so loyal that they will drag the over-eager ones to a halt. I could absolutely count on Comet and Streak, with their huge size, powerful bodies, and fiercely loyal dispositions, to stop the rest of the team, and later Arthur and Beau did the same.

Each dog is a trusted friend and companion, with his own special traits and little faults. To get the most from each, we must know every little quirk and mannerism as well as abilities and limitations. A few dogs are born leaders; some can be trained to lead, some cannot, and some could if they wanted to, but just won't. Sled dogs have a tremendous capacity and desire for work and, if handled properly, a tremendous desire to please as well. Occasionally we find an especially clever one, too, making him a double delight.

Tok was such a dog. He understood more English than any other sled dog I ever worked with. As an old dog, he lived inside the trapping cabins, sleeping unobtrusively in his warm corner. Every morning Julie made an extra pancake for him, the highlight of his day. Unless it had cranberries in it. Tok hated cranberries.

"Want a pancake, Tok?" I'd ask on berry-less days. The sober orange-brown dog would leave his corner to accept my gift with graceful dignity. Then one day I forgot about the cranberries.

"Want a pancake, Tok?" I asked, holding it out. He was halfway across the room when I remembered and quickly added, "It has cranberries in it."

A crestfallen expression crossed his face. The old dog didn't even come to find out for himself; he understood me, believed me, and sadly returned to his corner.

Tok's nephew, Rusty, was another hard-working dog, and smart, too — especially when it came to hiding how clever he was. Even though he knew all the commands and sometimes displayed contemptuous disgust for leaders who did not, if we tried to run him up front he usually stepped off the trail and sat down, looking back with a pointed stare. Only if he became thoroughly vexed with a leader's bad performance would he take over those duties.

Rusty had a rust-colored coat, tan markings, and a big white splotch across his chest. With his big floppy feet, ears that didn't quite stand up, and a ratty piglet-twist of a tail, he looked every bit a clown, and he played the part well. His big comical eyes expressed his whimsical curiosity, his self-created fear of anything he felt harbored the slightest threat to his personal well-being, and his bashful adoration of a handful of privileged people.

When he first joined our team at one and a half years of age, he kept getting injured because of his ludicrous incoordination. Rusty ran like a Raggedy Ann doll, long legs flying in every direction, feet flopping, each body part moving with apparent disregard for any other. But he was soon running a hundred miles a week on the trapline, and during his first four years in our team he logged about 8,000 miles. He still got into incredible tangles with the towline, but just before the ropes pulled tight around him he'd make a gangly, sprawling leap and miraculously land free, in place and pulling.

Not only was Rusty one of our best team dogs, but he also sired the best pups. At one year old, his daughter Amber ran on my team when I entered the Iditarod, and when I had to scratch halfway through the race, she was as strong and eager as any dog I had. The following year she finished the 1,000-mile Yukon Quest race in Julie's team.

Amber had a long-standing but friendly rivalry with our big black pet dog Pepper. When they were both younger, they loved nothing better than to race down the trail, Amber in the team and Pepper leaping alongside loose, both barking at each other at the tops of their lungs: "Arf! Arf! Arf!" Normally we don't tolerate such rude behavior, but they had so much fun I always had to laugh.

Then Pepper discovered something even better. She made a habit of darting ahead to crouch half-hidden in a certain clump of thick scrub spruce that grew at the trail's edge. Eyeing the pairs of dogs wickedly as they passed by, Pepper knew just where in the team her rival ran. When Amber trotted past unsuspectingly, Pepper leaped out right in her face.

"ARF!" she shouted.

Poor Amber! She fell to the ground in surprise, only to leap back up, laughter in her beaming face. I watched Pepper pull that stunt every time we passed that clump of trees, and every time Amber was startled out of her skin. But, quickly recovering, she always ran gaily on down the trail, Pepper bounding alongside.

"Arf!" they shouted gleefully. "Arf! Arf! Arf!"

Amber accompanied us on every trip, big and small, for ten years until old age finally caught up with her, and even then she looked more like a pup than an experienced old sled dog. Her sense of humor, perpetual smile, and big dewy eyes combined with her strong and loyal affection gave her a special place in our lives, and she spent her older years as a house pet.

Reuben, Rusty's son from another litter, grew into nearly a hundred pounds of power. A very tall, independent but devoted leader, he had striking blue eyes that shone brightly from a jet-black face set off by pure-white markings. Whenever we had to cover a twenty-mile trail buried under a foot of snow, we put Reuben up front, and he swung through the drifts like a long-legged bull moose.

The next litter of Rusty-pups gave us Cody, another blue-eyed leader but smaller and much faster except in deep snow. His two littermates were as different as could be. Joni, at seventy-two pounds, was one of our smallest dogs but a hard worker. Their brother Wiggles was born the runt of the litter but grew quite big with tremendously long legs nearly hidden beneath a five-inch-long mop of collie-colored hair — a powerful, whimsical dog and a strong addition to the team except when he overheated under that great fur-ball coat.

Now Rusty's kids, grandkids, and great-grandkids are running in our team, all proving their worth not only as hard-working dogs but as warm and loving companions chock-full of personality.

Our dogs' antics help break up the drudgery of mile-after-mile, day-after-day trapline work. Often I work outdoors in all temperatures for four to nine hours a day, mushing, snowshoeing, skiing, or hauling firewood. Trails must be kept open as the winter snows deepen, traps checked as often as possible, and furs picked up. In the evening I am busy cooking the rice, fish, and tallow for the dogs' dinner — which can take two or three hours when I start with snow instead of water. I need to cook my own food and perhaps a lunch for the next day, and promptly care for any furs that need work. Each animal caught needs to be thawed (if frozen), then skinned and the fur tacked inside-out on a shaped stretching board. After letting it dry for a few hours, I turn the skin fur-side out and brush it before it finishes drying. Most of our marten pelts are sold raw, so they need no further treatment, but if we plan to sew handcrafts from the fur, it must be tanned either commercially or at home later in the spring.

Finally, for each animal, I record its species, sex, and where it was caught, along with any notes of interest: whether it was especially fat or thin, any old injuries it had sustained, and the condition of the fur if it is damaged or less than prime. Marten are easily aged by examining the musculature of the skull, so we also can note whether the animal was a mature adult or a juvenile.

This way we can manage our traplines in the best way possible, trapping only if the fur is prime, and pulling a line if the population might be suffering. Catching older animals, with few young replacements, can indicate that the population is about to die off, and a large catch of older females is especially bad because it means we are taking breeding stock that would otherwise provide us with fur in the future. Either of these signs suggests that we'd better trap elsewhere. Scribbled under the glaring lantern light, these tattered records provide us with vital statistics that we can refer back to even years later.

The routine of traveling during the day and working in the evening often continues without a break for ten days to two weeks as I cover the trails, skiing or snowshoeing if the dogs are too tired. Finally I head for home, where I may get two weeks of relative leisure while, after giving the dogs a few days off, Julie goes back out to do it all again. Occasionally, if someone else can care for everything at home, we might travel together, but since getting horses that has been the exception rather than the rule.

Sometimes, during week after grinding week on the trail, the most exciting prospect of the day is figuring out what to have for dinner, especially if we aren't too tired to cook something ambitious. As all our food is hauled out by dog team, we have to keep its weight and variety to a minimum. Dehydrated foods — milk, eggs, vegetables, berries, and fruits — are standard fare, whether store-bought or home-dried. Lunch might be crackers and diced moose roast, or more often just some bannock cooked the night before. A typical supper consists of moose meat and garden vegetables cooked with noodles or instant potatoes, and berry pudding or bannock and homemade jam for dessert. When that gets too boring, we go to extremes to cook up something more exciting.

"Fruit Torte," Julie read aloud, examining a yellowing, tattered recipe folder dredged out of one of Slim's abandoned cabins. We were spending freezeup at the Birch Cabin, and since our six-week food supply for two people and four dogs had been paddled in by

Julie (sitting) poses with Miki and Reuben and part of the winter's fur catch: (from left) lynx, marten, wolf, red fox, and silver fox.

canoe, our diet was limited to dry goods, local cranberries, a large hunk of moose meat, and a couple of yellowing cauliflower heads.

"We have all the ingredients . . . well, *most* of the ingredients." She studied the recipe further. "Okay, we have *some* of the ingredients. I'm sure we can make it!"

We mixed together generous portions of precious butter, sugar, powdered egg, and water in amounts remotely paralleling those quoted in the recipe, and then added some flour and baking powder until we imagined the dough was the correct thickness for the alleged torte. (Never mind that we did not know exactly what "torte" was.) But what about the fruit part? All we had were cranberries and raisins. Not exotic enough.

We did have a bag of stale gorp: peanuts, chocolate chips, marshmallows, and dried fruit. Optimistically we dumped in most of the bag and poured the whole mess into a greased frying pan. Two hours of cooking atop the oven-less woodstove browned the Gorp Torte to perfection, and although rather dry by then, it proved just the thing for a couple of dessert-starved trappers.

Inventiveness has always played an important role in our trapline cuisine. After many long hard days, we just boil up some instant potatoes and dump in a small bag of moose roast and a packet of instant soup — the fastest real meal possible, even if the meat is frozen. If we're staying at the same cabin more than one night we have a few more options, and often boil up some moose meat and beans the night before so we can eat as soon as we tumble in the door after hours on the trail. Even when time allows, recipes don't help much when the only measuring gear we have is a two-cup Mason jar. We just make things up as we go along, and if it doesn't look right, we add more butter and sugar.

I do have a rule of thumb for bannock, the bread or biscuit substitute we eat when we don't have an oven for baking: three heaping spoons of flour, one level spoon of baking powder (Julie says less), two spoons of whole powdered milk, two spoons of sugar, up to one-half stick of melted butter, and enough water to make a thick dough. The size of the spoon is important. If I want a big bannock, I use a big spoon. For trail lunches I add more sugar, cinnamon, and a few raisins or dried berries to make a sweeter bread. The dough is cooked slowly in a greased iron frying pan elevated just above the surface of a slow-burning stove, and turned over once right before it starts smelling burnt.

With three to five line cabins and tent camps to keep stocked, running out of this or that, here or there, is inevitable. No baking powder? Pancakes work (sort of) without it. No sugar? Use jam to sweeten that raspberry pie. No powdered egg? Good! We can do without their peculiar flavor for awhile.

Because we travel from cabin to cabin, and each place is only heated during our brief stay, non-freezable goods like potatoes and raw carrots are either left at home or must be hauled along wherever we go. Julie and I once packed around a sackful of carrots in a bedroll in the dogsled everywhere we went, even sleeping with them in the tent camps, which fell well below freezing at night. Along with the carrots we kept a jar of mayonnaise, which separates and changes flavor if frozen. We decided to use up both nuisances by making a big carrot salad.

Because we had no grater, Julie spent half an hour slivering a huge stack of carrots with her knife. I dumped in a generous portion of mayonnaise, and Julie went to get the raisins.

We were out of raisins.

WHAT! Out of raisins! Impossible! We *always* have raisins! We *can't* be out!

We searched the tiny cabin, peering into every dark nook and cranny, prying open all the unlabeled and wrongly labeled cans and jars we use to mouse-proof our food.

We were out of raisins.

Wait — what's this? A box of raisin bran? Julie grabbed it. I said, "You gotta be kidding."

"I'm not eating carrot salad without raisins!" Julie insisted, hazel eyes flashing stubbornly.

For another half-hour she hunched over that box of cereal, picking out the shriveled little raisins, and finally we could eat our carrot salad . . . *with* raisins.

Once in a while not even our inventiveness can cut the craving for something really good, like Christmas cookies and candies and holiday feasts. Often I spend the last two or three weeks before Christmas alone on the trapline, harvesting fur and dreaming about all the goodies waiting at home. Even the time I caught the dreadful cold just before heading home from the distant Spruce Cabin.

Colds are usually unheard of on the isolated trapline trails, but my brother Ray had flown out from Fairbanks in his Super Cub with a cold-infested friend. They had spent a day with us, helping locate one of Slim's old trails that I'd had trouble finding. We didn't have enough dog power so I skied most of the twenty-four miles we covered that day, and ended up exhausted. Julie took the main team home while I stayed on to run the local lines once more before hightailing it home for Christmas.

When Ray flew back to Fairbanks, his friend forgot to take his cold along, leaving it with me instead. That was unfortunate because it was December 18. Christmas was just around the corner, and I was forty-five miles from home, with miles and miles of trail to check before the holiday. I had three half-broken pups and old Loki for a leader. And a cold.

Ah, well. I could have taken one day off, but I'd dropped my ax a little ways out on a trail, and I skied out to rescue it. The seven-mile mission didn't take long, but it was enough to set up my live-in viruses very nicely. They took up residence in high-rise establishments in my throat, sending urban sprawl up into my ears. I didn't have any throat lozenges, antihistamines, or all-night, sleep-tight cold medicine. I didn't even have any vitamin C.

By the next morning my ears were aching. This was unfortunate because I had a ten-mile side line to check. Ten miles, one way.

That was too much for the pups, so I had to do it on skis, packing my weighty cold along with me.

I jammed in ear plugs to keep my inner ears warm, tied down my fur hat, and submerged myself into a small, dark cocoon of hibernation, with only my legs operating automatically. At each set, I had to stop, stuporously clean out the snow that had accumulated in the trap, replace the little step sticks that prompted the animal to place its foot right on the trigger, and chuck a piece of moose gut into the back of the trap's tepee-shaped cubby. I didn't wake up until I was back at camp, seven hours and twenty miles later. By then the germs were residing in wall-to-wall mansions and condominiums in my upper airways, and it would have taken something stronger than Drano® to unclog my nose.

This was unfortunate because the following day I had to ski a fifteen-mile loop. That plus wading through and around a four-mile stretch of flooded creek in my ankle-high ski boots took me over seven hours. The urban sprawl spread into a massive metropolis surrounded by ever-expanding suburbs as viruses and bacteria set up shop lower in my airways and higher in my ears.

At least the hard part was behind me. Now all I had to do was get home, only forty-five miles away, before gorging myself silly on Christmas exotics. Luckily, Julie was coming partway out to meet me. I hitched up old Loki with the three pups and skijored a few miles toward the Birch Cabin, where my dogs collided headlong with hers in a joyous tangle of reunion.

Julie was full of news about what was going on at home and in the World, and who we had received Christmas cards from. One fellow who'd cared for our dogs the previous spring had made Christmas photo-cards of himself standing with *our* dog team.

"How dare he!" Julie shouted. "I didn't know whether to laugh, cry, or beat him up!"

"Doesn't he know our dogs are copyrighted, patent-pending?" I demanded with a wildly hoarse giggle. "By the way," I croaked. "I'm sick."

"Oh!" Julie waved me off, anxious to protect her own pristine lungs. "Get away from me!"

With a full-powered team, the rest of the run to the Birch Cabin seemed easy, and after I pulled a short side line the next morning we made the last run home to a cold, not-very-Christmasy cabin. Our folks were away vacationing, so for simplicity we stayed in Slim's old one-room cabin next door to the big house. At last, I could rest!

Of course, I still had ten hours of Christmas cards and other mail to work on the next day, but that was all indoor labor. By now, my throat was so raw I could not even talk out loud, limiting my communications to madly waving hand signals and an occasional hoarse whisper. And there was one more ski trip I had to make.

"You can't go," Julie declared. "You're sick."

"I AM going!" I whispered plaintively. "I've waited a whole year! I've skied miles and miles! And I'm NOT going to miss Stella's Christmas party!"

Stella Wildrick's Christmas potlucks were always special, with all kinds of luscious home-cooked foods, and nearly all of the thirty or so residents scattered around the lake converging on her house for the occasion. I had no intention of missing out just because of an overwhelming viral infection.

I lay around all day until it was time to leave. Then I grimly tied on my ski boots. The dogs needed their holiday, too, and this was before we had alternate transportation in the form of horses or a snowmachine that actually started. Julie and I headed out into the late-afternoon darkness.

Six miles away, we found Stella's cabin aglow with Christmas spirit, packed with friends, and flooded with the rich scent of good food. At least, I'm sure the rich scents were there, even if I couldn't smell them. I sat in a corner, glassy-eyed and silent, hardly able to taste the mountainous heaps of savory food spilling off my paper plate. A dark-eyed Santa Claus ho-ho-ho-ed his way in, and a half-dozen little kids swarmed shyly around him as he peered at the Christmas packages pulled from his big red bag, trying to read the labels without his glasses.

People laughed and talked and sang Christmas carols. Except for me. I just sat and nodded, or, when absolutely necessary, answered a direct question in a barely audible croak. Yet in spite of the internal war between the white blood cells clogging my nose and the viruses chewing into the deep recesses of my throat, I felt blissfully at peace. After the interminably long, stark days on the trail, all I needed was a good Christmas potluck to revive my drained spirits. The six miles of cold air on the ski home invigorated the viruses no end, but, belly full, I was without regret.

It was worth it.

We must have water regardless of the weather. One winter Lilja
and Miki hauled water up from the lake a mile away despite -60° F
temperatures.

CHAPTER 9

WEATHER
PERMITTING

Cold spells in January and February must be expected in Interior Alaska, where clear, calm weather allows the cold to settle so heavily it even weighs down the smoke from our fires. We expect to see fifty below once or twice a year, and every few years there's an even colder snap. By February, the returning sunlight forces warmth into the lengthening afternoons, but in January we adjust our plans to avoid traveling at risky temperatures, even if that means staying home for two weeks to wait out a cold spell.

One night I lay awake in a tiny canvas tent at the very end of our trapline, listening to a gusty wind boom through the low canyon, wrestling with the tall spruce that sheltered my camp.

That north wind carried the grainy dry snow which often presages a cold front, and in the morning as I mushed toward the Spruce Cabin on the first leg home, dense drifts topped off the trails. The wind rarely blew in that small canyon, and now the towering spruce trees shrugged off their heavy loads of accumulated powder. "Snow bears," Miki calls those packed lumps of snow that now slid from the branches and plummeted like meteorites, making craters up to five feet in diameter. Sadly I pictured all the just-serviced traps behind me already filling with snow. I thought it might be ten days before Miki got back to clean them out. I was wrong.

Two long days of plowing through drifts and clearing traps brought me to the Birch Cabin, where Miki waited with the horses. That night we called our parents on the radio to discuss the steadily falling temperature. "If it's colder than forty below tomorrow, we'll hole up here. Otherwise, we'll be home," I told them. By morning the thermometer read minus forty-four, but

Julie

before settling in for the day we tuned in KSKO, the McGrath radio station. They forecast fifty degrees below zero with no end in sight.

"Let's go home!" we chorused. A spell of fifty below would probably outlast our food supply; we'd be safer leaving now. Miki trotted out early with the horses, and when I overtook her later with the dog team, we switched and I rode the rest of the way. Afternoon temperatures peaked at a balmy minus twenty-eight but plummeted overnight to minus fifty. It didn't warm up to forty-five below for over two weeks.

That was January 1989, when temperatures across Interior Alaska ranged from minus fifty to minus seventy for days. Ice fog grounded airplanes; even instrument flights were canceled because airline altimeters weren't calibrated for the record-high barometric readings. Larger towns virtually shut down as cranky cars and thick ice fog made travel nearly impossible. Bush villages, dependent on frequent flights for fuel and groceries, felt the pinch as the cold stretched on. Accustomed to less frequent mail flights, our own tiny, independent village was well stocked, but after a couple of weeks neighbors began to barter for needed supplies. Everywhere, the long nights, reluctant machines, and ice fog added elements of misery to the bitter cold. For some, the cold snap became a terrible struggle.

Not so for us! We had been working furiously on the trapline for over two months; before that, the October fishing had given us no chance to recover from the September moose hunt or the August harvest. Now this enforced hiatus meant an enjoyable vacation. Like others around the lake, we had well-stocked larders and plenty of firewood. We spent a few days holed up just resting, but later took the dogs on daily walks to ward off cabin fever. The horses, too, were unperturbed, and even walked halfway across the lake for no particular reason. Although glad for a break from the routine, the dogs didn't fare as well as we did because even in their straw-filled houses the severe cold drained their energy.

When the mercury shrank down to sixty and seventy below, we worried about the horses, but with their little ears, compact bodies, and thick furry coats, the Icelandics seemed impervious to the cold. Although they ate extra feed soaked in warm water, they rarely drank from the bucket we offered them unless we baited the water with molasses. They spent their days foraging and walked home at dusk each afternoon, their breath condensing into ice crystals that lingered in a trail of fog a quarter of a mile long.

Ten days of extreme cold finished off the firewood in the shed and most of the water stored in the basement. In that weather Daddy's sno-go was a definite no-go, so we hitched Lilja to her sled and hauled water from the lake and seasoned wood from stacks in the forest. Leather straps, metal buckles, and wooden shafts snapped easily in the brittle cold, and even with gloves our fingers stung as we buckled on Lilja's harness, but she didn't mind the work. Worried that sweat might chill her, we worked the furry little mare carefully and blanketed her afterward, but she never lost weight or seemed cold. In the next few days she willingly hauled many loads of firewood, and brought 400 gallons of water from a hole we chopped through three feet of lake ice half a mile away.

The cold weather delayed our shipment of horse pellets, ordered a month earlier. Mushers across the lake were running short of dog food, too, so one afternoon we mushed our dogs to a meeting at a neighbor's home to see who had extra feed to share. After weeks of isolation we had a pleasant visit, the haves sharing with the have-nots. As a blushing sun dropped behind the crystalline haze that had settled over the lake, we headed home with two sacks of goat feed to tide over the horses. The dog team trotted easily, frothy steam rolling like smoke over their backs in the still air. At fifty-eight below the snow ground like silt under our sled, too cold to provide any glide. Dressed in so many layers of wool, down, and fur that we would have been sweating at forty below, we still felt the relentless penetration of arctic air slicing through our clothes. We took turns trotting behind the sled to stay warm, and the forty-minute trip didn't end too soon.

January drifted lazily into February and still the cold lingered, with nighttime temperatures falling to minus sixty and minus sixty-five, once to minus sixty-eight. McGrath, 150 miles southwest, hit eighty-six below. Yet every day saw a few minutes more sunlight, and by early February each passing week gained almost an hour extra light. As the sun rose higher each day, the cold finally dwindled to forty-five below, every day a bit warmer than the day before. Unable to contain our impatience, we hit the trail again with dogs and horses for another ten-day stint on the trapline. Two days later, the first plane in a month landed supplies and mail across the lake.

For us, it had been a warm and pleasant cold spell.

One year we had a very different wintertime event: puppies. Most of our litters are born during the summer, but Joni's pups came in December.

Unlike Icelandic horses, who can live half a century and often work into their thirties, our heavy trapline dogs begin to show their age at just seven years, and they often enter retirement by age ten. Since it takes two years or more for a youngster to reach his full potential, Miki and I must plan ahead to replace our aging canine workers. Many of our females are spayed to prevent accidental breeding, and most of our dogs are related, so we often have to bring in an unrelated adult to breed.

Almost all our team traces back to Casey, Rusty, and Legs, dogs we bought from long-distance racers who found them too big for competition. These three dogs produced pups in a variety of sizes, so we kept the biggest pups and sold the smallest. A series of breedings over a period of eight years gave us replacements for Loki and Tok, Comet and Streak, our cherished core team of older dogs who passed into a well-deserved retirement. Casey and Rusty produced Reuben, a beautiful dog and a fine trail leader. Casey and Legs begat Crystal and Toulouse. Crystal and Rusty begat Joni, Cody, and Wiggles. Joni inherited Rusty's hound build and her grandfather Legs's speed and wary reserve. Her blue eyes came from Crystal and Casey, and her puppies came from Bingo. An ex-race dog from Dawson City, Bingo came from an old line of Indian dogs. He was a happy dog, tough, compact, and solid. His puppies, Arthur and Beau and their two sisters Emily and Rosie, were born in the dark days of December.

At first, warm weather forestalled trouble. The four pups thrived in a log doghouse banked with snow for wind protection and insulation. But when the temperature plummeted to minus forty, our four wriggly puppies became four writhing problems squalling in the cold. Concerned, we moved the little family inside the Birch Cabin to keep them warm.

Hardly old enough to toddle, they didn't do much damage at first. Then their mother Joni stopping cleaning up after them. (She discovered we would do it for her.) Soon shredded paper, regurgitated blobs of scrap fur, and soft little piles of goo were all waiting to be stepped in by some bare foot on its way to the kindling box in the morning.

But the Birch Cabin is a good place for puppies. Grizzlies trash

With steam rising from water flowing over river ice, Miki and the team stop to ponder whether to get wet, go through the brush, or turn back.

the place every summer anyway, and though the pups do their level best, they're small potatoes compared to a bear that can pry up floorboards and pull down the stove. Joni's quartet spent ten blissful days inside before Miki set off trapping with the main team and I returned home, the puppies riding in my sled. That's when my four little problems became four *big* problems.

At seven weeks old, the pups could tolerate the forty-below weather in their doghouse with its burlap door and straw bedding, but I still brought them inside during the day while I worked at finishing a book manuscript. The book, *Dog Driver,* pointed out that seven-week-old pups needed socializing. And that's what I intended to give them. Our dogs lack exposure to other people, and by spending time with the pups myself, I hoped to minimize their distrust of strangers. Anyway, that was my excuse to enjoy the puppies. The writing and the cold weather trapped me inside, and the puppies offered entertainment and diversion.

I certainly didn't sit still much, not with all those puddles appearing. When I opened the door every morning and the puppies burst inside, they whirled about like so many little tornadoes, doing as much damage as possible before their breakfast of warm milk and puppy food. After eating, they played, then bickered, then fell asleep on my feet as I sat typing.

There was Beau, handsome, emotional, selfish. Emily, a bright little pixie full of energy. Shy, tender, affectionate Rosie. And Arthur, big, gentle, and enthusiastic, but not very bright. In that way he took after his father, Bingo, whose enthusiasm was exceeded only by his startling lack of brain cell connections.

Our big log home is no mansion, but it does have a sofa, hooked wool rugs on the tile floor, and parsley and flowers wintering on the windowsill. A puppy's paradise — and a babysitter's nightmare. The puppies were learning about life but not about propriety. They ate and drank and made puddles, played and fought, made puddles, and slept, and made puddles. I typed and wiped, typed and wiped. After using up a roll of paper towels in three days, I switched to a mop. That worked better. I tried paper-training, but the puppies were too young. I tried rushing them outside after their naps, but they never made it across the porch, where the puddles froze before I could wipe them up.

Beside making puddles, the pups also excelled at vandalism. Even if the house was neat (and it usually wasn't), they found things they oughtn't play with, like handcrafts and my wallet. They dragged boots and pillows against the hot stovepipe that rose through the floor from the basement wood furnace. Arthur ate the parsley plant. Emily fell down the ladder into the stone basement. They weren't supposed to get on the sofa, but they had jumping contests to see who could scale the cushions first. (Emily won, learning to dig in her claws and climb instead of jumping.) They pulled the leaves off the potted tuberose. They hauled around furs and skeins of yarn. And they leaked. They leaked on rugs, papers, mukluks, parkas, maps, and the sofa (Emily did that).

On my chilly afternoon jaunts, I left the puppies outside and sneaked away so they wouldn't follow me. Once they trailed me when I took Lilja across the lake to haul freight. The twelve-mile journey was much too far for them, so that night I let the exhausted pups stay inside. When I came down to check on them during the night, a toppled houseplant lay bleeding dirt on the rug, and the four pups lay sleeping peacefully in a row on the sofa.

For all their trouble, I enjoyed my youngsters no end. The best part came after their daily rampage through the house, when they finally fell asleep on my feet, well-adjusted, socially stable, healthy little puppies. Happy, warm, sweet . . . leaky . . . little puppies. I brought them inside as long as the cold snap lasted. Although it didn't dip below minus forty-five, it dragged on for days, and by the time it finally broke the pups were old enough to spend the day outside anyway.

In time Emily and Rosie grew up into good workers, but they were too small and eventually we had to sell them to an appreciative family. Although Arthur delights in annoying the other dogs while Beau sees danger lurking behind every bend, the two of them have become major powerhouses in our team.

In 1990, the year after our winter of the bad cold snap, we saw extremes of snow instead of cold. It started in October, when I was shopping in Fairbanks. My overnight trip stretched to six days before the weather cleared enough to fly home. November continued snowy, with short intervals of unusual cold for variety. By early December the dogs were worn out after breaking out eighty miles of trail every week.

"I'm going to ski the trapline this time," Miki announced. "The dogs need a break."

"Just plain ski, no dogs at all?" I asked skeptically.

"Yes. Pep can pack for me."

Pepper was horrified. At eighty-five pounds, the glossy shepherd-lab-husky mix pet outweighed several of our sled dogs, but the suggestion that she carry a load sent her cowering to the floor in stunned disbelief. But Miki was determined, so off she skied with Pepper hang-dogging along wearing a little blue dog pack I had sewn up just for her.

The weather remained quiet and warm for ten days — the only good weather all winter. Miki skied our entire trail, and I picked her up at the Birch Cabin no worse for the wear. By then Pep had learned to wear the pack with responsibility and pride, if not pleasure.

The team logged plenty of ten-hour days that year, especially on the twenty-one-mile slog from the Birch Cabin to the West Line tent. On three trips in February, the dogs pushed through ten-inch snowfalls over a soft base; on a fourth trip it dipped to minus forty. When I returned one last time to pull the traps, the last fifteen miles of trail from the tent to the Spruce Cabin lay under nearly two feet of heavy snow. The dogs found faint traces of the trail the first five miles, but then I had to snowshoe ahead, breaking out the trail as the dogs plowed along behind pulling the sled.

The work raised a damp sweat but a tart ten-below breeze made me shiver within moments of stopping. So I didn't stop. Just a minute now and then let me catch my breath or drink from the water jug I kept insulated in a sock. All day and into the night, my snowshoes drove through the deep snow one heavy step at a time. *Squish, squash. Squish, squash.* We moved painfully slowly, and as the frosty scenery crawled by and the hours passed, I felt as though I was watching a very beautiful but very familiar video in slow motion, one frame at a time. *Squish, squash. Squish, squash.* I crossed Whisper Creek as the last light faded, grateful that for once the gurgling stream lay silent under solid ice. By then I was reaching the limits of my endurance. With only three miles to go I pushed wearily on, finding the trail in total darkness only because the snow there was knee-deep instead of waist-deep under my snowshoes. My pace slowed from a trudge to a crawl as exhaustion set in. *Squish . . . squash. . . .* Half a mile out the dogs lost patience, shoving past me and lunging through the deep snow to break trail as I slogged behind.

It was eleven at night. I had been snowshoeing hard for fourteen hours, and when the cabin finally peeked out from a huge heap of snow I felt dangerously tired. An awareness of the danger sharpened my senses; I quickly traded my wet coat for dry clothes, and crunched up crackers in my dry mouth. The dogs pushed into the cabin and collapsed. I flopped on the floor, lying beside the stove to light the fire. It smoked, unable to draw air.

I guessed the problem, and tired as I was, I scrambled onto the roof to knock the snow off the stovepipe. That done, the fire burned freely and soon warmed the cabin. I melted snow and drank two pints of Tang and a pint of cocoa, topping it off with some cereal and a couple aspirin. I hurt all night, but I had gotten our traps pulled by the end of the legal trapping season.

Meanwhile, Miki tired herself out pulling traps on the spur trails near the Birch Cabin. We were both so worn out that we didn't even go on a dog sled trip that year. That was the hardest trapping season of our career — until the following year, when the snow began in November and didn't stop until February. The first heavy dumps caused huge overflows in swamps and lakes as it weighed down the ice, but later the snow lay so deep that we rode high above the water. Record snowfalls inundated the whole state, but we had learned from the previous year. We set fewer miles of trail and broke up the longest run with a tent at Wolverine Crossing, halfway between the Birch Cabin and the West Line tent.

While some years we never step into snowshoes, that winter I snowshoed the entire line not once but twice, with old Hector or some other faithful dog pulling my camp gear in a tiny plastic sled behind me. Once I traveled fifty miles in three days, the last day at fifty below. We didn't catch much fur as the traps were constantly buried and re-buried under the snow, but by the end I didn't feel as chubby and I was genuinely enjoying snowshoeing the more leisurely distances of ten or twelve miles.

Between the heavy snows and bitter cold come rare periods of "hot" weather, when icy rains glaze the trail and soak the snow. The warm, wet air feels like the breath of spring, but it makes sledding or skiing sticky, wet, and uncomfortable. If possible, we avoid traveling until the weather stabilizes again. One year we spent several days at home waiting for a heat wave to pass.

Taking advantage of the warm weather, we let the fire die so we could clean the stovepipe, a complicated procedure since the pipe rises from the basement through two floors, a stack robber, and the roof.

"You can go up on the roof," Miki offered.

"I did last time," I protested.

"So you know how," she whined.

"Okay, if you clean the stack robber."

"Okay," Miki said brightly.

I scaled the high snow-covered aluminum roof and scanned the river delta, the small bay below, low hills to the east, and broad willow flats swirling beyond, reaching out into a drippy fog that veiled the mountains. "We should have a treehouse up here!" I shouted down to Miki.

"I'm going in now," she replied.

"No, you have to stay out here and give me moral support," I called back. Carefully backing out the screws securing the top joint, I removed the top piece of pipe and cleaned it before setting it aside.

"Now you can go in," I told Miki. Our chimney-sweeping was

unorthodox but serviceable. I weighted a long string with my pocketknife and lowered it down the pipe. Miki took apart the pipe above
the stack robber on the main floor and caught the knife, pulling
down the stiff-bristled brush which I had tied to the string. Then I
pulled the brush back up and reassembled the top section of pipe.

Going inside, I supported the stovepipe while Miki detached the
stack robber, a box of pipes that dissipates heat from the smoke-
stack by means of a fan — a brilliant contraption, but a mess to
clean. Miki carried the thing, drooling soot, out the front door to
clean it with a whisk broom and a bristled bottle cleaner.

"Chim-chiminee, chim-chiminee," Miki warbled as she scraped
away. "Chim-chim-cher—HAK!" I heard her choke on the black
dust. After sweeping the last section of pipe below the stack robber,
we screwed it all back together again.

The warm weather made another chore easier, too: trimming
the horses' hooves. The hooves can grow brittle and crack when
trimmed in cold weather, so during the heat wave we took time to
nip off the excess growth, tossing the clippings to the dogs to gnaw
on. The huskies enjoyed this chinook, too, with no work to do and
no cold to fight. Still, one does tire of abnormal weather, and it was
a relief for all when winter returned.

While we rarely put off trapping for anything but the most severe cold, bad weather can indirectly interfere with our plans. One
year we set an extra-long trapline, with three cabins and two tent
camps, so we had to plan our late-season schedule carefully to be
sure we pulled all the traps on time.

We expected to split up to pull different trails, but at the last
minute our parents got weathered in Fairbanks and couldn't fly out
to keep the house from freezing. We reworked and replanned our
schedule as the lowering weather continued, but in the end I went
out alone, dreading the chore of closing up five camps by myself.
Miki promised to join me if Marmee and Daddy arrived soon. "I'll
at least make it out to help you close the Birch Cabin and the Twelve-
Mile camp," she promised.

"Okay," I said gloomily.

Three days of travel, springing traps as I went, brought me to
the Spruce Cabin. Arriving early, I took care of my dogs and began
storing food in buckets and carrying them to the suspended platform

cache outside. Everything edible or breakable had to be hidden or put above the reach of grizzlies for the summer.

The next day I hitched three dogs to a little plastic sled and skijored around the twenty-four-mile Hilltop Loop, pulling traps and picking up fur. We dove down ravines, crashed through brush, and skittered along glazed ice, my little sled whipping along between the dogs and my skis. At the tiny Grayling Creek cabin, I stopped to clean up and pack leftover gear onto my sled. After burning the trash, I hung the lantern and a few tools in a bucket on the wall and then continued on to the Spruce Cabin.

That evening I skinned fur, cooked dog food, and began cleaning up the cabin. The work continued the next morning as I packed more gear up the eighteen-foot ladder to the cache, stowing food, bedding, tools, tarps, gasoline, and dog food in buckets weighing up to forty pounds each. All the food and equipment we could leave here now meant that much less we'd have to haul out on the rough fall trails next year.

I stocked the cabin with firewood, shoveled ashes from the stove, scraped the dirt floor clean, burned trash, hid tools and books in a wooden chest under the bed, cooked dog food, and rolled up the sleeping bags. Then I picked up outside, fed the dogs, and made one last trip up that wobbly ladder to cover the cache with plastic sheeting. Finally, I removed the clear plastic windows and hid them under the bed. Now when the bears scrambled through the windows, they wouldn't destroy the plastic. I looked around the clean, bare cabin and thought how sad it would be to return next fall and find the table pulled down, stovepipe knocked over, floor scratched up, and woodpile toppled, all the handiwork of the bears. Still, leaving the cabin open and mostly empty was better than sealing it shut and full of goodies that might tempt the most respectable bruin to dig through the sod and pole roof. It was a lot easier to fix a broken table than a shredded roof.

A cold breeze flooded through the empty windows. It had been a long day, and at dusk it started to snow. But the dogs were rested if I was not, so I hooked up and traveled back to the West Line, arriving at 11 P.M. Morning chores included cleaning up the camp, packing gear to the camp's cache, and hanging the little airtight stove under the platform that stood high in the trees. I packed the eight-by-ten canvas tent and sleeping bags into my overloaded dog sled, leaving only a couple lengths of stovepipe, firewood, and water cans for the bears to tamper with.

Back at the Birch Cabin that evening, I contacted Miki on my little ham radio. Marmee and Daddy were still stuck in town. She was still stuck at home. "Weather permitting" had not cooperated. Groaning inwardly, I spent half the night packing gear into water-tight buckets and hanging them on a high wire strung between two stout trees. In the morning, I headed out on the Twelve-Mile spur. The weather was fine here; a sparkling sun filled the day with color, the blue sky setting off the deep green of spring spruce and the sparkling white snow. On a good trail my dogs trotted and loped happily despite the long miles behind them.

Cutting off the main trail, we headed up the Twelve-Mile Slough. Two miles below the camp, the creek ice suddenly disintegrated under my dogs. Dazzling water flooded around the huskies and they panicked, scattering to reach safety. Half leaped past the gaping hole; the rest strained to jump on ice pans to avoid the racing black water. They struggled frantically, falling and splashing in the icy current.

I leaped backwards, abandoning the sled as it sank into the hole. "Okay, hike!" I shouted. My leader, Legs, surged forward, dragging the team dogs hopping and bouncing over the shattered ice, only to have more ice crumble under their feet.

"Hike! Hike!" The ice fractured again, black water swirling over the broken ice floes. Gamely the dogs rushed over the ice pans, my little sled bobbing and skipping from one floating plate to another. Finally all reached safe footing a hundred yards above me. I drew in a deep breath.

"Whooaa," I called in a deep, resonant, this-is-the-boss-speaking voice. The dogs stopped. They dove and rolled in the dry snow, shaking off their fear along with the flecks of ice that glinted in the sunlight.

"*Oh-dee-oh-dee-oh!*" Streak bellowed.

"*Eee-dee-eee-dee-ee!*" Comet replied joyfully.

"Yeah, we have to move the trail off this creek next year," I panted as I circled the open holes. I never did learn just how deep that water was.

At the tent camp I snacked the dogs, pulled traps on a half-mile spur, ate a quick lunch, and collapsed the tent. Folding it tightly, I squeezed it into a sack and with a breathtaking struggle hoisted it high between two trees. (It was a vain effort — when we returned the next year, bears had destroyed it and we had to sleep out.)

Four camps done. With a sled load of bedding and gear, I headed back to the Birch Cabin, skirting the bad ice. Slaving into the night, I cooked dog food, sawed wood, cleaned the cabin, and packed food. By morning I had five loads of bedding and food packed up to the tiny platform cache, and six five-gallon buckets strung on the wire cache. I hid the dishes, books, lantern, and windows, swept the floor, dumped the ashes, picked up outside, and scrubbed the split-log floor with water and bleach (a bear deterrent, unreliable at best). Finally I was done. Four sleeping bags, a tent, boxes

We carry a handheld two-meter ham radio so we can communicate with home during our wanderings. Julie checks in while mushing in Denali Park.

of empty jars, a stove, a twelve-volt battery, furs, skis, snowshoes, and extra clothing filled my trapline sled and a second smaller sled towed behind.

Whew.

I hooked up the dogs, hanging up their picket chains so they wouldn't rust. The team waited eagerly. Eight days, five camps, and 115 miles on the trail were enough. We were ready for home, a good rest, and then a nice dog sled trip to reward the dogs, and ourselves, for the winter's work. Yet looking back at the forlorn cabin, I missed it already. Eight months was too long to wait for next season.

Although we stop trapping at the end of February, or sooner if fur loses its prime early, the winter is far from over. Trappers traditionally turn to wolves and beaver after marten and lynx seasons end, but we take advantage of the warmer weather and brighter days to vacation with our dogs. Sometimes during heavy snow years or when Lilja is expecting a foal, we stay closer to home. A short trip can be fun too, with North America's tallest peak just beyond the end of our trapline. A trip we made in 1990 to the base of Denali held just as much excitement and mystique as the longer journeys we have made.

We had only twelve days of free time that year and our parents were away, but despite the heavy snow we were determined to make the most of it. Letting the house freeze, we buried our potatoes under quilts so they would last until our return. Our friend Becky, who lived across the lake, eagerly volunteered to tend the horses. Although they normally do well foraging loose, the deep snow and numerous wolves that year made us wary of leaving them alone.

Penny, Becky's mother and our close friend, came out to help us settle the horses in a corral by their cabin, along with a few pups too young for a sled trip. "Don't do anything rash," Penny warned. "I'm just telling you because your parents aren't here to do that."

"We'll try not to," I assured her, grateful for her concern.

Mushing south to the end of our trapline, we spent two days in the Spruce Cabin while I snowshoed toward the towering rock that crowns the Alaska Range. In the clear sky it sparkled like a jewel, drawing me ever nearer. Despite waist-deep snow, I made quick tracks thanks to a mid-winter thaw which provided a solid crust under just one foot of snow. I snowshoed seven miles before turning back. Just before I turned around, I spotted a moose cow and calf standing in an open channel of the shallow stream. Browsing on willows that overhung the water, the moose stood hoof-deep in the current to avoid the billowing drifts that could trap them like so much wolf bait. The cow looked ornery, stressed by the unpleasant conditions, so I gave them a wide berth.

Dense clouds obscured the mountains the next morning as we ran nine dogs, hitched single-file, up my narrow snowshoe trail. Toulouse forged ahead of the team in loose lead to pack the trail, while Pepper and old Rusty jogged loose behind the sled. Despite the poor trail the dogs moved well, hurrying across perilous ice bridges and fording shallow water where no bridges could be found.

"I'm going to photograph those moose," I told Miki when we came upon the cow and calf in the same spot. Miki kept the dogs quiet as I crept up to the big animals, crouching behind willows to snap a few shots. The cow rumbled deep in her throat, moving to block my view of her calf. Reluctant to bother her more, I backed away and we pushed on upriver.

Two days of heavy going brought us to treeline. We camped in the last good timber and that evening snowshoed a couple of miles upstream, delighted to find the wide creek bottom solidly packed with hard snowdrifts that allowed fast going. Just after sunset the clouds peeled away from the Alaska Range and the 20,320-foot peak cut into the darkening blue-gray sky above us, twenty miles south and almost four miles straight up from our camp. In the growing darkness the high wall loomed a clear white against the sky, a ghostly line of fog shimmering halfway up the sheer slope of Wickersham Wall.

"Wow, wow, oh . . . wow," I breathed.

"Gawking like gol-danged tourists," Miki added, repeating a familiar refrain.

The clear night turned cold, twenty below, but by morning clouds had closed in again, leaving only the rounded Peters and Jeffery Domes visible 10,000 feet below the top of Denali. The creek spread wide before us, its left flank bristling with scattered, stunted spruce trees, the right edged with steep banks overhung by massive corniced snowdrifts, with barren tundra hills gently rising beyond. Our map hinted at a patch of timber high up in the stream valley, and while suspicious of its accuracy, we aimed for the spot as a tentative campsite.

A few hours' trek up the drifted streambed found us climbing into a forked basin valley four miles wide and five long, bisected down the middle by sharp conical hills and skewered with the twisting ridges of glacial eskers that drove down from the sheer mountain walls of rock backing the valley.

I spotted a low bank of round granite stones blown free of snow beside the drifted creek, and put two five-pounders into the sled. They'd be handy later on.

The trees on the map must have sprouted from someone's imagination, for this valley was barren except for thinly-scattered patches of waist-high willows, twisted and stunted by wind. At six in the evening we stopped to reconnoiter our position. The scoured hills, deeply drifted ditches, and arching cornices gave stark evidence of the brutal winds that battered this place. To camp here, with no shelter and no proper gear, could be unpleasant or even hazardous.

"If we go back to treeline tonight, we won't be able to explore this valley," I said. "I'm game to take a chance and spend the night here. We can look around tomorrow and get back to our lower camp in the evening."

Meeting my dare, Miki agreed. She built a twig fire while I dug a pit three feet deep in the snow for us to sleep in. Putting my five-pound stones into the fire, we heated them thoroughly to tuck inside our sleeping bags for extra warmth. Before turning in, we hiked along a winding gravel ridge up to a house-sized boulder, dropped here by glaciers a millennium ago. A deep cavity worn into its base on the uphill side suggested that torrents of water had once rushed down the ridgetop back when the valley floor was plugged with ice. That angular base would have cut through the water like the prow of a ship, so we named it Ship Rock.

Near dark, we snuggled into our heavy sleeping bags, heated by the granite cobbles. After the last light dwindled away, a gentle breeze sprang up, sprinkling loose snow over us.

"I'm scared," I whispered.

Miki tittered. "Me, too."

We crawled out to scan for incoming storms. The soft wind drifted away, leaving the valley still and silent. Then a small, strong light flashed on the horizon.

"Look!" I cried. It flashed again, green this time instead of yellow. "It's the runway beacon at home!"

"I'll be darned!" Miki exclaimed. Steadily, silently, the light flashed, yellow — green — yellow — green. The beacon stood fifty-five miles away and 3,000 feet below us, yet it gave us a sense of security and comfort up in this bleak valley. We slept well that night.

At dawn, we left the dogs and climbed a 4,800-foot dome above the valley. Wolf, caribou, and sheep tracks were sprinkled across the rounded top of the mountain. The descent into the west fork of the valley was steep, and the moosehide soles of my mukluks skidded perilously on the wind-blasted slope. I remembered Penny's warning, but down we went. Slipping and sliding down the 800-foot drop, we hit the upper end of the forked valley, glad to be on safe ground again.

Two miles farther, an old mining camp stood below the angular mountain walls. Drifts capped the old cabin's roof, and wind had scoured the snow away from one corner. Built with old-fashioned squared logs, with three rooms stuck together, it stood sturdy and unmolested by bears. Rusting tractors sat nearby. We knew the mine had been occupied in years past, but had heard that Denali Park personnel had decided to "rehabilitate" it, returning the digging to a natural state and destroying the short local roads. While I regretted the original destruction that the mine had caused, it also seemed silly to spend money forcing the place back to nature.

The valley sloped steeply down toward our camp, and all too soon we arrived back at the dogs after a glorious, marvelous morning. Bolting down a quick lunch, we headed back to our treeline camp. Now at last the peaks behind us began elbowing through the clouds, and scattered rays of silvery sunlight glinted off vertical ridges thickly painted with blue ice. The sled, pulled by our long string of dogs, snaked down the creek, pulling steadily away from the mysterious valley, and we craned our necks to stare back at the mountains.

"Gol-dang tourists," Miki repeated as we regretfully left the beautiful valley behind.

Heading homeward the next day, we wound down the narrow creek between towering spruce trees, crossing the snow bridges and open water once more, and then spotting those same two moose in the dashing water.

"It's my turn for the photos," Miki said.

"Don't go too close. Remember, I told you she's mean," I warned.

Miki cut upstream for a better angle as the big animals walked on gangly legs in the shallow, churning water. The cow thought Miki was cutting off their escape route and charged her. Twice.

"I TOLD you not to go too close!" I shouted as Miki beat a hasty retreat. "I TOLD you she was mean!"

"I wasn't as close as YOU were!" Miki panted, scurrying back to the sled.

I groaned. "Don't you remember what Penny said? We've crossed open water and snow bridges, climbed a mountain, camped above treeline, and got charged by a moose. I thought we told Penny we wouldn't do anything rash!"

We vowed to return to that special valley below Denali, but the next time we mushed up that way, a storm pinned us below treeline. With a tent for shelter, we made ourselves at home as windblown snow ripped over the canvas roof. The dogs curled in the lee of a few stunted trees, and we waited for the storm to blow over. But time ran out before the wind, and reluctantly we headed home. "Weather permitting" had not permitted.

During our sled trip up the Porcupine River, our team encountered battering wind, blowing snow, and bitterly cold weather
above the village of Old Crow.

CHAPTER 10

THE
ENDURANCE

Dark current swirled, sucking ominously along a gaping hole before slipping away again beneath the Yukon River ice. Pinched between a cut bank and the long, wide line of open water, the snowmachine trail zigzagged treacherously over steep, jumbled shore ice, its hard-packed surface slanting sharply down to the very brink of the hole.

From my position on the gee pole between the dogs and the long heavy sled, I could see gravel beneath three feet of clear rushing water, but that river still looked mighty cold and wet. With over a week's worth of dog food and supplies loaded in our sled, if it fell in we'd have an awful time getting it back out. As the dogs scrabbled over piles of broken ice, the sled repeatedly slid down toward that hole. I hoped it would not end up like its namesake the *Endurance,* a brave ship crushed and sunk in the ice pack of the Antarctic.

Levering against the gee pole, I pried the weighty craft back up onto the trail as Julie leaned grimly against the handlebow in back. The runners kept skidding within inches of the water's edge, but with one of us at each end we managed to keep the sled out of the water, if not quite under control. Finally the black water receded behind us and the trail led us on smoothly downstream.

The Yukon River between Circle City and Fort Yukon has, in the past century, been notorious among winter travelers for its wicked holes and treacherous ice. Challenging it for the first time, we were not without trepidation — death by drowning or freezing remains a real possibility on the Yukon, even in early March.

Miki

153

Thirty-four years earlier, our mother had kayaked down the Porcupine River from Old Crow, Yukon Territory, to Fort Yukon. Now we planned to reverse her trip, first mushing downriver to Fort Yukon from the road's end at Circle, and then traveling up the frozen Porcupine to the Gwich'in Indian village of Old Crow. Then, by going 200 miles farther east to the Dempster Highway, we could mush south to Dawson City. And why stop there? A short hop of 150 miles would get us back to Tok on the Alaska Highway, making a semicircle of about 900 miles. Although not as long as our expedition to Nome and the Kobuk, on this trip we'd face uncertain trails and only four feed pick-ups, requiring a lot of heavy loads in the sled.

After an uneventful trip along the winter trail to reach the road system at Nenana, we trucked into Fairbanks and spent several days doing the same extensive preparations that had preceded our trip to Nome. This time everything was complicated because we were going into Canada, but finally the details fell into place, feed was shipped, and we were ready to truck to Circle City and strike out down the Yukon.

We'd heard conflicting reports about trail conditions to Fort Yukon: some people told us there was a virtual highway, while others reported no trail at all. Leaving Circle City, we scooted along a hard-packed trail for the first twelve miles, making good time in spite of our load. Then, abruptly, the whole trail swerved up the bank into the yard of Albert Carroll's trapping cabin. As we halted uncertainly outside, several men poured out, looking over our team of big working dogs and answering our first question with distressing certainty:

"You can't get to Fort Yukon on this trail!"

Julie stared in dismay as another trapper appeared and offered his advice. This trail did continue on downriver, he told us, but not very far.

"You aren't the Collins girls, are you?" one of them asked, recognizing us from the stories we'd written for the regional newspaper, which had given us a certain amount of notoriety. (A fellow once wrote us to say how much he enjoyed our stories because we were "always getting into trouble!" This trip looked like no exception.)

There were more handshakes and a jumble of names. "Come in and have tea," the trappers invited.

"This trail goes on down a-ways," one added.

They all talked eagerly without regard for what anyone else said.

"They want to go to Fort Yukon."

"Come in and have tea."

Dismal head-shaking. "You'll have to snowshoe forty miles," one put in.

"How far does this trail go?" Julie asked in consternation. Snowshoeing would cut our speed down from six or eight miles an hour to one or two.

"Big dogs!" they exclaimed, looking over our team more closely.

"I have a tent camp at Twenty-two Mile," Albert said. "You can stay there tonight."

"Come in and have tea."

We packed into the small cabin with all five trappers. Sunlight blazed in the window, striking a colorful carpet covering part of the floor. "You can stay here tonight if you want to. We're all going up to Circle."

"I'll tell you how to get to my tent camp." They sat down as Albert started explaining the trails to us.

"You go down this way. Stay on this trail all the way. You'll go down a bank onto a slough with lots of beaver dams on it."

"Here's some tea. There's two cups on the table. They're dirty; we don't have any housewives here!" one laughed.

"Keep to the right. Always keep to the right."

"I ran my dogs to Fort Yukon a few years ago," someone broke in. "It took me ten hours."

"Old tent camp on the left . . ."

One of them started drawing a map on a scrap of paper.

"Spent the night and went the rest of the way . . . ninety-seven mile!"

"Don't turn right!"

"No, it was a hundred and six miles that year," someone broke in.

"Go upstream from that tent, keep right — always keep right — it goes across the river and on down to Ike's camp down there."

"My dad built this house."

"How far is it?" Julie ventured.

"You want some of this?" one asked, holding out a bottle of whiskey. I shook my head, trying to listen to the instructions.

"Here's a map of the trail — "

Someone poked a button and suddenly Bruce Springsteen was singing right there in that cabin.

"Bo-o-rn in the U.S.A.! I was . . ."

"No, this is all wrong," our advisor said, snatching away the sketch just before it reached Julie's eager fingers. "I changed the trail."

"Born in the U.S.A.!"

"Why do you want to go to Fort Yukon?"

"We want to mush up the Porcupine River into Canada," Julie answered.

They stared at us as if we were stark raving crazy. The momentary pause was broken only by Bruce's yowling.

"I was BORN in the U.S.A.!"

"Go back the way you came from tent camp and then turn right, upriver," Albert said finally.

"Yeah, don't come all the way back up here!" one laughed.

The volume of the tape player sputtered, and Bruce elevated his voice by several decibels. "I WAS *BORN* IN THE U.S.A.!"

"Always keep right — don't ever turn left."

"Just ten hours for me to go to Fort Yukon, but there was a trail then."

"Except when you leave the tent, that's just a beaver trail," Albert went on, meaning a snowmachine trail leading only to a beaver house he'd been trapping.

"I WAS BORN IN THE U.S.A.!" Bruce bellowed.

"Beaver set on the left — "

"You'll have at least twenty miles of trail to break out."

"You have snowshoes?"

"You might only have two miles, just from Ike's across the river."

We assured them we had a good pair of snowshoes, and heaven knew we'd done enough snowshoeing in the past. Two miles sounded a lot better than forty.

Albert shook his head worriedly. "It'll take you four hours to get to my tent."

"Oh, they can do it in two."

"BORN in the . . ." Bruce's voice dropped back to its previous level.

"I just came back from Ike's place. He might have a trail on down."

Bruce Springsteen started another song. I gulped down my tea. They were all talking at once, and then there was a sudden pause. Finally Albert said:

"You got that down pat?"

Julie gave him a thin smile.

But we took every reasonable right turn. We went past the old tent camp, down the slough with the beaver dams, and spent the night at Albert's tent camp. We found Ike's the next morning, and he did have a trail going on down. He also warned us about that open hole we'd have to squeak past.

We had only six miles of trail to break out, and just a day later we trooped into Fort Yukon, much relieved to leave the hazardous Yukon behind as we swung east to follow a well-used overland trail to Chalkyitsik, an Indian village on the Black River. We'd heard stories of drinking and alcohol-related problems in this village, but the day we arrived it lay quietly under the March sun, a bunch of men working to pump water to town from a hole cut in the river ice. The only excitement occurred when our dog team, with powerful Comet and Streak in the wheel, charged suddenly into someone's yard, chased a Lab into its house, and roared on through without stopping — this in spite of the chains we'd wrapped around the runners to slow down the dogs and keep them under control.

We picked up 300 pounds of supplies in Chalkyitsik. With 200 miles of questionable trail to cover before our next resupply at Old Crow, we relied on our team to haul over ten days' food for the two of us and the ten dogs, in case the going proved slow. Locating the overland trail, we swung north toward the Porcupine River, with Julie steering the sled and me being towed on skis behind it.

The *Endurance* was a new sled built for this trip, and we did not have the loading figured out yet. Under that heavy load, it refused to steer properly, and every few hundred yards it nosed off the hard-packed snowmachine trail into deep, soft snow, dragging the team to a halt again and again.

"Do you want to put on a gee pole?" I finally asked, standing on my skis as Julie angrily heaved the sled back onto the trail.

"No!" she shrieked. By her tone I knew she was too frustrated and tired to want to mess with one. Although a gee pole can be a big help in steering, it was always annoying to stop, cut down and limb a small, straight tree, and tie it onto the sled. I could also tell from her voice that it had to be done, so I cut the tree and tied it on myself while she rested with the dogs.

Under way again, we slid along the trail, the *Endurance* tracking beautifully with the help of the gee pole. Later we would learn to load the long sled with the center of gravity farther forward, allowing it to swivel more easily, instead of putting more weight in the back, as we must do in shorter sleds.

We reached the Porcupine by evening, camping in the alders at its edge. As we sat around our fire in the deepening twilight with stars sparkling overhead, a feeling of utter contentment pushed aside the day's weariness. At last, we had reached the mystical Porcupine, a clear-water river north of the Arctic Circle.

"There's nowhere else I'd rather be than right here, right now," Julie mused, poking the fire to watch a small shower of sparks go up. Our anticipation of exploring the reaches of the mighty river was more delicious than ever.

"From Circle to Fort Yukon, and up the Porcupine . . ." I chanted, then wondered how this new verse of our traveling song would end.

After years of taking trips together, we find our evening chores slip easily into a pleasant routine, with dog care taking highest priority. We picketed each dog on a short drop line attached to a long cable strung between two trees, and checked out any suspicious health problems. Julie hauled in firewood cut from dead standing spruce or alders, while I lit the fire and started cooking our dinner and melting snow for the dogs' food. On some trips — when we are rich and also can afford the weight — we feed the dogs frozen meat, thawing it in hot water and adding suet or tallow and enough premium dry dog food to soak up the excess water. This time, traveling long distances and unable to carry the sheer weight of raw meat, we chose a top-quality dry dog food, formulated for racing sled dogs, for the bulk of the diet, although we still melted in some tallow when they needed the extra fat. On really long hauls, we'd pack over a week's worth of dog food, so besides commercial feed we'd depend on a condensed diet of rice and tallow, adding meat meal, powdered egg, or dried fish for protein. Because rice takes an hour to cook, this is most inconvenient, but it beats running short of food.

After finishing our own dinner of instant food rounded out with home-baked goodies, I unloaded the sled while Julie fed the dogs their hot dinner. Two mattress pads were laid end-to-end in the long basket of the sled, followed by our heavy-duty sleeping bags. Although we were only slightly damp, we stood around the smoking fire until completely dry, knowing from bitter experience how chilly any moisture can become.

Done with their hot supper, the dogs lifted their voices in song, and we listened for answering sled dogs or wild wolves passing within earshot. The evening silence returned double-strength, and finally we each crawled into our respective sleeping bags, Julie facing the front of the sled, and me with my head buried beneath the handlebow, our legs overlapping for warmth. Weary but content after the day's journey, I took one last peek at the quiet dogs, the softly moving aurora, and the distant stars promising a chilly night, then nestled down with my coat as a pillow, letting my mind stretch into sleep.

The towering, craggy cliffs of the Lower Ramparts only hinted at the scenery ahead as we sped upriver the following day. My short, wide skis skittered happily across patches of deep, clear ice as I gripped the gee pole. Far, far below, shiny cobbles lay locked in the glassy clutches of the frozen river.

The windblown trail dragged hard on the runners, and by afternoon some of the dogs were developing foot problems because of the abrasive surface. Still, they seemed light-hearted and as eager as we were to see around each bend. Whenever we stopped for a break or to put booties on a sore-footed dog, Streak threw himself down to roll in the snow.

"*Oh-dee-oh-dee-oh!*" he shouted with delight.

"*Eee-dee-eee-dee-eee!*" Comet shrieked, hurtling his 110-pound bulk down on his equally large brother. Squalling with glee, the pair spent the better part of each short break thrashing on their backs, feet kicking wildly in the air.

Fifty windblown miles on the river made a long day, but ample reward awaited at our journey's end. Richard Carroll Jr. had invited us to use a cozy guest cabin at his father's Porcupine River Lodge, and the warm house with real beds and a gas stove seemed quite a luxury after camping out.

Richard Jr. joined us later that evening after a long haul by snowmachine from Fort Yukon, and the following morning he entertained us with tales of trapping the rich Porcupine area. He told of a dark night at a trapping cabin when a wolf came into his yard and tried to kill one of his dogs. The creature spit out the dog to turn on Richard, who shot the wolf just as it leaped at him. Although I'd heard many reliable accounts of wolves killing and eating chained sled dogs, I had never before heard a first-hand account of a wolf attacking a human. The idea that wolves never attack humans comes from the lack of substantiated accounts — that is, there are no witnesses because the victims are always alone. I found Richard's story all the more believable because we had been warned about the aggressiveness of wolves in the Porcupine River area.

Just beyond the end of Richard's trapline a half-day's travel upriver, we hit a windblown dog team trail. From the unusually narrow toboggan tracks, we knew it must have been made by Paul Jagow. We'd heard about him.

"He's a lawyer from New York," one trapper had told us. "He lives in a hole in the ground."

Whether he was a lawyer or not we never knew, but upon reaching his trapping camp we were greeted by a friendly, slight, dark-haired man who invited us inside his modest home. It was reminiscent of an Eskimo sod-and-driftwood igloo: a sunken entrance acted as a cold trap, and the interior, lined with sloping walls of neatly peeled aspen poles, was surprising bright, lit by March sunlight pouring in an overhead window. With its narrow, compact construction, the tiny room looked more like a ship's cabin than a trapper's winter home.

With his slender white hands and curious speech, Jagow seemed oddly out of place. He told us tales of hunting — "It was a wow, man, it really was!" — and hardship — "It was ridiculous, man, it really was!" But he said he'd been trapping the Porcupine for ten years, and that's a long time for a New York lawyer.

We continued toward Canada, breaking our own trail up the wind-packed river canyon. Jagow's trail only led partway up, and even it was so windblown we could hardly follow the faint scratches left by his sled runners.

We were running young Toulouse up front. The big brown son of Legs, Toulouse had a burning desire to do good. He was so sure of himself that he didn't always listen to our commands, but as a trail leader he soon outshone both Sky and Legs, our two veterans. Every time he lost Jagow's trail, he cast resolutely back and forth until he cut across it, and then stuck to it until it disappeared beneath the drifts once more. When we finally left the end of the trail behind, Toulouse didn't understand. He kept switching back and forth across the drifted canyon floor, searching for it. Finally I skied ahead, cutting a straight line upriver. But my progress over the hard-packed drifts was so much slower than the dogs, I soon allowed them to pass me.

In surprise Julie and I watched Toulouse as he drove forward, straight ahead. He no longer wasted time and effort searching for a nonexistent trail, having learned what to do after just a few minutes of watching me.

That afternoon, March 10, we crossed the border into Canada, passing by Rampart House with its big buildings standing weathered and empty. This was the last location of Hudson Bay Company's trading post, operated by fur buyers. First located at Fort Yukon, the Canadian company was discovered to have been accidentally built within Alaska, so it was moved to Old Rampart. Twenty years later, that too proved to be on American soil, and once again the trading post was moved, this time to Rampart House, before the turn of the century. Both the Old Rampart and Rampart House settlements are now abandoned.

Just upstream and across the river, we halted for the night, setting up our little seven-by-eight wood-heated wall tent. During our pre-trip research, one trapper had advised us to carry a wall tent as protection against the wind and severe weather the Arctic could throw at the Porcupine. Although we usually travel light, we bowed to local wisdom, and greatly appreciated the temperature-controlled environment. We didn't always bother setting up the tent, but every few days we'd take the extra time to pitch it so we could dry everything thoroughly and treat ourselves to a day of rest in relative luxury.

In spite of having no trail, we traveled fairly fast on the wind-packed river because we did not have to break trail ahead of the dogs. Steep walls pinched the river into a narrow, deep canyon slicing between towering pinnacles and rocks colored red and yellow. Scrub spruce scrabbled for footholds in small pockets of loose soil on the broken walls; what lay above was hidden from our view by the sheer depth of the canyon. Further upstream the canyon opened up and the snow became deeper and softer until eventually I had to ski ahead to break trail for the team.

"Look," Julie said, pointing at the map as we sat on the sled during a rest stop. "See this big oxbow bend we're coming up on? I betcha there's a portage trail cutting across it — watch for it."

Sure enough, a few minutes later I spotted a bit of a cut in the trees. Even more thrilling, I could just make out a faint mark leading from the cut, the remnants of a weathered snowmachine track; we had reached the trails spreading outward from Old Crow.

We camped in the trees at the upper end of the portage, and as we cooked supper over a little fire, Steven Frost, a well-known Canadian trapper from Old Crow, drove up on his snowmachine.

"I've got a cabin a few miles up," he told us. "The schoolteacher is staying there. You should stop and have tea."

Being shy, we've always found it difficult to stop in with strangers, but this time it turned out to be a big break. Peter Harms, the teacher, and his wife, Joanne, were originally from Edmonton — urban Canada. They marveled at our dog team and our trip. Then they gave us the key to their completely modern apartment in Old Crow.

"We're spending Spring Break here," they said. "You might as well stay in our place!"

What a blessing that proved to be! That night, as we rested in the spacious, warm, clean, fully equipped apartment, a blizzard swept in from the north, bringing gritty snow pushed by forty to fifty mph winds, and the temperature sank to twenty below. We holed up, watching sheets of snow blast past the window and stack up in high drifts along the town's frame buildings. On short forays out to check the dogs, who were sleeping in the lee of some willows on the riverbank, I could hardly stand against the gusts.

After two days the wind abated somewhat and we loaded up, harnessed the dogs, and headed upriver. Well-rested in spite of the cold, the team plunged eagerly into fifteen below temperatures made bitter by a thirty mph wind.

This next 200-mile leg from Old Crow to the Eagle Plains Hotel, a solitary outpost on the Dempster Highway, was the most uncertain part of the trip, with unusually deep snow and no trail in the middle section. Heavy drifting completely buried much of the trail leaving Old Crow. We heard that a fellow named Randy was supposed to bring a snowmachine in from Eagle Plains. If he made it, we'd have a good trail. If he didn't, our success was questionable.

Tiring from pushing ahead through heavy drifts, Sky and Legs gave out early in the day, but in single lead Toulouse quickly learned to feel for the trail even when it was invisible. Time and again he stumbled off it, and time and again he cast around until he felt the hard surface beneath the drifts. Although slow on gee and haw commands, he never became discouraged from the constant struggle or our repeated orders. But soon the snow drifted so hard he couldn't tell a packed drift from the packed trail. Half the time I had to ski ahead with a poke stick, pushing it down through inches or even feet of snow to feel for the hard-packed trail surface hidden beneath — and buried drifts often fooled even me. This was the easy part, too; once this trail ended, we'd be on our own. How we hoped for Randy's success!

The temperature dropped steadily as the sky cleared and the wind calmed. We set up the tent every night; the extra effort of scooping away the snow, stringing up the rope ridge pole, and sawing stove-length wood was worth it to avoid a battle with the cold.

Two nights after leaving Old Crow, a dreadful uproar among the dogs jerked me from a dead sleep.

"Something's out there!" Julie hissed loudly in my ear.

I shot out of bed, vague images from Richard Carroll's wolf stories lingering in the dark corners of my mind. Canadian law prohibits handguns so we had no firearm. Barefoot and clad in long johns, I burst into the bitter cold, snatching up the ax.

"HEY!" I bellowed in my most awful, throat-ripping yell.

Instant silence fell. A quick investigation proved the ruckus had only been a couple loose dogs fighting over a piece of caribou meat Steven Frost had generously given us, with every other dog eager to join in or at least cheer on their favorites from their pickets. Disgusted, I crept back to bed.

"Well, it happened!" I shouted the next morning, peering at the frosted thermometer.

It was fifty below, and the nights that followed were no warmer. Because of the severe cold, we traveled at a more relaxed pace, taking advantage of warmer afternoons and fully enjoying the panoramas of steep, rolling, white hillsides thinly skirted with spruce above the endless ribbon of river, now only half as wide as when we'd first hit it.

At this slow pace, if Randy didn't show up soon with a trail, we would not be able to safely stretch our ten-day food supply long enough to reach the highway. We plowed on hopefully, but our concern grew. What would we do if he didn't show up? By stretching our rations too far, we could get into real trouble if another storm wiped out our back trail, and the last thing we wanted was to be the target of a search-and-rescue effort. But if we were forced to return to Old Crow — what then? We had no dog food there either.

Five days out of Old Crow, including one day of rest, we passed a cabin called Salmon Cache. Although tempted to cut the day short and stay, we mushed on a little farther, breaking trail ahead of the dogs. Finally we called a halt and camped for two days, not daring to stretch our back trail any thinner.

Lying on our backs on our heavy sleeping bags, we stared up at the white canvas ceiling holding back the cold, chanting together:

"Come on, Randy! COME ON, Randy!"

Randy didn't come.

After waiting as long as we dared, we headed back for Old Crow. (We later learned that the snowmachiner had only made it a few miles before the deep snow forced him to turn back to the highway.) To lighten the gloomy, anxious mood, I finished the verse of our song.

From Circle to Fort Yukon,
And up the Porcupine,
All the way to Salmon Cache
And there we drew the line, boys,
  There we drew the line.

Deep and drifted was the snow
'Twas fifty-three below
We tucked our tails, turned and ran
And raced back to Old Crow, boys,
  Raced back to Old Crow!

Now what? We arrived back in Old Crow with a slim supply of dog food, ten dogs, and a twelve-foot sled that was not about to fit on the six-seat Cessna 206 which flew into the village from Eagle Plains.

We spent a suspense-filled night with the Harmses. Wind whistled around their apartment and over the big red school, kicking up gray snow and flinging sheets of drift across the Porcupine River. In the lee of the huge Public Health Station, our dogs rested quietly on the riverbank.

Lady Luck arrived in the morning, flying a Hercules. The huge plane from Inuvik roared overhead, loaded with fuel for Old Crow. It had been freighting all week, several flights a day. We walked down to the little airport terminal and found the pilot, a graying, broad-shouldered man commanding respect.

"*You* go first," I whispered to Julie.

She twisted her battered marten fur hat in her hands as she approached the pilot. "We have a dog sled we need to get over to Eagle Plains," she began timidly. "And we were sort of wondering if you could maybe fly it up to Inuvik for us and put it on a Points North truck. We'd be glad to pay for it."

"Can't you get it over there on a charter?" the pilot asked.

"No, it's too big to fit on the plane."

"I can take it," he said, to our profound relief. "But I couldn't accept any money. I wouldn't want to take the business away from anyone, but if it won't fit on the other plane, we'll get it there. Where are you from?"

"Alaska. We ran our dogs up from Fort Yukon."

"How long did that take?"

"About ten days." We couldn't even remember for sure any more.

"My father ran a dog team as a park ranger before the war." The pilot, whose name was Murray Dunn, told us about his father, and we told him about our sled trip, realizing we would be forever in his debt.

Although the sled traveled on the Herc for free, the two trips on the chartered 206 cost $510 and nearly wiped out our supply of cash, but at least it got our gear, our ten dogs, and ourselves to the highway. With implicit trust, our faithful companions climbed into the small plane, quietly riding as we soared effortlessly over deep snow, spruce-covered flats, and bald, windblown hills. In just two hours we traversed the wide country that had defeated our crew.

To our profound relief, a generous trucker delivered our sled from Inuvik, safe and sound, to Eagle Plains shortly after our arrival.

The truck stop was an oasis in the wilderness, with a tourist-quality hotel and restaurant. Set atop a long, high ridge, it overlooked miles and miles of lowlands and, far to the east, the Richardson Mountains. After days on the trail, it seemed an incredible, if expensive, luxury to sleep in a hotel bed and eat real hamburgers. The wilderness called, however, and we had to answer, leaving the next morning to strike south toward our next stop: Dawson City, 230 miles away.

Now instead of breaking trail, we traveled on the snow-packed highway, dodging semi rigs en route to Inuvik. Once again our dogs' faith in us paid off. Even though the dogs had never before been exposed to traffic, as each huge truck roared past, they believed our reassuring words, sitting quietly at the edge of the road, squinting against the blast, until the way was clear. Fortunately traffic was light, and some days only four or five vehicles came along. Still, as we twisted through the hills, every time we rounded a blind corner we dreaded running unexpectedly into a rig. Bad ice, blizzards, and deep snow all seemed trivial when stacked up against getting squashed by a semi.

Legs helped us avoid that fate. If we put Toulouse up front, the big brown dog took us straight down the middle of the road — a life-threatening tendency! What did he, bold dog, care for giant tractor trailers? Legs, though, was a devout edge-of-the-roader. He wore booties to protect his tender feet, but the gravel on the road bothered him, and he, clever dog, quickly learned that the shoulder had softer snow for padding. Always agreeable, little Sky followed the lead of whichever bigger dog ran beside him.

We traveled fifty miles that first day. But the farther south we mushed, the less snow covered the gravel. Mile after mile, we ran and walked behind the sled to save wear and tear on the runners and lessen the drag for the dogs. Eventually we loaded my skis; I just couldn't stay upright. Sometimes we used the "ride and tie" method, Julie driving the dogs a little ways and then tying them at the edge of the road to walk ahead, while I walked behind, reached the dogs, and mushed past her to repeat the process. Although this was faster than one of us walking all the time, it was dangerous to get too far ahead of the dogs because of traffic.

Every bend unveiled another awesome scene, with river ice of

When we reached the Dempster Highway, we found we had new problems to cope with!

the deepest blue, and on both sides of the road ridges and passes climbed into craggy mountains that drove up into the sky. Ptarmigan patted out their little trails through the willows, and a black fox crossing a treeless hillside paused at our arrival, sitting down to scrutinize the passing of this odd vehicle. He sat there still, sharp little ears pricked toward us and thick, full tail folded neatly beside him, as we disappeared around the next bend.

We paralleled the Peel River for a while, then climbed into the Ogilvie Mountains, drinking in the scenic peaks, sharp and white against the deep blue late-March sky. Each river reached and range gained became a small triumph; every valley crossed took on a special significance. Not traveling the highway in an isolated capsule of store-bought air, we were aware of the sounds and scents as well as sights — gurgling water and sulfurous odors near Engineer Creek, and the pure silence and fresh, clean smell of cold mountain passes.

Pushing through the Ogilvies, we reached the historic gold-mining areas made famous during the great gold rush at the turn of the century. Up the headwaters of the Blackstone River we mushed, gazing at the pinnacle of Tombstone Mountain and other increasingly jagged peaks as we climbed a spectacular pass before descending the North Fork of the Klondike River.

After several days of running on the hard, unforgiving road, some of the dogs started getting gimpy, with transient lameness and choppy gaits from stiffness and minor sprains. But the slight problems didn't seem to bother them much, and we eased up on the mileage to keep them happy. Anticipating bad feet due to the gravel and pavement, we'd sent an extra bunch of booties along with our food shipment to Eagle Plains for this highway run, but to our surprise no serious foot problems materialized.

My skis did not fare as well. As I skied ahead of the dogs along a small boulder-strewn creek to detour around a section of bare road, one ski snapped in half right under the binding, ending my skiing for a time. Likewise the *Endurance* suffered. Dragged along miles of gravelly road, the 3/8-inch plastic shoeing on the wooden runners abraded away. Then, as I trotted beside the sled, I sniffed loudly.

"I smell smoke!"

Julie sniffed too. "Oh!" she shouted. "It's the sled!"

The gravel, grinding away on the wooden runners themselves, had created enough friction to heat the wood to near-burning. By the time we reached Dawson City at the end of the Dempster Highway, six days after leaving Eagle Plains, the tail end of the inch-thick ash runner had worn completely away, and the gravel had chewed up half of the false runner as well.

Friends in Dawson put us up — and put up with us — for two days. Mimi Elliot was throwing the dinner party of the year, but if our smoky, well-used trail clothes offended any of the elitely dressed guests, no one let on. Mimi's musher friend made sure our dogs had everything they needed. They lay around happily, healing up from their little hurts while I healed up from a cold.

Before heading on, I sawed off the broken half of my ski and moved the binding forward. For the rest of the trip, I traveled on a ski and a half, which worked fine as long as I stayed out of deep snow and narrow holes punched by moose.

With 130 miles to go, we felt home free as we headed down the mighty Yukon into a blizzard that obscured the high bluffs and threatened to obliterate the trail. The Taylor Highway, which we planned to follow, was rumored to be bare of snow south of Chicken, so instead of mushing clear to the Alaska Highway we decided to truck from the little mining community. Following the Yukon and Fortymile Rivers brought us to the bridge where the Taylor crossed the Fortymile, and from there we were gritty-grinding over gravel again. Our runners were disappearing faster than ever as the back ends of the false runners wore away and even the back stanchion pegs stubbed along the ground.

A few miles from Chicken we dodged down a snowmachine trail that followed a creek paralleling the gravelly road. The farther we went, the snowier the trail became. Then we started breaking through into overflow.

"Hike!" Julie shouted.

The dogs drove forward, splashing through eight inches of water and slush. Frigid icicles of ice water drained down into my ski boots, soaking my feet as I towed behind the sled. By the time the dogs scrambled onto a firm trail, we were all getting wet. At least the April weather had brought temperatures up to the freezing point. A few hundred yards on, we hit water again, and this time our dubious trail disappeared completely.

We didn't want to go back through all that water behind us, but we sure didn't want to break trail through snow water, either. As we pondered our fate, I spied another fresh track just ahead. Half an hour later our team was merrily chasing loose dogs in downtown Chicken, so enthusiastically that Julie had to tip over the *Endurance*. It fell with a massive boom ("Like a downed mammoth," Julie said), dragging our misfits to a halt.

Julie caught the mail plane to Fairbanks the next day to pick up our truck. Not sure when she'd get back, I waited in our tent camp just outside town, peeling pieces of diamond willow to kill time. Inside the bright wall tent the following morning, I shaved bits of bark from the half-frozen wood while the dogs lounged on their picket line. Comet was free to wander around camp, but even he preferred snoozing on the bare ground under a big spruce tree.

Suddenly I heard a collective gasp from the dogs. "ARF!" Amber shouted as Comet tore off for the road with a thundering beat of huge paws. The rumble of our truck had not registered with me, but it sure had with the dogs: they knew their 900-mile journey was over.

But we weren't home yet. After driving from Chicken to Nenana, we still had to make the 130-mile trip home and once again faced a jaunt fraught with the perils of breakup.

Star-light, star bright,
First star I see tonight . . .

Staring up at a star-studded sky until my neck cricked, I almost fell off my skis as I glided along behind the dog sled. Darkness had not come until nearly eleven on that night of April 13. It had hit fifty degrees in the afternoon, and we had traveled only a short distance out of Nenana before the sun turned the trail to slush. The dogs' eagerness dwindled in the heat and we camped for the rest of the day, heading on at 8 P.M. when things started cooling down. The dogs knew this trail home well, and despite the slushy trail they trotted willingly into the increasing darkness.

We mushed straight through the night, crossing flooded sloughs and bare gravel bars in the dark, casting about for the trail which no longer showed on the far side. On and on we trekked, the great canopy of a moonless sky filled with the glitter of stars near and far.

Stopping at dawn, we made a quick breakfast. When I walked among the dogs to pat them, I spied a smear of blood on the crusty snow. Inspecting a few feet, I isolated the problem: Amber had a badly swollen, abraded toe. Although she limped a little, any pain she felt did nothing to dampen her happy-go-lucky attitude that matched her furry golden-tan mask and loppy ears so well. I took off her harness, and for the rest of the trip she cheerily scampered along loose.

We chugged on until the trail began to thaw in mid-morning. Camping for the day, the dogs sprawled on bare ground under spruce trees as Julie and I dozed the afternoon and evening away, cozy in our dogsled. At 3 A.M., when the faintest hint of dawn in the north-eastern sky promised enough light to navigate the flooding rivers ahead, we harnessed up and headed out as Julie sang:

Through the mountains of Denali
Across the Dawson Hills
On the flatlands of the Kuskokwim
I'll travel where I will, boys
    Travel where I will!

The dogs had run more than a thousand miles in the last seven weeks, and after blizzards and fifty below temperatures, snow drifts and glare ice and semi trucks, the thought of nice, dry doghouse roofs to lie on under a warm spring sun pulled them onward across bare moss, deep water, and slushy trails. Sometimes we traveled for a mile without benefit of snow, taking turns mushing ahead and walking behind, or sharing the runners. We had covered this trail enough times that even the difficult parts seemed familiar, and if we lost it, we knew how to pick it up again.

Just twenty-five miles from home we got lost, wandering around some beaver trapping trails. Eventually we backtracked to the mouth of the stream we trap on, and headed up it instead, splashing through mile after mile of shin-deep water. Gratefully I exchanged my ski boots for rubber boots. Once again Toulouse shone, plunging through the flood when the others balked at the deep water. Picking up another overland trail, we cut out across the flats, through miles of scrub spruce and tamarack, willows and a myriad of small lakes and marshes. Thirteen hours of traveling brought us to the muddy shores of the lake, and after slogging through a quarter-mile of mud, we hit solid lake ice.

The heat of the afternoon slowed us all, but the dogs never faltered on the last two miles of spring ice, their boundless heart and drive overcoming their fatigue. At last we reached the final impasse of our odyssey: a half-mile of bare, rocky beach.

This time we didn't have to wreck what was left of our sled. We just turned those ten good dogs loose and, all together, we merrily walked home.

I wish I may,
I wish I might . . .

No, I thought, I don't need a lucky star this time. The dream had already come true.

After splitting and stacking several cords, Miki stands trium-
phantly atop a pile of firewood that will heat our main home for
about half of the seven-month-long winter.

CHAPTER 11

CHORES

With the coming of spring, Miki and I turn from trapping and winter adventures to harvesting. We harvest firewood in May, rhubarb in June, berries in July, vegetables in August, moose in September, and fish in October, which brings us back to trapping in winter. Of course these chores do overlap; woodcutting, for instance, often starts in March and may not be done until October.

In fact, of all the chores Miki and I do, woodcutting is among the most tedious. Even with a chain saw, we spend several spring days at each trapping camp, cutting wood for the next year. Then we return home to start the real job: cutting wood for the big house. Heating it may require eight cords of firewood per winter, which takes several weeks to cut, split, and stack. Luckily, when Daddy is at home his firewood heats the house, but Miki and I keep our own woodpiles as well. At least we try to. To burn efficiently the birch wood needs to be seasoned for two years, and when we fall behind it means burning green wood or rotten stumps.

One year I ran completely out of wood right before heading out to the Birch Cabin to trade places with Miki. Rather than use Daddy's wood, I scrounged a big pile from the forest for her to burn when she came down. However, I left a disclaimer on the table:

Here is your WOOD.
Some of it is DRY.
Some of it is WET.
Some of it is GREEN.
Some of it is ROTTEN.
But it is WOOD.
So don't COMPLAIN.

Scrabbling for wood every winter was frustrating. Then one year we had to forgo our spring dog sled trip

Julie

because Lilja was expecting a foal, and suddenly we had several extra weeks to cut wood.

"Every year we cut wood to use when Daddy's away, and every year we run out," I told Miki. "This year we've got time to cut more, and I'm going to do it. I'm going to cut down forty trees so we never run out of wood again!"

"Go ahead," she said.

I bought a brand-new Husqvarna chain saw and after two weeks cutting wood on the trapline I started cutting wood at home. Miki didn't like using the chain saw, so every day I went out to the wood lot by myself. With the snow still hip-deep, I shuffled from tree to tree, stomping out escape paths in case a tree fell the wrong way. I cut down forty of the biggest birch trees I could find, crawling and wading through wet snow to saw them into stove-length blocks, then leaving them where they lay until the snow melted. By the time the last tree fell, the retreating snow made it easier to split the blocks. Miki came out with her splitting maul, steel wedge, and sledge hammer to split the wood so it would dry faster. Sometimes I helped her, but mostly I stacked the wood in tall piles, where it would dry for two summers before we hauled it home with Lilja's big sled.

WHACK! The maul bit deeply into the red heart of a knotty log. Miki's strong hands wrenched it back out for another try, dusty hair drifting freely above her mussed braids. I bucked a couple split lengths toward a growing pile. In the distance the long single note of a varied thrush rang out, and the buzz of the first mosquitoes promised months of torment ahead. As we worked, the sweet, light scent of fresh birch drifted gently on the spring breeze. Clear, clean, faintly sugary birch sap was rising in the trees, oozing from the new stumps, dripping from twigs, and running down fresh scars. Cutting the wood before the sap rose made the blocks lighter, and they would dry more quickly. Already tiny leaf buds had appeared on the crooked red branches, covering the gray woods with a fuzzy green haze, and the cut trees, too, tried to green up, with buds swelling on the twigs. One morning a moose wandered by, found our cut trees, and stayed for breakfast, not bothering to leave when we arrived. The friendly barren cow preferred munching on twigs from our cut trees because the high branches lack the bitter, oily flavor of those lower twigs moose normally can reach; this clever anti-browsing chemical protects the lower, more accessible branches but not the high tops of trees.

In the summer Lilja sometimes pulls a cartload of driftwood to burn under the dog food cooker.

My forty trees stacked into ten cords of wood, a good average. Many saplings remained in the half-acre wood lot to grow and refill the area, so in another forty years we could harvest it again.

Of course, cutting firewood is not the only item on our List of Spring Chores. Most of these tasks are time-consuming but pleasant — cleaning and raking the lawn and dog yard, raking and composting horse manure, planting the garden, collecting meltwater for tanning furs and spring housecleaning, and starting a new crop of chickens from little peepers we buy in town.

One spring chore, however, is time-consuming but *not* pleasant. Income tax.

It's one thing to compute taxes with an accountant or a simple W-2 form, and quite another when you're 150 miles from help and have no phone and you need to report on two shaky businesses as well as investments you didn't know you had until their tax slips arrived. Also, when the mail plane comes in only once a week, you don't always have until April 15 to finish your taxes. You have until April 15 or the second Tuesday in April, whichever comes first.

"Don't report any interest off our joint savings account," I warned Miki one bright spring morning as we sat laboring at the same desks where we once studied for grade school.

"Why not?" she demanded.

"Because the bank reported it to the IRS under my social security number, not yours. If you report it, they won't like you, and if I report any less than both our halves, they'll put me in jail."

The sun beat eagerly through our open bedroom window, beckoning us to join it outside. Though work was piling up, our tools sat idle. Instead of being productive and having fun, we sat inside puzzling over our respective forms. "Why did I make so much more money than you did?" Miki wailed.

"I bought more photo supplies," I said. "I bought so much stuff, I hardly made any money writing this year."

"But you reported all that interest on the savings account," Miki fumed. "Give me your form!" I handed it over and she compared it to hers. With similar investments, and being partners in several ventures, we report very similar amounts to the IRS, with many identical entries.

"Oh!" Miki exclaimed. "I added my IRA deduction to my income, instead of subtracting it!"

I laughed. "Isn't that just like you! Where would you be without me?"

"In jail!" she shouted.

Then I got stuck. Schedule B said to enter capital gains distributions on line 6 (and line 13, Schedule D) and add it to line 7, subtract from line 5, and enter the result on line 9 and on Form 1040, line 9. I knew the IRS wouldn't want me to subtract my capital gains, but that's how I interpreted their instructions.

After fuming for half an hour I had a flash of inspiration. I entered the capital gains somewhere else entirely and skipped Schedule D. Miki copied my improvisation.

"They shouldn't care how you do it, if you end up paying the right amount," I said hopefully.

We scribbled and added and compared. "What's the answer to 8a?" Miki asked, and telling her gave me the uneasy feeling that we were cheating on homework.

"Why am I still paying so much more than you?" Miki wailed with frustration. "Oh! I added my business expenses to my profits, instead of subtracting them!"

I laughed and laughed. I hadn't made any mistakes — yet.

"Why don't we deduct for operating a business in our home?" Miki inquired.

"Because . . . because it's too much trouble," I sighed.

I was all done. We double-checked. It looked fine. I wrote my check. We always ask an expert — Daddy — to review our work, but just before heading downstairs Miki realized that we had forgotten to consider our biggest expense — the dog team. Since the team provides us with essential transportation on the trapline, we deduct most of their expenses just as other trappers can deduct snowmachine expenses.

"Are we really going to change all these papers?" Miki asked ruefully.

"It'll save an awful lot of money," I said. I did some rough figures. "Would you do fifteen minutes of work to save $700?" I asked.

Miki looked miserable. "I guess so."

We erased and crossed out, scribbled and refigured. In the melee I forgot to add my Schedule C page A (trapping and handcraft profits) to my Schedule C page B (freelance writing profits). By the time I realized my error, I had to go back once again and change my Form SE lines 2, 3, 7, and 8, and my Form 1040 lines 12, 23, 31, 32, 35, 37, 38, 40, 47, 48, 53, 62, and 64. I would have copied the whole form onto a fresh sheet, but we had no extras and it wasn't worth the two-hour sled trip to the post office to get a clean form. Well, if the IRS couldn't read what I wrote, they couldn't prove I did anything wrong, could they?

As usual, the forms took an hour to complete the first time and half a day to finish after correcting all the mistakes.

"What a disaster," Miki groaned. "Why don't you write a story about it for the *Northland News?*"

"If they knew how we did this," I told her, "We'd get audited for sure!"

The *Northland News,* a monthly newspaper sent to Bush Alaska villages, publishes little stories we write, providing a small but reliable source of income. We sell bigger stories for more money to regional and national magazines, but they appear less regularly. Writing is just a sideline for us; the sale of furs and handcrafts, while variable, usually outstrips the income we make as authors. In the spring and early summer we do much of the handcraft work: tanning furs, brushing the dogs, and spinning the fur they shed. Once we complete these preparations, we can work on finishing the products during any leisure time we have throughout the year.

The soft, woolly fur that keeps our huskies warm during the winter makes a thick yarn, which we knit into warm hats and mittens. Any trapline furs that we do not sell also go into crafts. Fox, lynx, beaver, wolf, and marten make hats, mittens, overmitts, and mukluks, while the leftover scraps make cute little fur animals, fur flowers, baby booties, and key chains.

The problem with making things is that then we must sell the darn stuff. This reclusive way of life hasn't honed our ability to mingle with others — actually, we never had that talent in the first place. While gift shops and winter-supply stores buy some of our products, we also attend one or two craft fairs each summer in Fairbanks, and it took us a few years to feel comfortable doing that.

One summer I strolled through the Bentley Mall in Fairbanks, examining the many booths set up for an indoor craft show. Shiny baubles, embroidered handiwork, and wooden doodads lay attractively displayed on tables guarded by smiling, talkative artists. Then I saw our own table, fur crafts hanging from antler hooks and piled high on a red cloth. Behind the table sat Miki, tense and silent, showing the whites of her eyes.

"Smile!" I ordered sternly. "Everybody else is smiling, and you're sitting there looking scared, sad, and slightly hostile. You're supposed to smile!"

Some years nothing sells, fueling an intense homesickness and frustration over the time wasted. Other years can get really exciting. One summer half the ladies in Fairbanks were expecting babies and the other half were looking for gifts. We started with seven pairs of baby booties at the start of a two-weekend show, and by the end of the second weekend we had sold twenty-four pairs. Every day I'd walk down three booths to buy rabbit skins from our friend Glenn Stoneman, and sew up more booties just as fast as I could. Another year we trapped more fox than usual so we offered fox hats for $99 that summer. We sold an awful lot of hats, but some of the more discerning ladies were suspicious. "How come they're so cheap?" they demanded, and they didn't always believe our explanation.

Then there are the duds — the leather vest, the fur pillow, the little bags, the moosehide mukluks, that sat for years until we gave them away or used them ourselves. There are also surprises. One woman asked Miki to make a moose-thong hair tie with fur pompoms. Miki whipped one up and charged three dollars. Then she made a bunch more and sold eighteen in three days.

Most of our summer work doesn't involve money at all. We spend our time caring for our animals, gathering food and other resources to see us through the year, and doing jobs that can't be done in the winter, like cement work and digging post holes. One day we preserve rhubarb, weed and water the garden, hill potatoes, pick strawberries, mow the lawn, fill a handcraft order, and trim the horses' hooves. On another day we might harvest and freeze broccoli, roll over a compost pile, pick one or two gallons of blueberries and make jam, rake out the horse corral, and move the fish net to a better location. Or we might haul freight by boat and pack horse from the post office, brush out a trail, type out a story, and attend a community meeting. Daily chores include rustling up something for dinner; a baked whitefish from the net, crisp vegetables from the garden, and a fresh berry pie for dessert are common summertime fare.

With all the work to be done, the worst problem is deciding what to do first. "Shall we be good little girls and weed the garden?" Miki wonders at breakfast. "Or shall we be good little girls and finish stacking the firewood?"

"We have to kill chickens today," I remind her. "And you have a fur hat to make, and I have to print some photos for that magazine."

Timing is crucial for some chores, so we try hard not to put them off. The harvest demands special attention. If not preserved at the peak of maturity and ripeness, our food supply will be inferior until next year's produce is ready. We often postpone other jobs, like building a puppy pen, repairing a fence, or completing a sewing project, but even so, our best-laid plans to pick strawberries before they mold, or Swiss chard before it bolts, often fall apart. Maybe a colt needs a gash stitched, or we catch so many fish they have to be cut for drying so they don't spoil, or the mail brings a demand that must be met *now*. Then, too, nobody is hanging over our shoulders to shout "YOU'RE FIRED!" if we fail to finish our work. Bush life requires endless self-discipline as well as stamina.

Luckily, Miki and I are pretty easygoing about dividing the labor. Sometimes we work together or take turns with chores, while other chores belong exclusively to her or to me. For instance, Miki always picks up the dog yard, lights the fire under the dog food cooker, and doctors sick dogs. I always check the fish net, water the dogs, and restrain wiggling critters while Miki medicates them.

This division of labor is especially important for chores that take practice and skill. Miki always trims the horses' hooves, for it takes practice to make them level. I do most of the small engine repair because I finally made a little headway in figuring it out. But many unassigned jobs are divided by compromising.

"I'll cut down some trees for fence poles if you hitch up a horse and drag them in," I'll suggest.

Miki, thinking of other pressing demands, counters my suggestion. "I'll plant those last rows of carrots if you cut the poles *and* drag them in."

Those microscopic specks called carrot seeds put me in a sweat not just because they're so small but because Miki complains about the uneven way I plant them. Today, I end up hauling the poles. Miki plants carrots. And we work into midnight's soft light to finish it all.

Of course we quarrel sometimes, but usually the system works. When it doesn't, arguments swell hot and furious, but seldom last long. "What'll you do if I pump water?" I asked one day.

"I'll work on the compost pile," Miki offered.

"You'd do that anyway," I said.

"Then I'll pump water and *you* do the compost."

"The compost is your job, and the strawberries are more important. They're getting too ripe."

"You always pick strawberries," Miki retorted.

"Well, this time *you* can pick the strawberries!"

"Huh! Then *you* can clean the dog yard!"

"And *you* can check the fish net!" I shot back.

"*You* can water the garden!"

"*You* can run the chain saw and the motorboat and the lawn mower!"

"*You* can run the tiller and the chipper and the Skil saw! And *you* can sew up the hurt dogs!" Miki sniffed.

"Well . . . well, *you* can make the custard and the white sauce and pie fillings!"

"And *you* can make the pie crusts and bread and biscuits!"

"And *you* can sew the mitts and kuspuks and dog harnesses!"

"*YOU* can sew the trapper's hats and baby booties and slippers!"

"*YOU* can write my *Northland News* story!"

"*YOU* can write mine!"

By now we are laughing and shouting. "*YOU* can feed the chickens!" I bellow.

"*YOU* can feed the horses!" Miki roars.

"I'll git you!" I shout.

"No, *I'll git you!*"

By now we have forgotten the original problem. The argument peters out. I go off to pick strawberries. Miki retreats to her beloved compost. The water waits for another day.

Besides the food we gather, both wild and cultivated, we use a wide range of other natural resources. Some outsiders think the subsistence way of life means harvesting wild animals, but that is only a small part of it. With no nearby shopping centers, we've always turned to the land for a variety of supplies. As children, we used twigs, roots, birch bark, alder cones, and shells to make little crafts. We filled tiny snail shells with wax for doll candles, glued alder cones into little animals, and hollowed out conch fungus plucked from birch trees to make cups for flowers or candleholders. Now, as adults, we use that same imagination to envision finished products when we look around at the resources provided by the wilderness.

Spruce logs, birch bark, flat stones, and sand are all good building materials. The ubiquitous spruce poles can be found in cabin roofs, garden fences, fish racks, chicken coops, dog houses, tent frames, and compost cribs. We use them to anchor fish nets and dog chains, for sled repair along the trail, for trapline cubbies, and to secure beaver traps. Birch bark makes good fire-starter, waterproof shingles, and lightweight baskets. Abrasive goose grass works well for scouring pots on camping trips. Dry grass insulates mukluks and mitts if we're caught without good gear, while moss insulates our roofs and our outside freezer.

Willow wands mark our winter routes along open swamps and lakes so we don't have to make a new trail every time wind or snow obliterates the old one. The saplings, set upright every hundred yards, can also lead us home in fog and snowstorms, and on black nights. Our lead dogs learn to "connect the dots" when they can't see the trail. If we shout "Trail!" and they don't see it, they'll veer off toward the nearest wand. Willows make good riding whips, too; often just snapping off a branch in a silent threat will liven up a pokey horse. The tiniest willow twigs are best for "caging" either side of a snare to guide a lynx or wolf through the loop.

I learned long ago to note potential resources during my travels. I remember the locations of distant berry patches, Christmas trees, cabin logs, or spruce burls. Ten years ago I spotted a thick patch of currant bushes two miles above the Birch Cabin. I never made it up there again, but I haven't forgotten it. I know where to find the small flat stones I use as ballast in the little fur animals I sew . . . where birch saplings grow in dense thickets, easy to harvest for beaver bait and sled railings . . . where to search for straight, mature birch trees to mill into sled runners . . . and where to find red dock for a colorful winter bouquet.

Using these resources does more than save us money. It makes us more self-sufficient and independent, and it keeps our brains working as we ponder how to best splint a broken sled or repair a leaky sod roof. We feel at home just about anywhere in this country because we know where to look for what we need, whether it's along sandy ridges for cranberries or on riverbanks for tall spruce trees.

Of course, sometimes our use of these resources is challenged by other critters. Bears and wolves have scavenged our moose kills. Ravens, fox, and mink work havoc on fish caches. Bears, mice, grouse, and smaller birds vie for the berries we plan to pick. Even the wind and rain, snow and water can work against us. The glacier river that flows into the lake has changed course to silt up our bay and our water supply. Rain knocks ripe blueberries from their bushes; snow covers late cranberries; wind topples some of the finest spruce trees and creates winter silt storms that bury our strawberry patch. It's disheartening to shovel silt dunes off the strawberries, or to lose fifty fish to the ravens or five marten to a wolf. For the most part, though, we protect what we can and accept the losses with a shrug, saying "That's the way it is." After all, they were here first.

Our hectic lives become even more frantic as the short summer pushes toward fall. The harvest climaxes in August, with berries and vegetables going into the freezer almost every day. Other chores get pushed aside as the pace speeds up; luckily, we can involve our animals in some of the work so they aren't too neglected. Several dogs accompany me, running loose, when I check our fish net two miles away, and I use a horse or two to pack fish the last half-mile up the silted bay from the boat landing. We also ride the horses to the cranberry patches, bringing along a couple of dogs to secure the area against bears.

Routine medical chores such as vaccinations, worming, and toenail and hoof trimming often get put off until moose-hunting is nearly upon us, but we take care of emergencies on the spot. Porcupines move around in late summer, so we keep pliers and tranquilizers handy for the inevitable encounters. Some dogs learn to leave porcupines alone after a run-in, but a few will settle for nothing less than complete revenge.

Other minor problems need immediate attention so they don't become serious. The dogs occasionally suffer from summer eczema, which can turn into ugly sores if not treated. Lilja's light skin and eyes make her vulnerable to minor eye irritations that occasionally lead to infections. One year Pepper became so lame that we opted for a painful knee surgery to repair torn cruciate ligaments. Her recovery took months of gentle rehabilitation, during which Pep was not a happy doggie, but the operation considerably improved her life, justifying the pain, time, and expense.

Emergencies are the worst. One night, checking the dogs, Miki found one of them bloated. We worked on him all night. When Miki was unable to push a tube down to his stomach to relieve the gas, she sedated him and inserted a large-bore needle through the abdomen into his stomach. This released the pressure, but only temporarily. We knew the stomach must have twisted. Even if the stormy weather had allowed us to fly him to a vet, it would have been too late. When the bloat increased again, our only option was to put him down with a bullet. This ended his pain, but not ours. Just like that, he was gone. It was one of those occasions when we pay a heavy price for our remote lifestyle; immediate access to a veterinarian might have saved his life.

Worse yet was when we lost Legs. He suffered not for hours but

for days. At first we didn't
realize how serious the problem was. He went lame, and
two of his feet felt cold. Then
he developed a high fever, a
systemic infection. Antibiotics did nothing. Injecting him
with penicillin offered only
temporary relief. A vet we
consulted by phone could offer no solution. The cause of
the infection became apparent
only when the skin on those
two feet broke open: a mysterious blockage of blood in
both feet had resulted in gan-
grene. Skin sloughed off

**Julie and Comet were especially
good friends.**

muscle; muscle sloughed off bone. Amputating both feet would have
left him miserable beyond endurance. With grief and frustration,
we faced the inevitable: the only way we could help him was to help
him die. Fighting tears, Miki and I gently carried the big white dog
away, but when we laid him down to do the dreadful deed, he was
already gone.

Then there was the day Comet got mauled by a porcupine two
miles from home. While I restrained the huge squalling mutt, Miki
pulled out as many bristling quills as she could with her fingers before we headed home for the pliers. The quill pig had lashed his
stickery tail against Comet's loose jowls, and by the time we reached
home the loose skin had swelled up around the quills, making many
of them impossible to remove. Still, we weren't too worried. Quills
can work through flesh and bone, but often make their way back
out without doing serious harm. I have even seen a dog eat part of a
porcupine's prickly skin without suffering.

However, we did keep an eye on Comet. I noticed right away
when the big dog began squinting and twisting his head in pain.
Suspecting a quill might be burrowing into the back of his eye, I
made a late-night flight to Fairbanks with him huddled in the
back of our little Cessna.

Dr. Karin Schmidt removed his pierced eye, and several quills along with it. Shortly after I flew him home, another quill exited right beside his remaining eye. He gradually recovered from the trauma during the next few days, apparently unhampered by the loss of his eye.

One evening a week later, when Comet and Streak were loose, I noticed that the big buffoon was oddly reluctant to play with his brother. He acted subdued. "Almost like he has a headache," I commented to Miki. That night he couldn't hold down his dinner. In the morning he seemed better, but by afternoon he was staggering and pacing with pain. Miki had flown to town, and I managed to contact her by radio. "I think the quills might be working into his brain," I told her. Miki made a quick visit to Dr. Schmidt and flew straight out with steroids and antibiotics. Sick with anxiety, I hurried down to meet her as she pulled the boat ashore after the trip across the lake from the runway. Our eyes met and her face fell. I didn't have to say much; she could read it in my expression.

"He's going down fast," I said. I wanted to say, "We're losing him," but I couldn't.

We rushed back to the dog yard with the medicine. When I last left Comet, he had been lying stuporously, unable to move although I thought he was still aware of my presence. Now when we reached his side, a seizure had gripped him. Medicating him would be impossible unless the seizure stopped. We could only kneel beside him, holding him as the violent jerks racked his powerful body. The minutes passed like years until after a full hour the contractions grew weaker, dwindling slowly to rigid tremors. Then his great body lay still. Miki placed a hand over his heart as the last quivering faded away. Then she began to cry, then we were both crying. I looked at Streak. He was sitting very still. I knew we could never again speak Comet's name in front of him, for Streak would know it and look for his big brother, and he would not be there.

Who now would run beside old Streak? Who would help him drive away bears? Who would escort the horses on our rides? Who would *eee-dee-eee-dee-eee* for Streak's *oh-dee-oh-dee-oh?*

Comet left a gaping hole that no other dog could fill. I will miss him always. Sometimes it hurts so much to lose such a fine friend, the only explanation that gives any comfort at all is that maybe God needed a good dog.

These two moose took refuge from the deep snow by standing in a shallow creek. The cow, threatened by our approach, warned us off with raised hackles, laid-back ears, and nose poked out.

CHAPTER 12

CLOSE ENCOUNTERS

"Wipeout!" I shouted. "Double wipeout! WHOA!"

Skiing behind Julie's sled in forty-below cold, I had fallen down just before a right-angle snap turn in the trail sent my sister catapulting away as well. The sled promptly tipped over, plowing the eager team to a halt. Panting, the dogs looked back impatiently as they waited for us to brush the snow from our clothes.

Back in control, Julie let the dogs charge onward as I gripped my skijoring rope, trying to see the trail through thick layers of frost coating my glasses. The dogs had been plowing through deep snow all day, and we thought their sudden enthusiasm lay in their desire to reach home and their warm, hay-lined doghouses just a mile and a half away. But actually their ambition was sparked by something closer at hand.

With Toulouse blazing along in the lead, the team burst out of the alders onto a small, grass-lined slough glazed with frozen overflow. On the far side stood a couple of moose.

Because of the snowed-in trail, our nine dogs ran in single file on a double-length towline. Running loose were three mostly grown pups, our pet dog Pepper, and Streak and Rusty, both retired by then, bringing our total to fifteen. The pups, sprinting ahead, had already reached the moose, and their hysterical barking excited the team dogs even more. Any chance Toulouse had of dragging the others down the trail dissolved as the momentum of the whole pack carried one and all toward the big animals, Julie's steel-pronged sled brake rasping futilely across the impenetrable surface of the ice.

"Toulouse!" Julie shouted first at the big leader, *Miki*

and then she called to the other trained leaders running farther back in the team. "Reuben! Cody!"

The cow melted back into the brush on the far side of the slough, but the half-grown calf hardly moved from his spot on solid footing. Although not even a year old, he already approached six feet in height. Toulouse, swinging around behind the calf, cut off his escape, and the rest of the pack closed in from all sides. Their voices raised a loud clamor as they surrounded the wretched little fellow.

"Hector! HECTOR!" Julie roared as one of the more powerful team dogs drove forward, dragging sled and driver along with him. Tipping her sled over in a last-ditch attempt to stop the team, Julie slowed the back three or four dogs to a halt. Rusty, aging and running loose, kept his distance, as did Pepper, her courage as small as she was big. Old Streak, the pups, and the working sled dogs — thirteen in all — had no such qualms.

Even with dogs barking wildly at him from every angle, the calf didn't seem too perturbed. He simply took a few circling steps and kicked out halfheartedly a few times. Chunks of ice, probably collected by walking in overflow and soft snow, clung to his back legs.

Although not actually trying to bite their captive, the dogs were about as thrilled as they could get. They had caught themselves a moose! Golly! Toulouse circled the animal, dragging his long towrope around the calf's feet.

"You watch for the mother!" I shouted to my twin sister. If that cow charged back to extricate her youngster from his dilemma, we might all get stomped out. But the forty-below cold had iced Julie's glasses, limiting her vision, and I wasn't sure she'd even see the cow before it was too late. Popping off my skis and stuffing my own worthless glasses into a pocket, I rushed forward.

"Don't go up there! Do NOT go up there!" Julie shouted at me over the racket.

I wasn't about to approach the calf too closely. Even though he looked rather harmless and had even given up his ineffective kicking, I didn't want to find out how much clout he could pack into one double-pronged hoof. Some moose act so tame that ignorant people walk right up to them — occasionally getting a half-ton kick. Other moose aggressively attack people and dog teams that try to use "their" trails, especially during deep snow years like this one, when moose think a hard-packed surface is the safest place from which they can make a stand. The moose in our isolated area almost always give us right-of-way, but I didn't want to push my luck. Grabbing the towline ahead of the wheel dog, I hauled back. "Toulouse! Joni! Reuben!" I shouted sternly.

Averaging over eighty pounds apiece, hardened and strong from days of breaking trail, the dogs had the advantage. They did not want to leave that moose, and I wasn't making a dent in their determination. The befuddled calf had stepped free of the towline twice now but still showed no interest in leaving. He didn't want to follow the cow into brisket-deep snow, nor was he keen on moving away up the slough.

Then, dancing and dodging, Toulouse hitched a full wrap around one skinny moose leg. I groaned inwardly and kept hauling and shouting. As I gained control over the back dogs, Julie grabbed them so I could work my way up the towline without approaching the moose too closely. "Pike! Bingo! Wiggles! WIGGLES!"

After several minutes of calling girls and barking dogs, I had freed most of the team, dragging them back from their victim. The calf took a careful step and miraculously the towrope fell away from his leg.

"Toulouse!" I snarled. "Come gee!"

The big brown leader finally decided the game had stalled out. He came away, bringing the remaining team dogs with him. Straightening them quickly, Julie mushed around the corner so they couldn't rejoin the fray. That left me with the three youngsters, audacious old Streak, and one dog who'd accidentally come unsnapped from the towline.

"Streak! Cody!" The two adults came reluctantly when I called, and I dragged them away. "Arthur! Beau! Emily!" Only one pup responded, but I knew the younger ones wouldn't stay long without adult backup.

"Shooo-eee!" I sighed in relief as I rejoined Julie. Once away from the excitement, the adult dogs made far-apart tracks for home, and the pups had sense enough to get back in time for dinner. None of the dogs had been hurt; we've always been lucky (so far) and even after twenty-plus years of mushing, we've never had a serious moose-related injury.

Although not wounded by the dogs, the calf had acted lethargic, possibly weakened by disease, starvation, or the effects of the winter's unusually deep snow. Several weeks later I found a wolf-killed calf just a hundred yards from that spot, and I always wondered if it was the same one. We'll never know; that winter we found four moose kills within two miles of our house, the work of a wolf population expanding to feed on vulnerable moose bogged down, exhausted, and hungry after several winters of heavy snow.

As trappers, we harvest the renewable resources offered by the land. Killing an animal is sobering, but I recognize it as part of the natural cycle of life and death constantly and violently taking place in the wild. Realistically, a steel trap or snare is no more cruel than normal death by disease, starvation, or predation. All animals get eaten sooner or later, and when they're trapped at least the precious pelts are not torn and scattered to the wind. We feed palatable carcasses to our dogs and place the untasty ones out as bait, where they often end up in the bellies of hungry fox, marten, and other scavengers who have no qualms about eating their own kind. I have always felt it better to harvest from a wild land than to tame and overcrowd the country, growing meat in a feedlot and furs in a cage, or wearing products from environmentally destructive petroleum and chemical industries.

Unlike predators who must kill or die, we can choose not to harvest an area if it shows signs of depletion. Our country has been trapped almost continuously since about 1900, yet still shows no signs of damage or depletion, thanks in part to its isolation and inaccessibility. Far greater swings in animal populations are caused by natural forces than by trapping. One year a rainy summer might grow a lot of grass, feed a lot of healthy mice, and give a boost to the marten population. Another year an influx of lynx might drive every marten out of the lowlands, and we find them overcrowded in the spruce hills where lynx rarely venture.

Unlike marten, which tend to be both curious and incautious, wolves usually shy away from any suspicious alterations, even a cleverly disguised snare or a trap hidden under a month of snows. Because of their skill in avoiding sets, and because they pass through our area unpredictably, often we don't even try to catch them. In fact, in our first ten years of full-time trapping, we never caught one. But we enjoyed listening to them serenade back and forth with our sled dogs, and on rare occasions we spotted a pair on some distant corner of a lake or stream. During the deep snow years of the late 1980s and early '90s, they became a more frequent sight.

One night as Julie and I settled down to sleep in the Birch Cabin at the start of trapping season, the wolves sounded so close we got up and slipped outside to listen. Our dogs, leaping into a tizzy on their chains, barked and howled, yelped and yowled at their wild cousins, and the wolves howled right back as Julie and I stood in lightly falling snow, peering upriver through the darkness. Were those dark spots wolves gliding across snow-blanketed sandbars, or were our eyes playing tricks on us?

Half an hour later our dogs again broke into riotous barking but not howling this time, and by that we knew the wolves were passing silently by upwind, very close. I've heard of dogs crying and hiding, terrified at the sound or scent of wolves. In some cases their fear is justified, as wolves have come right into dog yards to kill and eat a husky. But our dogs had never witnessed such a travesty. They were ready to race out and either make friends or drive the intruders out of the territory — they weren't sure which.

The next morning Julie and I debated which one of us should carry our only firearm, our Ruger .44 revolver. I planned to mush out a side line making marten sets with a small team; Julie was heading up another trail on foot. Because the dogs would offer me some protection from late-season bears, Julie won the pistol. We had never run into a bear this late, but the tracks of wandering grizzlies often caught our attention in the first week of November, before deepening snow and lack of food sent them into hibernation.

I mushed out for eight miles, banging along the rough trail over tussocks not yet padded by snow, through scrub spruce, open grassy marshes, and the blackened stumps of an old burn barely starting to regrow even after thirty years. Finally I tied up my tiring team, leaving them to rest for the return trip while I walked another mile, digging out and setting marten cubbies. As always, the dogs greeted me with relief when I came back, barking and crying and telling me how worried they'd been.

Halfway home, I stopped to clear out a section of trail where the forest fire had allowed saplings and brush to grow up on the land — and the trail. I paused when my five dogs alerted me with a few small woofs, and then I heard the thin, pure tones of howling wolves, close but not in sight.

I howled once myself to get the dogs singing; often wolves come up close to check out a vocal dog. After five minutes with the dogs alternately howling and listening in intense silence, I spotted one drifting through burned-over scrub spruce a quarter-mile away, heading farther off.

I gave up. Not that I could win a pelt without a firearm anyway, but it was fun just seeing one. As the white wolf slipped out of sight I started the dogs for home, heading back across the mile-long frozen lake.

Halfway across, I glanced back and almost fell off my sled. Just behind me and off to one side of my trail trotted a big gray wolf.

Only a hundred feet away, he moved with a wolf's characteristically long, swinging gait. His back was light gray, his legs almost white, and his face wore the most distinctive mask I've ever seen on a wolf, dark gray accenting the nearly pure white muzzle.

It took me a moment to recover from the start he gave me. Then I glanced at my unsuspecting dogs. Somehow, until they saw him, I felt as though I was alone with the wolf, and although I wasn't really afraid of him, I didn't want to be alone with him, either.

"Look, look," I said, not loudly.

Usually that warning causes a couple of dogs to look sharply about, especially the old-timers like Streak and Amber. This time, all five furry heads snapped around in every direction. The wolf was almost abreast of me now, and just as I looked back again the team spotted him. As one, they spun toward the big predator.

Less than two inches of snow covered the glassy surface of the frozen lake, and the claw brake on my sled made no impression on either the ice or the dogs. As the wolf coolly changed course to avoid an imminent collision, I dragged my feet to slow the dogs, finally tipping the sled onto its side and sitting down on it.

The increased drag and my quiet "whoa" slowed the dogs. They stopped and stood, rigidly staring at the wolf. He stared right back with melting-pitch eyes, thick handsome coat unruffled as his long skinny legs carried him with graceful dignity to one side. I estimated his weight at ninety to one hundred pounds, about the same size as my bigger dogs except for 110-pound Streak.

When he started to circle again, the dogs couldn't stand it. They strained forward together, and I didn't try to stop them. The sled, dragging on its side, kept them from gaining on the wolf too fast.

We scribbled a jagged line in the snow for a quarter-mile, alternately chasing the unconcerned wolf and standing still to watch him. Finally the big fellow had seen enough. He turned and swung off toward the scrub spruce. Enraptured, the dogs and I stared after him in awe, and then at my command the team headed willingly for home.

From the sign on my backtrail I saw that the wolves had followed me most of the way out from the cabin. Just a mile from home, as I passed a marten cubby, the dogs hesitated, unsure whether I wanted them to stop.

"On by," I told them cheerfully, glancing at the undisturbed tipi of sticks over the bait. Obediently the team got back in gear and picked up the slack towline, only to suddenly spin around with a collective gasp. Following their staring eyes, I slammed on the brake.

Fifty feet behind the cubby crouched a wolf. Caught in the little marten trap. By one toe.

"Oh-h, my gosh," I whispered.

After ten years, this was the first time we'd caught up to a wolf before he escaped from our trap. And me without a firearm.

Fortunately Julie had tossed some extra traps into my sled, and I picked out one attached to a long cable. Tying up my dogs, I tiptoed over, careful not to panic the big animal. The small pole anchoring the trap, meant to hold a marten, was too small to stop a wolf, and he'd pulled it away without disturbing the cubby. But then the trap had snubbed up short, its chain wrapped around a twiggy little tree. One hard jerk from the wolf would either free the trap from the tree or the toe from the trap.

Although the wolf looked big, I could see by his overgrown leg bones, ivory teeth, and short face that he was not yet full grown, and obviously not trap-wise. I tried not to feel sorry for him; so many young animals don't survive their first year anyway. He crouched on the ground, snarling a dangerous warning, brown face wrinkling threateningly. After some maneuvering I backed him into the spare trap, and he didn't even seem to feel it snap shut on his hind foot. With the wolf thus immobilized, I was more safe from his powerful jaws, and one quick blow with the back of my ax finished him.

Our first wolf! The pelt meant money in the bank, or trim for mukluks and fur for the thick ruffs we need to protect our faces from the cutting winter wind. I did feel a little guilty about killing him. But the loss of a youngster does not affect the stability of the pack as much as that of an older, more experienced and respected member. Studies have shown that a major cause of death among wolves is being killed by other wolves, and that is particularly true of younger ones as they mature and disperse to new territory, only to be caught when they infringe on strange packs.

When I got home, at first I explained only about the wolf I'd seen on the lake. "I sure wished I'd had that pistol," I told Julie. Then I added dramatically, "Especially when I found this." Flipping back the sled tarp, I showed her our first wolf.

I had seen Julie surprised before, but I had never seen her look as if she actually didn't believe her eyes. She stared at the big animal, too amazed for words.

Although an accidental catch, it was still a triumph. The wolf population in our area had been growing explosively, and we had started to fear for the local moose population. This one wolf alone could have killed five moose each winter over his lifetime — thousands of pounds of meat.

When predator levels outstrip the moose, we stand to lose not only our meat supply, but other creatures as well, when the hungry wolves turned to eating smaller prey animals that feed the fur supply, even consuming fox, lynx, and marten. And, perhaps, horses. Although so far the wolves have left our livestock alone, they present a constant threat.

"Even so," I told Julie, "if it came right down to it and I had to decide whether Alaska had wolves or horses, I'd have to side with the wolves."

She agreed without hesitation; giving up horses would be a terrible blow, but sometimes the wild ones must be given priority.

Streak had been starting to age that day when he saw the wolf trailing us across the lonely lake. Several years later, at ten and a half years old, his once-proud body suffered from arthritis. He traveled at a hobbling walk, sometimes crying in pain when he first rose in the morning. Even running loose Streak could no longer keep up with the main team. Although he enjoyed a pampered retirement, tottering around loose and coming inside at will, it broke his heart to see the team head off without him. Still, I treasured his

Streak was an outstanding bear dog. Even at age eleven, he was willing to tackle one alone, but this old black bear was too aggressive so Miki shot him. Streak was very proud of *his* bear.

companionship, taking him on walks or rides with the horses whenever I could.

One early winter day, he was delighted to come with me on a two-mile hike to check a fish net set under the frozen lake ice, especially as Pepper came along. The two dogs gamboled about or lay on the drifted snow as I chopped out both ends of the net. As I hauled it from under the ice, the far end dragged a length of rope underwater behind it, to be used later to pull the net back into place. Using a fish pick made from a bent nail driven into a five-inch section of old ax handle, I pulled fish from the net, glad for the rubber gloves protecting my hands from the wet. Finished at last, I reset the net under the ice, anchoring each end to an upright pole. Loading my catch into a small plastic sled, I straightened my stiff back.

"Okay, you guys," I called. "Let's go home!"

Pepper and Streak danced eagerly ahead as I pulled the sled myself. Pepper had decided she was *not* a sled dog, and Streak's arthritis prevented me from asking for his help. But the sled moved easily, and I did not mind the extra work.

We followed the lakeshore home, staying on the smooth,

windblown ice below our birch-covered hill that juts into the lake. A mile from home, just before I turned into our bay, Streak decided to inspect our second fish net set 200 yards offshore. He knew Julie had been there earlier, and maybe he'd find a few tasty, frozen, golden-orange whitefish eggs scattered in the snow. I let him go; he'd come along when he was good and ready.

Then I saw the wolves. As Streak poked around the net, three of them materialized from a low draw across the narrow mouth of the bay, heading straight for the old dog.

"Streak!" I shouted. "Streak!"

I knew a lot of wolves were around that year, and not many moose. They might be hungry, and they considered dogs fair game. A lone wolf had killed some half-grown husky pups across the lake the year before, and I didn't want my retired old friend to be the next victim.

Streak lifted his massive, furry, black and white head to stare at the intruders, tail aloft and not a particle of fear in his big old body. A small hump-backed black wolf, probably just a pup, ranged in advance of the others. Scanning the snowy scene, I saw another pair appear, and then two more, making seven in all.

I dropped my sled rope and headed for Streak, shouting loudly. The wolves didn't even glance my way. I had never been afraid of wolves before, but these looked like they had blood on their minds.

The first wolf whipped past Streak. The old dog spun at it, sending the pup cowering away. As I looked anxiously toward the approaching pack, I saw four more trail out of the brush, for a total of eleven.

I stopped, heart in my throat. Suddenly I wasn't so anxious to rush over to Streak. I could almost hear Julie's sharp words echoing in my head: "Don't go up there! Do NOT go up there!" Those wolves showed not the slightest fear of either me or my dogs. Without a weapon, I was helpless.

The next two wolves had no qualms about tackling Streak together, closing in swiftly as he boldly faced them. These two looked much bigger than the first, intense as they aggressively charged their prey.

A confirmed old bully, Streak knew how to use his 110-pound bulk to put down an attacker. But against two wolves, with more on the way? I stood rooted, staring in horror.

Both wolves leaped at once, hurtling at the aged dog in well-coordinated unison. As they lunged, Streak reared on arthritic hind legs, towering above the low-slung, lithe predators to drive down on both of them with his massive chest and jaws.

From my distance I couldn't tell exactly what happened, but it was all over in an instant. With a roar and a snap, Streak squashed both wolves to the ground at once, beating them in a flash. Wolves make an offensive attack only when they have the advantage, and, abashed, these two abruptly retreated toward the hesitating pack.

Streak stared arrogantly after them. When he was good and ready, he turned and strolled serenely back to me, tail aloft, just as cool as could be.

The pack doubled back in retreat, not hurrying but with their interest in Streak doused as they filed toward the brush at the mouth of the bay. Counting again, I came up with twelve, and a few minutes later I saw two more back in the low-lying willows — fourteen in all, the biggest pack I had ever seen.

I don't think Streak realized how close he came to losing his life. Age may have ravaged his imposing body and stolen his nimble speed and splendid strength, but it could not dull his aggressive, loyal heart nor dampen the spirit shining from his golden-brown eyes. Because of that, he lived on to hobble regally among the chained sled dogs, squashing the disrespectful and shouting for joy when I greeted him every morning.

Bringing the dogs home, I left them there, got Julie and our rifles, and headed back out. We found the wolves inspecting the fish net again. I didn't count them, but Julie thought she saw at least sixteen. The entire pack started to retreat while we were still several hundred yards away.

I've never done any long-distance shooting, much less at a moving target, so I wasn't surprised that neither of us knocked one down. I was mad, wanting to teach them a little respect for humans!

After the last wolf disappeared into the brush, we inspected their tracks. It didn't look like we'd poked a hole in any of them, although we saw one set of tracks with a fourteen-foot spread between each bound. Curiously, one of the wolves never even broke out of a trot.

We learned later that these wolves were well fed. A pilot spotted a fresh moose kill just a couple of miles away that same day, not

even cleaned up yet. Possibly the first black wolf was just an ignorant pup, and the two adults were merely trying to extricate him
from danger. *(Junior! How many times have we told you not to talk to
strangers?)* Most likely they were either defending their territory or
just went after Streak because he was alive, solitary, and vulnerable
— reason enough for almost any predator to attack, hungry or not.
Streak was just fortunate that the majority of the pack did not reach
him at once.

Many misinformed people think of wolves as spiritual, much-
maligned dog-like creatures living harmlessly on mice and other small
varmints. They may find such an image mystical and enchanting,
but I consider it an insult. Wolves are so much more than that, intel-
ligent and socially adept enough to team up against a prey animal
ten or twenty times the weight of a lone wolf, taking it down even
if that means injuring the poor beast and letting it weaken for days
before ultimately slaughtering it. Like us, wolves kill for a living,
and not as safely as we do with our rifles and traps. With each hunt
comes the risk of being kicked, bitten, or mauled, possibly causing
crippling injury or death. While I respect and admire wolves for
their talents, I also appreciate the harm they can inflict both on
individual animals and on whole populations.

We don't see wolves very often, although they frequently use
our dog team trails for easy travel, especially when the snow lies
deep and soft elsewhere. One time as I stopped to make a set along
the edge of a creek, the dogs started woofing. Then Beau, always on
guard and quite the scaredy in spite of his eighty-five tall, handsome
pounds, growled a bit, something I always take seriously.

Right away I thought: *Bear!* This was my first trip out in early
November, and in the lead spunky, blue-eyed Cody had been following the tracks of a late grizzly wandering up the creek. I was
hastily digging out my .308 Winchester rifle, carried for just such an
emergency, when the dogs' alarm intensified. I looked up just in
time to see a slim, silvery-gray wolf break out of the timber a few
hundred feet away, drifting out onto the open creek to watch us.
Apparently the dogs had heard the wolf without winding it, for as
soon as they identified it, their concern melted away, replaced by an
alert interest.

I had to take a shot at the wolf even though it was so beautiful I didn't really want kill it, and I guess my guardian angel was on duty and sent that bullet astray. The wolf dodged back into the trees unharmed, only to return momentarily to trail us for a mile or two, staying out of my range.

Because of that missed shot, I carried the rifle with me on my next trip out. By then, November 11, I figured the big bears should all be asleep, and I could have switched to the lighter, less cumbersome (if less effective on bears) .44 revolver we use to dispatch bigger trapped animals. But I might get another shot at a wolf, and I also liked the rifle because I could easily shoot grouse with it. Abundant in the cottonwood growth along the creek, the birds made a nice change from moose meat, and I always aimed at the head so the heavy bullet would not damage the succulent meat.

Running an eighty-mile trapline by dog team is never easy, but that next trip out seemed especially tough. The sixteen-mile trail between the Twelve-Mile Camp and the Spruce Cabin lay buried under six or eight inches of fresh snow on top of an already soft surface, and my small team of seven dogs was still tired from yesterday's long hours coming up from the Birch Cabin.

At seventy pounds, my little leader Cody was not really tall enough for such heavy going, but he was the only lead dog I had that day. A stocky but well-built dog with a beautiful slate-gray and white face and kind dark blue eyes, he loved to run but found slow work disagreeable. Two other dogs concerned me as well. Smokey Joe, also a small dog and only a year old, could be ruined by too much work at so tender an age. Amber would be ten next spring, aging and sore in the back but always puppy-like, cheerful and ready to go.

Beaver trapping and caring for the horses kept Julie close to home, so as usual I traveled alone. The snow already lay two feet deep here on the north side of the Alaska Range, and it looked like we might be in for another tough year. The last three years had brought record levels of snowfall, and we had two generations of dogs who thought trapline work meant day after day of pushing through deep snow on bottomless trails. Their speed had dropped each year, along with their attitude, and more and more I brought all the dogs into the cabin at night to keep them better rested and a bit happier. Now we were going through it all again.

Well, I was feeling pretty sorry for myself as I pedaled and walked behind the loaded sled, heaving it over to bang the ice off the runners every time I crossed the shallow, still-open creek.

Once past the predictable open sections of the stream, I stopped in frustration to chop down a straight young cottonwood and tie it to my sled for a gee pole. Using the pole to steer the sled from the front, I could ski along straddling the towline, taking my weight off the dogs. We moved a bit faster then, but the skis slowed me down every time I stopped to clean off a trap.

The dogs and I were near the spot where we'd seen the wolf when I stopped at a trap set under an alder stump on the edge of a long, narrow, willow-lined slough. We had already used up four hours of the short winter day mushing the first ten miles, and we had six more miles to go. As I swept the snow from the trap, replaced the step sticks, and flipped a piece of rotted moose gut into the cubby, I figured we could still reach the snug, well-stocked cabin before the early evening caught us.

I figured wrong.

As I turned back on my skis to my dog team, Beau, in the wheel, started giving an alarm bark. When a couple of other dogs joined in, I paused at the back of the sled, my eyes following their gaze upriver. I thought about that wolf, and leaned over to extract the heavy rifle from where it lay in its case, lashed inside the canvas tarp enclosing my load.

Before I even reached the knot, I glimpsed a dark shape moving rapidly down the creek just around the bend, mostly hidden by a screen of cottonwoods and brush. A wolf, I thought. But it wasn't moving like a wolf. The color was wrong, too — a dark brown, more like a wolverine. The dogs stared intently, barking a little. I was reaching for my rifle again when the animal cleared the bend.

It wasn't a wolf. It wasn't a wolverine, either.

It was a big old grizzly bear. And he was running right at us.

My heart dropped right down into my boots. Before I could move, the dogs charged forward with a burst of excitement, heading straight at the oncoming bear seventy-five yards away, ready to tear him apart. Still on my skis, I automatically grabbed the handlebow of my sled, sliding along behind. I could have let them go, but they were taking my rifle along with them!

I couldn't believe that the bear would not stop. Bears often bluff-charge, sometimes running to within a few feet, and this one was up against seven dogs, as big and strong as a pack of wolves, not to mention the rushing seven-foot sled and myself. I just couldn't believe it.

"Whoa!" I shouted angrily, sternly, to my dogs. If I let any nervousness into my voice, the bear would pick up on it. "Whoa! *Whoa!*"

The dogs didn't stop because of my order. They stopped because they suddenly realized something was terribly wrong. This monster was ready to tear *them* apart! And he didn't stop. He kept right on loping, silent, intent, right straight at us, his long, heavy, dark coat rippling shaggily over powerful shoulders.

Quickly I popped off my skis so I could at least dodge. Then I yanked open the sled tarp and unzipped the rifle case, trying to watch the charging bear as I worked. I knew that if he didn't stop when he reached the dogs, I'd never get the gun in time.

The grizzly covered the seventy-five yards in seconds. As he closed head-on with the team, Cody sprang sideways into the deep snow beside the trail, out of the bear's path. As the grizzly overshot him, the next pair of dogs likewise dodged aside. Had they been loose, they would have then closed in from behind, getting his attention away from me. But between the restraining towline and the deep snow reaching their chests, the dogs couldn't move any farther than their initial leap. That was enough; the bear, still running in great bounds, overshot them too.

Smokey and Amber, next in line, swung aside as well, barely clearing the side of the trail. As they did, the grizzly skidded to a halt right beside them, spinning to stare silently into their terrified faces, just twenty feet from where I stood behind the sled, working frantically to retrieve my rifle.

The dogs huddled in the snow, frozen and wild-eyed as the bear stared at them. From where he stood he could have reached out and easily hooked Amber with a big front paw, or flattened both dogs with one pounce. The little old dog, with young Smokey crouched low behind her, did her best to melt right down into the snow.

Finally I yanked the rifle clear of its case. Jacking one of the four shells into the chamber, I threw it to my shoulder. The sights of the .308 lined up on a huge wall of dark brown fur. I aimed just behind the shoulder, not wanting to risk a head shot when his nose was only two feet from Amber.

As the sights closed on him, my shock drained away. This rifle, my trusted moose-hunting gun, had never let me down, and suddenly

I felt in control. For just an instant, I hesitated. I didn't have a bear ticket. Was this defense of life and property? He had not actually hurt any of us yet, but that could change in a split second. Once he got onto the dogs — or the sled, or myself — I might not get another clean shot. I might hit a dog, or injure the bear, possibly making him even more dangerous. All this ran fleetingly through my mind, culminating in the thought, "Should-I-shoot-*yes.*"

Gently I squeezed the trigger, firing right over Beau's head and past the team dogs by about four feet.

The grizzly reeled, almost falling as the 180-grain bullet slammed into him. Seven frightened furry heads snapped toward the sound of my rifle, and then snapped back at the bear. Staggering, he turned away from the team as I sent another bullet into him as fast as I could. At a wavering walk, he started back up the trail. When I fired the third shot he was about down, and the fourth one hit him as he collapsed into the snow at the trail's edge, fifty feet beyond Cody.

I started to breathe again, digging a reload from my pocket. I didn't move from behind the sled until my rifle was fully loaded. By then the bear lay motionless, the majesty flown from his body.

The whole thing had taken less than thirty seconds.

That's when I started getting shaky. It had happened so fast. What if I hadn't been carrying the rifle? What if the grizzly hadn't stopped? In over thirty years of bush living, never before had I been charged by a bear.

"Oh, you guys," I breathed to the dogs. "You guys, you guys . . ."

They barked warningly as I tottered over to the big, inert form. They knew I was in control again, but they still did not want me to go over to that bear. No way!

Rifle ready, I was prepared to send a bullet into the grizzly's head if he so much as wiggled a whisker. But my first shot had been fatal, the other three only hastening his death.

Because I didn't have a grizzly ticket, I had to turn in the hide and skull. With darkness just a couple hours away and the dogs already tired, the thought of skinning that huge animal and loading the sled down with another hundred pounds of hide, skull, and feet made me sick. At least with the temperature well above zero working bare-handed was not a problem. Still trembling, I dug out my pocketknife.

The dogs waited, subdued and shaken, barking worriedly

whenever I heaved the bear over or so much as lifted a massive, long-clawed paw. As I skinned him, I saw that instead of carrying a thick layer of fat for his winter's sleep, the bear had virtually no stores at all. Close to starvation, he had probably charged out of desperation.

Looking at his tracks later, I saw that as soon as he'd heard Beau barking, he had broken from a trudging walk into a lope, which had not faltered until he stood nose-to-nose with Amber. Perhaps he had thought we were a pack of wolves on a kill, and hoped to drive us off to claim the meat for himself. Although I had a freshly killed grouse and fifteen pounds of rotted moose gut bait in my sled, the wind had been quartering toward me, and I don't believe he smelled it before he started his charge.

Humans seem to always stereotype animals, trying to put each species in a slot and assign to it predictable traits and behaviors. We forget that every animal is an individual, so when one doesn't behave the way we think he ought to, we find it most disconcerting. When a moose calf doesn't give ground, when wolves attack a pet dog, or when a bear shows himself in winter with two feet of snow blanketing the ground, you realize that animals are in a sense like humans — individuals and not always predictable.

Skinning up the bear's neck, I found a radio collar completely hidden in his long, dense fur. This bear was being tracked by the National Park Service; he was one of the Denali Park grizzlies.

Judging by what I found inside him — heaps of raw rice and a small scrap of yellow wrapping paper reading "Made in California" — I knew he'd trashed the Spruce Cabin ahead. When I arrived there, hours after dark and exhausted from the added load, I was prepared for the damage.

Our little cabin lay in ruins, lantern glass shattered, plastic windows torn out, table smashed, outer door yanked off its hinges, a five-gallon metal bucket ripped to ribbons. The bear had even opened the door to the stove, pushed in his long, hairy arm, and dragged out a pawful of ashes. Everything edible had either been consumed or scattered across the dirt floor, mixed generously with matches, push pins, and broken glass. Tired though I was, I stepped outside to make sure the stovepipe was intact, only to find it knocked down at ceiling level. If I had lit a fire before replacing it, I could have burned the cabin down.

For the next two days I lived off the incidental supplies I'd packed along, and when I found a dirty lump of chocolate on the floor, I popped the whole ounce into my mouth. It sure tasted good.

Stretching out the bear's hide, I measured it to be roughly seven feet long with an eight-foot arm span, a big bear for this hungry country. The soles of his feet were cut and ragged, and his teeth yellowed, some worn to the gum line, others rotted with deep areas of decay.

Information sent to me later by the Park Service proved enlightening. Recognizing the gravity of my situation, they did not question the killing of "their" bear. Of the twenty-two grizzlies being monitored, mine was one of only two not yet in hibernation. Although well past his prime at eighteen years of age, he had still weighed 550 pounds earlier in the year; only one other bear had been larger. He ranged over an area fifty miles long, and radio-tracking biologists sometimes spotted him thirty-five miles from his location of five days earlier.

At the request of the biologist, I sent in the bear's femur. Tests showed that at the time I shot him, the grizzly had already started burning fat stored in his bone marrow, the last energy reserves left before starvation.

"He was in very poor physical condition and likely would not have survived the winter," park biologist Jeff Keay wrote me later.

I felt comforted by that. If not forgivable, his actions were at least understandable. And I had not needlessly destroyed a mighty monarch with years of life left; if anything, this death was less cruel than one of slow, desperate starvation.

As for me, it was one of the worst scares I ever had. I never even had time to get scared until it was all over, but for days that charging bear was the last thing I thought of when I went to bed, and the first thing that came to mind when I woke up the next morning.

I reckon I'll be carrying that trusty .308, with its open sights and battered stock, until the end of November every winter from now on.

This creek had broken up, but the well-used winter trail made an ice bridge solid enough to lead the horses across. Icicles hang from the underside as Miki leads Dropi carefully over.

CHAPTER 13

HOME

"We're in trouble! Big trouble! Major trouble!" I shouted.

Miki had just ducked out of the Birch Cabin to catch my dogs as they rolled in. She seized my coat and dragged me close to her ruddy face. "What?" she demanded.

"Serious trouble! A real catastrophe!" I jabbered.

"WHAT?"

"You can't cross the Spruce Crossing without a canoe!" I reported, throwing out my arms dramatically.

Miki stood stunned. The rivers close to home never went out before mid-April, and this was only the ninth. Sure, it had been forty degrees, but that wasn't uncommon this time of year. Just last week we'd crossed the creek, ten miles beyond the Birch Cabin, on solid ice, and today rushing water filled it instead!

This year of all years, we needed that trail passable. The cabin permit we had applied for so long ago, the one that would allow us to replace our Twelve-Mile tent camp, thirteen miles beyond the Birch Cabin, was almost approved. The tent that we used there instead of Slim's collapsed cabin had served us well, but something more permanent would be safer; we could take better care of our fur, bring the dogs inside on cold nights, and stay warmer ourselves. We wouldn't have to worry about hauling the bulky tent out every fall, we wouldn't have to cut as much firewood, and we would have shelter there during summer treks.

Building a cabin required moving feed and building supplies to the remote site thirty miles from home, quite a job with snowmelt in full swing and now, unexpectedly, with creek ice breaking up. Staying out for two months with all fifteen dogs and three horses — Lilja, Dropi, and the yearling Andi — meant a major freighting job. We had spent the last two weeks *Julie* stockpiling materials at the Birch Cabin and now, after moving only three of perhaps twenty loads to the Twelve-Mile, we met this awful predicament. How could we transfer 2,000 pounds across an open creek? Though only hip-deep, the channel lay in a gaping chasm three feet below the thick shelf ice. If I stood in the water, the top of that ice would be chest-high.

"What'll we do?" Miki asked in horror.

"What can we do? We'll have to get the canoe!"

"How'll we get the horses across?"

"I . . . I don't know. Maybe we can find an ice bridge somewhere. Otherwise, we'll just have to wait until after breakup! They can't possibly jump off the ice into the water."

"We couldn't chop a ramp?"

"Not right now, for sure. The ice is overhanging the river with up to a foot of air under it. Even if it didn't collapse, I'm sure the horses would never jump, and I'd be scared to force them."

"Oh . . . oh, holy smokies."

Towing our eighteen-foot aluminum canoe from home out to the Spruce Crossing turned into twenty-six miles of uncomfortable work. The trail to the Birch Cabin was easy, but the last ten miles beyond the Birch Cabin cut through dense spruce forests with sunken potholes and rough, partly melted trails. Miki had to ski on a gee pole, steering my dog sled so that I could concentrate on dealing with the unruly canoe lurching over the snow behind the sled. Twisted sideways on the sled runners, I jerked the rumbling craft around corners, steadying it on the bumps and squalling angrily each time the sled swooped down a bank and yanked the canoe's bow forward into my back.

Once at the crossing, however, the dreaded chore of ferrying freight across the water proved surprisingly pleasant and only slightly complicated by the problem of lowering each fifty-pound sack down a vertical wall of ice to where the canoe lay in the water. On the opposite side the ice had slumped into the water, making a nice ramp for unloading. We cached everything at the crossing, for trails were melting fast. The last three miles to the Twelve-Mile camp would be passable throughout the spring, so the freight could be moved the last distance later when we had more leisure.

"What a huge lot of extra work," I sighed. "These unexpected problems are sometimes blessings in disguise, but I can't imagine *this* turning out for the good."

The freighting of our supplies from the Birch Cabin to the far side of the Spruce Crossing progressed in fits and starts. Worn down from trapping, our dogs were tired of slogging out the same old trail. The weather grew steadily warmer, and to avoid the mushy, melting trails we only traveled from 6 A.M. until noon.

On Easter Sunday we gave the dogs a holiday and spent a pleasant afternoon riding Lilja and Dropi upriver from the Birch Cabin, with Andi trotting merrily along behind. Overwhelmed by springtime, the creek was alive with runoff dripping and soaking into the heavy snow, but the ice supported the horses easily as we jogged along. Here and there we spotted holes where beavers had broken through the river ice. They made broad, scooped paths into the willows, looking for fresh twigs to supplement their depleted underwater brush piles. Tufts of yellow grass poked through the snow, luring the horses toward the banks. Unencumbered by a rider, Andi stopped often to nibble on grass and twigs, his red topknot bobbing as he plucked the choicest bites. Then, whinnying shrilly, he galloped to catch up, white legs flying and multicolored tail streaming behind. Grosbeaks, red polls, and chickadees danced through barren brush and gay pussy willows, enjoying seeds exposed by the snowmelt without the competition of other sparrows that had not yet returned north. A shifty sky warmed our backs with sunshine, then cooled us with the damp, shadowy breezes so typical of an Alaska spring. Winter floods had left rough ice with only a little snow, so we made good time and traveled several miles before turning back.

April 21 was the last day we spent at the Birch Cabin together. Miki had just made one final sled run home, fighting mud, slush, overflow, and running water on her return trip late at night. We had to move soon, before the frozen swamps turned to liquid muck, but we regretted leaving the cozy cabin that had been our home for so many weeks, with its sunny yard where horses and dogs were equally contented. Miki loaded the horses with light packs and led them out on the trail toward the Twelve-Mile, traveling in the afternoon heat to avoid the nightly crusts of icy snow that the horses found so unpleasant. Slogging slowly through deep, wet snow, she took two days to reach the Spruce Crossing just ten miles away. Meanwhile, I made two early morning dog sled trips with the last of the freight, arriving at the crossing with the final load at 8:30 in the morning. Unlike horses, dogs work better at dawn, when cooler air freezes the trails enough to support them.

Moving the entire crew to the crossing was only the first hurdle. The next challenge was transferring everything across the creek. First, we hauled the dog harnesses, saddle panniers, and remaining freight over in the canoe. Then I donned hip boots and jumped off the shelf ice into the water two feet below. Miki threw in our dog sled and I dragged it, half floating and half dragging on the sandy bottom, to the far side. The dogs clustered along the ice edge and with a little encouragement they toppled in and swam across. (Ever eager, Toulouse swam across several times.) Then we inhaled deeply and turned to the horses.

The ice canyon had continued to melt and wasn't quite as deep as before, and just upstream a gravel bar now peeked out below the ice edge. Miki chopped steps two and a half feet down to the narrow rim of gravel, and we sprinkled them liberally with sand so the horses wouldn't slip. The ice ramp on the far side looked more risky, but with chopped footholds and more sand, we thought the horses could climb it.

"I think they *can* do it, but I'm not sure if they *will* do it," Miki mused. We thought the horses would balk at the ice, the drop-off, the soft gravel, or the speeding, frigid water. But no! They hopped carefully down the steps and plunged eagerly into the clear, sparkling water. They *wanted* to get wet! Lilja, who usually goes where *she* wants to go, knew of the hidden dangers lurking beneath the swift water. She listened carefully as Miki guided her briskly down the creek a hundred yards and then across to the ice ramp. Dropi and Andi followed close behind, skirting underwater logs and deep holes. The horses scampered up the ramp, well pleased with themselves, and we shouted with joy and relief.

I hitched up the dogs and loaded my sled, leaving first with the team. Miki followed with the horses. Halfway to the camp, a black, swampy little stream we call Icky Creek was mostly open, but a narrow ice bridge, strengthened by a natural arch, offered a safe crossing over the shallow water below. One last creek, the Twelve-Mile, might have flooded too. Worried about that possible problem, when I broke onto the riverbank and looked far across the willow bar and the broad creek, it took a moment for me to realize that the tent itself was — gone!

"Awright! The creek is solid! Oh — my goodness! The tent!" I thought. Had it collapsed under snow? No, it hadn't snowed. People trespassing? Never! The only other possibility hit hard.

A bear.

Stopping the dogs, I pulled Miki's .308 from its scabbard before moving warily across to the camp. The tent lay in a tangled heap. Books, food, and bedding lay twisted through shredded canvas. More gear was widely scattered along the riverbank. Churned up with the torn canvas and bedding was a hideous mass of oatmeal, instant potatoes, and brilliant red Kool-aid.

I turned the dogs loose. They scouted for the bear and found nothing. Searching for sign, I found only week-old evidence. The grizzly had not caused as much damage as he might have. He destroyed, ate, or packed off a week's worth of our food and fifty pounds each of dog food and grain. He had entered the tent through the front door and made his own back door and two side exits. He then wadded up the tent and scratched it apart like a kitten with a ball of yarn. Our gas-crate cupboard and spruce-board shelf had been crushed, but the stove and pipe, though bent, were still usable.

Had the Spruce Crossing not broken up early, forcing us to stock-pile food there, our freight would have been waiting at the Twelve-Mile for the bear to destroy. With spring conditions, crossing the main rivers to get home was impossible, and without that food we'd have been in trouble. The open creek, so worrisome those last two weeks of freighting, proved to be a blessing after all.

That night Miki and I lay in the shredded remains of our tent as the dogs woofed and growled at bear scents lingering in the gloom of a short spring night. Miki's rifle rested ready beside the bed. "This is going to be great!" she said cheerfully.

Luckily, we had plenty of dental floss — our standard thread — which we used to stitch together the shredded tent to make it a usable if well-ventilated shelter. We found it handy to poke a hand through the wall to grab a jar of jam or pickled beets stored just outside. To replace the food we did lose, Miki made an unscheduled and somewhat hazardous sled trip to the Birch Cabin. We were still short of milk, sugar, and potatoes, but our parents, flying to Fairbanks for the rest of the spring, air-dropped us enough to eke out our meager supply.

So we settled into our new home and life at the Twelve-Mile.

We freighted in the last of our stockpiled feed and finished a small corral for the horses. In the fine spring weather, the dogs needed no shelter and were parked along the sunny riverbank to enjoy a well-deserved rest. Of course we had no neighbors, but loneliness was out of the question with all twenty of us living together. Our parents were out of radio range in Fairbanks, so we had no outside contact unless the rare plane flew over that we could call with an aircraft radio. The extreme isolation might have made some people feel trapped, but having spent a lifetime in this country we settled in easily and contentedly. Except for taking extra care to prevent serious accidents, Miki and I felt as comfortable and secure here as in the cabin where we grew up.

On the first of May we moved the last load in from the crossing. By using local resources — logs, poles, gravel, sod, and moss — we could limit our hauled-in materials to spikes, nails, plastic sheeting, stove, and stovepipe. Our tools included the chain saw and axes, shovel, hammer, maul, and wedge. A drawknife, peevee, scribe, and other logging tools would have been helpful, but all-purpose tools such as the ax made adequate substitutes.

Then we began work on the cabin in earnest. This was not easy, because the promised permit had not materialized. Back in November, the man handling our cabin permit had assured me that we could count on building the cabin in the spring.

"That's what they told us in 1987, and that was five years ago," I had said suspiciously. "We don't want to haul feed out and then spend breakup out there with no permit."

But the permit was firmly promised, even if the dedicated fellow had to air-drop it. So we made our plans and because our outfit had to be moved before breakup, we stuck with them, hoping for the best while the permit stumbled through a maze of bureaucratic thickets.

We did have a permit to cut logs, so we began immediately. White spruce logs, straight but not too big for two girls and a small horse to handle, fell before my sturdy old chain saw. After we peeled off the half-frozen bark with axes, Lilja dutifully dragged in the larger logs, fearlessly crossing sagging creek ice as gaping holes melted and expanded along the shallow stream. Dropi, more timid about working in harness, hauled in the smaller logs.

We made a staunch effort to respect the government guidelines.

Slash had to be scattered, trees cut flush with the ground, camp kept tidy, and Slim's rotten old cabin and his historical legacy left undisturbed. Scattering the branches and bark was no problem, but with deep, wet snow still covering the ground in early May, cutting trees flush proved so troublesome that I returned after snowmelt to shave down the stubble. Slim's "legacy" included widely scattered tin cans, leaky buckets, old drums, tools, and rusted stovepipe. Keeping a tidy camp without disturbing his trash was just not possible!

With over thirty logs drying in the lengthening days of May, we turned to roofing materials. Short logs split with a chain saw, wedge, and maul made half-round slabs for the roof. This was Slim's way, and made a brighter, cleaner cabin than the more common pole roof. We peeled the logs before splitting them, having learned that if the bark stripped off in a spiral the grain itself was twisted; this meant using the saw often to start a new split whenever the crack spiraled off course.

Mid-May came, but the permit did not. Except for the suspense of not knowing when or if it might arrive, our wait passed pleasantly, even joyfully. I used the chain saw to slab spruce planks for furniture. Thick sheets of lush moss, free now of winter's snow, parted reluctantly from the forest floor and were piled into a dogsled and hauled out by horse for the sod roof.

Our building materials thus assembled, we suddenly had time to kill. We cut firewood and brushed trail. We washed laundry, pecked on the typewriter, and groomed masses of shedding hair from the horses. We picked fermented cranberries, last year's crop, to mix in our sourdough pancakes.

We went on picnics, walked the dogs, and sought wild grass for the horses. Nearly every day we rode up or down the shallow creek, searching for forage to supplement the horses' pelleted rations. The horses eagerly looked ahead as new scenery unfolded on either side of the willow-lined sandbars. Ducks and other waterfowl took flight at our approach, and just a bend below our camp we found a smelly, torn-up hollow where the grizzly had bedded down. At first we rode on the frozen creek, crossing open channels on ice bridges. Later, the horses grew adept at jumping off the rotting shelf ice down a foot or more into the shallow water, and if the ice disintegrated under their feet, well, so much more fun.

Of course, a few dogs always came along. Some days we all went a mile downriver so the horses could graze in a tiny pasture by a pond. Joni and her grand-puppies, Peter, Dusty, Barki, and Smokey, loved playfully chasing phalaropes as the tiny shorebirds twirled around the little pond.

On one hike, Peter, Barki, Arthur, and Beau tackled a startled black bear. We had a few seconds of high excitement while I beat a hasty retreat. The glossy black animal leaped and spun to face the dogs, who swirled around it like angry hornets. My dogs gave up when I called them off, except for young Barki, who was beside himself with the glory of battle until he realized his comrades had abandoned him. He scuttled after me, and for days afterwards he sounded the alarm every time he saw Pepper's shiny black coat gliding through the forest.

Old Streak dutifully treed squirrels and a porcupine, which helped stretch the meat meal and rice we cooked for the dogs. Toulouse's favorite game was to grab Andi by his bushy tail, swinging freely as the colt galloped off — a pastime we soon ended by leaving the big dog at home when we went riding. A highlight for Wiggles was the day when he pushed into the tent to eat not just our moose meat dinner but a bag of carefully hoarded Oreo cookies. Andi, meanwhile, served as Camp Pet and Pest, tripping over tent strings, drinking from the water bucket, and chasing the dogs.

Life was marvelous! The enforced leisure came as a welcome rest after the hard winter's work. One gloriously sunny day we tied the tent flaps wide open, built a roaring fire, and cooked up sizzling hot golden lumps of deep-fried whitefish. We sat in the open door eating as the wind thumped and billowed against the canvas tent and a warm, beaming sun wrestled with the cold gusts.

A heat wave broke the unusually cold May weather, melting the last snow away and making walking easier. While I waited at the tent in case the ever-elusive permit appeared, Miki made a day-long sojourn. Crossing the creek to seek out a shortcut from one of Slim's old trails, she headed off into the boonies. To determine where she was relative to camp, she called me on a radio regularly so I could fire the rifle as a directional aid. (The horses came running at the first shot, of course.)

Every time Miki called, I had a bit of news. "The creek is coming up." "The creek is coming up FAST." "The water is up three more inches, and it's dark brown now." "The creek is up over a foot since you left." When Miki finally reappeared, the water almost spilled into her hip boots, and by morning it was impassable. It remained high for over a week until the spring flood subsided.

The clear, cold water we once drank succumbed to a churning mass of brown runoff boiling with flotsam. Confident the shelf ice would melt slowly, we planned to use that for drinking, but in two days the flood had washed it away. Rather than drink the ugly floodwater, we tapped birch trees. The crystal-clear sap, with its pure, faintly sweet flavor, was our water and our nectar for many days. To stretch our dwindling sugar supply, we also boiled gallons of the sap to make a thin but flavorful syrup for our pancakes.

The horses, used to crossing the creek for forage, continued making the trip even when they had to swim. During the height of the flood, Dropi headed boldly into the river, expecting an easy crossing, but the current swept him away, spinning him swiftly downstream and then dashing him against the looming roots of a large grounded drift log. The snag's twisted gray fingers caught the young chestnut, who fought to keep his head clear as he struggled to escape.

Andi had followed Dropi into the water, but quickly turned back and scrambled ashore. By the time Julie and I grabbed some rope and raced down, Dropi had freed himself and swum across, where he stayed for quite some time before venturing home at a safer crossing.

On a clear, calm evening in late May, Ray flew overhead in his plane to check on us, dropping a sack of fresh fruit and meat that splattered across the sandbar — narrowly missing one of the dogs! Glad to hear on the radio that all was well, we scraped up the sandy hamburger and celebrated with another picnic. A few days later, Ray landed on a gravel bar two miles away with a load of supplies. On May 29, another airplane droned overhead and the streamer shooting out its window bore a far more valuable cargo: the cabin permit. Moments later we broke ground, and by morning a layer of gravel and bone-dry loess substrate provided a suitable foundation.

Although Miki and I had helped Ray and our parents build several cabins and we had repaired a few others, we had never built one alone. Undaunted, we fitted the logs with ax and chain saw, aiming for a paper-thin fit but settling for any gap smaller than a little finger. I notched the top of the logs instead of the bottom, a

This was the first cabin we'd built by ourselves, and when we started constructing the gable ends, we had to make things up as we went along. Julie cut the slant for the roof with her chain saw.

professional's no-no, but a much faster method. In this dry location and under a good roof, moisture was unlikely to accumulate in the face-up notches, and with our food dwindling rapidly, time pressed harder than the desire to do perfect work.

Moving logs only ten to fourteen inches in diameter and fifteen feet or less in length, we suffered only a few kinked muscles and never had to resort to ropes, planks, or horses to lift them up the ever-growing walls. In five days we finished the walls and suddenly had to face the fact the we had no idea how to erect the gable ends, which had to balance atop the walls, yet be secure enough to bear the ridgepole and two purloins which supported the roof. Making things up as we went, we spiked in short logs, slanting the ends with my chain saw for the roof angle. We popped sweat and cracked bones raising the heavy purloin logs and ridge pole. Roughly eighteen feet long, the ridgepole would extend the roof to provide a protective overhang in the rear and a sizable porch in front of the ten-by-twelve cabin. After spiking the ridgepole and purloins, I drove the chain saw through the front wall, making two vertical cuts and shoving out the center: a door.

The next day, June 6, I left. Because of our dwindling food supply, we had to start the tedious process of moving our crew back home, so I headed out on foot with Toulouse, Joni, Cody, Wiggles, Reuben, Peter, and Barki. A long two-day hike across rivers, bogs, and thickets brought the dogs home where Marmee and Daddy, also recently returned, could tend them. After three days planting the garden, I walked back out. During my absence Miki chinked the logs with moss and nailed on the split-board roof, and when I returned she left with Streak, Amber, Bingo, Dusty, and Smokey. Only Arthur, Beau, and Pepper remained. They would accompany us on the final trek home with the horses on a circuitous route to avoid the swamps.

With only three dogs left, the yard around our new home felt sad and deserted as I finished the roof with layers of plastic sheeting, dirt, sod, and moss for insulation against cold winter nights. I made quick work of banging together the door, a shelf, a table beneath the tiny front window, and a slab bed against the back wall. Finally, the stove pipe safety: the top third of a steel drum with a five-gallon bucket centered in it to secure the stovepipe in the roof.

When Daddy landed Miki on the gravel bar a couple days later, the cabin was essentially finished. Miki and I spent one night together under the solid roof — but only after pitching our mosquito-proof pup tent inside!

Our great adventure in cabin-building over, we turned our attention to the great adventure of getting the horses home without drowning them in the meandering swamps that barred our path. A 130-mile detour should do the trick.

We decided to stay on riverbanks, where traveling was easier and safer for the horses. By hiking out our trapline and into the foothills of the Alaska Range, we could cross the highlands to two other rivers that flowed back toward home. This would take us into some unfamiliar country, but we would be within radio range of our parents for most of the loop. And by staying on rivers, we hoped to find a safe route for the horses to follow.

By now we'd had horses for six years. Katla had died. Kopur had failed. Lilja had raised three foals, counting the one we'd sold before bringing her home. We had trained Dropi and expected to train Andi in a few more years. Although we still didn't count ourselves as experienced with horses, we'd had a good start. At least we knew what might happen out there, and what we needed to deal with it. We carried rubber horse galoshes, Easy Boots®, in case the horses' unshod hooves became bruised or sore. For wounds, we carried a first aid kit including surgical scrub, tranquilizers, antibiotics, eye ointment, and anti-inflammatories. A complete sewing and repair kit held tools and spare parts in case of breakdowns. If a horse got bogged in a swamp or quicksand, we had plenty of rope and an extra horse to pull it out. If (heaven forbid!) one broke its leg, a pistol offered the final, desperate solution.

The pistol, coupled with pepper spray and the three dogs, also would serve as bear protection. If the dogs ran into a porcupine, we had the tranquilizers and pliers. If one of us was injured, we could dip into the horse-repair kit. If the rivers flooded, I had my flotation coat. This journey, then, could test our newly wrought and still-expanding range of horse sense.

Closing up our new little home with some regret, we loaded our gear on the horses, leaving for the Spruce Cabin late to give Lilja and Dropi an easy first day. Carrying two weeks of supplies, including 160 pounds of horse food and forty pounds of dog food, they'd have a heavy load until we consumed some of it. Andi gamboled behind and the three dogs ranged ahead with smaller packs of their own as Miki and I marched out the trail, each leading a pack horse. To stretch our horse food we traveled slowly, stopping at grassy patches so the horses could forage.

At night we removed the packs and let the horses roll and browse before tying them up. Pepper pounced on the tent as soon as we unloaded it, silently pleading for me to set it up. The tiny tent protected her from the tormenting mosquitoes and also gave the insecure dog a sense of home and comfort. After chores and meals, we joined Pepper, crawling inside to sleep on saddle blankets and sleeping bags.

We fell easily into a comfortable routine, thrilling to see old familiar trapline vistas under the new guise of summertime greens, blues, and grays. The few troubles that cropped up were managed without difficulty: a little saddle sore, tender hooves, a few porcupine quills in Arthur's nose. We reached the Spruce Cabin in two days and spent the evening cleaning up and repairing the camp. A day later we reached treeline and made a lovely tramp across the foothills to reach the river that would lead us back toward home. A lone wolf, one moose, and a gorgeous blond grizzly provided excitement but no immediate danger. The mountain range lay under turbulent gray clouds that cast a steady sprinkle of rain on our crew, but the silent, invisible presence of Denali, rising beyond the clouds, radiated over us as we passed below its base. Even in unfamiliar country, with the mountain there we always felt within the sanctuary of our own backyard.

The next few days of traveling downriver led us into gradually deeper waters. Sometimes we crossed chest-deep channels; other times we followed dry sloughs or pushed through alder thickets made hazardous by sucking little drainages. On a sandy island at the west end of our trapline, we gave the animals a day of rest while I hiked down to check our West Line tent camp. Our second night there was the only time the dogs failed to alert us to an intruder. Instead Dropi sounded the alarm first, with a loud snort and alert ears.

The dogs leaped up as we scrambled out of the tent into the soft glow of the June night. All eyes were riveted on the riverbank, and noses suspiciously tested the wind. As Miki and I tiptoed through the willows, we spotted a black bear standing by the water of a thin slough, hesitating over whether to cross and visit.

Brandishing the Ruger, Miki boldly informed him that there were many of us, and we were well armed, and he should take himself elsewhere. The dogs loudly backed up her demand, and after an uneasy pause the bear reluctantly faded back into the alders.

Morning brought a terrific storm cloud hovering ominously on the southwestern horizon, a boiling black monster bearing steadily closer as we ate breakfast.

"Shall we load up and head out, or crawl back in the tent to see if that rainstorm misses us?" I wondered.

"Let's wait," Miki suggested. "It does look awful dark."

The towering, hideously dark storm gradually slid east, narrowly missing our camp. When it appeared to be pulling away, we once more loaded our gear into horse packs, dog packs, and backpacks, and set out on the daily trek. I walked first, leading Lilja and Dropi, while Miki followed shouldering a pack with our sleeping bags. In a few minutes we emerged from a portage onto a broad field of glacier-like aufeis, made by winter floods freezing in deep layers that still lingered despite the heat of late June. A mile upstream, the rugged bulk of a low mountain jutted against the river, paling behind the mist of the storm cloud.

"What was all the dust in the woods back there?" I asked Miki. "Was it spruce pollen or windblown silt?"

"I don't know," she replied, pulling spruce twigs from her braids. "It didn't look like either." We picked our way down the braided glacial river, across the crumbling ice and a wide flat of gravel and quicksand. The gray mist swept slowly toward us again, lowering visibility.

"Look at the cloud now," I said, peering uneasily over my shoulder. "Doesn't it look awful brown around the edges? Like dust. Or smoke from a forest fire. But it's been too wet for fires and I don't smell any smoke, either."

"Maybe it's a dust storm," Miki offered doubtfully.

"Where from? And where's the wind?" I asked. "And that looks like rain." I pointed upriver toward the gray haze now flowing rapidly toward us. "We're going to get wet soon."

Then I looked closely at my sister. Her cap seemed sort of . . . dusty. I looked at Pepper. Gray dust streaked her glossy black face. I looked up at the thickening mist. It had enveloped us now, but . . . it wasn't wet. The air felt dry and . . . creepy.

"That's not rain," I stammered.

Miki stared at the heavy haze. "Then what is it? Major meteorite strike? Nuclear holocaust?"

I shook my head. "I doubt it. A volcano?"

We stared at each other. "It must be fallout from a volcano!" we chorused.

The nearest volcanoes lay far to the south, but we could think of no other logical explanation. Though doubtful, we were still alarmed by the idea. Was the stuff dangerous? Should we stop? The haze grew thicker. Now we could see ash falling, a fine, light powder sifting ominously through the silent air.

We started walking. Fast. But we couldn't outstrip the storm. Inexorably it swept down to cover us with a smothering atmosphere of heavy ashen air. The haze grew thicker until we could barely see across the river. Birds fell silent. The normally persistent fog of mosquitoes dwindled and vanished. Then it began to get dark.

With growing anxiety, we dug out wraps for our faces. With bandannas, bill caps, and jacket hoods pulled tight, we felt more protected from this . . . stuff. A layer of ash now covered the ground, turning the gray glacial silt an ugly brown. We didn't know whether to stop or not. If it lasted over a day, we couldn't possibly wait it out; we barely had enough food to get home, and our usual fallback plan — an airdrop from a bush plane — was impossible in this sooty weather. The horses might be able to find forage, but we knew that eruptions in Iceland had killed thousands of horses. Would eating ash-covered grass hurt our horses? Could the animals travel safely through the thick ash? Would the gritty, abrasive fallout damage their lungs? Or scratch their eyes? And what if it wasn't volcanic after all, but something else?

Finally I unpacked our little ham radio and turned it on. "KL7IS, KL7IS, this is KL7RD mobile," I called.

Daddy answered my call immediately, and I explained the mysterious storm. "I think it's volcanic ash," I said.

"Yes, it's from Mount Spurr," he told us. "It erupted early this morning. The weather's fine here, though."

"Is it dangerous?" I asked.

The radio fell silent while Daddy consulted Marmee. As the geologist in the family, she would have the best advice. "The ash shouldn't be dangerous," he reported after a pause.

Mount Spurr lay west of Anchorage and 150 miles south of us. Apparently the winds aloft had concentrated the ash in our area. Heartened and hoping the silent storm would soon dissipate, we trekked on through the weird gray twilight. We felt isolated by the oppressive, palpable heaviness, unable to see beyond one river bend. Here and there flowers glowed in the darkness from under layers of ash — soft, pink wild roses and brilliant yellow tundra roses in the forest, and the brighter red of shrubby dwarf fireweed on gravel bars — the only bright spots in the gloom.

By afternoon every leaf of every tree bore a thick layer of the pale ash. Dust poured over us as we pushed through thickets along the riverbank. Layer after layer built up on the horses as we struggled through the choking stuff. The gritty air did not bother the horses, but the dogs coughed frequently as their rapid panting drew ash into their throats. By the time we camped, a sickly brown hue tinged the normal gray of the silty river. When our animals shook the dust off, they disappeared in flying powder. But the sky looked brighter, and we could no longer see the particles drifting down.

The worst was over, but for two days we bushwhacked along the river through clouds of the abrasive dust that fell and rose and swirled from tangled alders, gnarled willows, and waist-high dwarf birch. Then, thankfully, a gentle night-long rain washed the ash into the ground. The only dust left was on us — in our hair, our clothes, the tent and sleeping bags, in the animals' fur and their packs, clogging zippers, coating hair, and etching the cracks in our chapped hands.

"They look like burnt wienies," Miki mourned, inspecting her wrinkled, blackened fingers.

Reaching the Burn, we camped near the spot where we had vacationed with Kopur and Lilja so long ago, and fought the quicksand to cross the river in the morning. Traveling through the Burn with Kopur, we had worried constantly that the spook would panic and bolt into the forest. Two years later, Lilja had guided Jim and Dropi down this same route; this time it was Dropi and young Andi who followed her toward home.

By now Miki and I knew more about what we were doing. Our diamond hitches still went together slowly, but they turned out more snug and shapely than before. We had camped out enough to know what to bring and what to leave behind. We had shuffled our small herd until the horses were just suited to our needs: gentle, friendly, reliable, and willing. We knew the horses now, well enough to read in their faces whether they were contented, worried, or annoyed. And we had learned which sled dogs enjoyed horses for companionship and which preferred horses for chasing, so we could choose appropriate ones for the trip.

As we poked through blackened tree stumps and clambered over heaps of burned logs, circled bogs, and slogged across mossy drainages, we knew which obstacles the horses could handle and which they needed to avoid. The learning process had been long and sometimes painful, but with the knowledge came security. Disasters could still befall us, but with ignorance no longer a major factor, we were less likely to be unwitting instigators. After two months spent alone with our horses and huskies, we could travel the last miles knowing that we had finally taken them on a major expedition and *not* gotten into trouble!

One day we climbed tall sand bluffs above the river and as the panorama unfolded below, Lilja suddenly balked. We wondered if something was wrong. No, nothing was wrong. She just wanted to take in the view. Her gentle white face softened as she gazed across the broad, tree-covered flats toward the Alaska Range, the country she was now so familiar with. Denali and other local mountains had little perceptible accumulation of volcanic ash, but fallout had cloaked snow-covered 11,670-foot Mt. Russell and other southern mountains in a gray-brown mantle.

Lilja's curiosity satisfied, she soon nudged us onward, but for us the sight was of more than passing interest. The ash on those snowy peaks and glaciers would absorb the sun's heat, melting ice and snow and possibly causing a major flood that might block our way home. Indeed, one night the river did rise almost a foot, but the water didn't actually spill over the riverbanks until the last day in. After several days underwater, the silty ground might have turned into the same quicksand that had trapped Lilja on her very first trip down the Old Channel, but this flood came too late to saturate the banks before we slipped quickly by.

A mile from home we stopped at a small stream to clean up so we wouldn't arrive too dirty and shabby. We scrubbed and splashed and scrubbed and scrubbed, but it was no use.

"I can't get any more dirt off without a solvent," Miki said finally. The ash had mixed with sweat, silt, and insect repellent to form an insoluble glue.

"I thought we were ready for anything," Miki mused. "With the first aid kit, repair kit, rain gear and extra clothes, pistol and pepper spray, pliers, Easyboots®, and all that other junk we hauled along, I thought we were well prepared."

"Next time, we'll have to be prepared for volcanoes!" I laughed.

One final barrier, a deep, narrow creek, barred our way. Miki checked a shallow mud bar across the mouth, and her stick poked down five feet into the quicksand. We decided to swim the horses across the deeper water instead. The bank dropped off vertically and Miki stood in shoulder-deep water, urging Lilja in. The little mare knew home lay only a mile away, so into the water she plunged. Miki grabbed Lilja's head, but couldn't keep her nose from dipping momentarily underwater. Snorting, Lilja swam swiftly across and scrambled through deep mud to the firm ground beyond. Dropi wasn't so sure, but after thinking it over he too toppled in. Miki seized his saddle and he towed her strongly to the far bank. As Dropi slogged through the knee-deep mud to the trees, I let go of Andi and he sprang into the water. With a terrific splash the colt was completely submerged but he bobbed up, snorting and puffing, to race after the older horses. The dogs swam readily across, and Miki and I